The Psychology of Terrorism

The Psychology of Terrorism

◆

Volume III
Theoretical Understandings
and Perspectives

Edited by Chris E. Stout
Foreword by Klaus Schwab

Psychological Dimensions to War and Peace
Harvey Langholtz, Series Editor

 PRAEGER

Westport, Connecticut
London

Library of Congress Cataloging-in-Publication Data

The psychology of terrorism / edited by Chris E. Stout ; foreword by Klaus Schwab.
    p. cm.—(Psychological dimensions to war and peace, ISSN 1540–5265)
    Includes bibliographical references and index.
    ISBN 0–275–97771–4 (set)—ISBN 0–275–97865–6 (vol. I)—ISBN 0–275–97866–4
(vol. II)—ISBN 0–275–97867–2 (vol. III)—ISBN 0–275–97868–0 (vol. IV)
    1. Terrorism—Psychological aspects. 2. Terrorists—Psychology. 3.
Terrorism—Prevention. I. Stout, Chris E. II. Series.
HV6431 .P798 2002
303.6'25—dc21   2002072845

British Library Cataloguing in Publication Data is available.

Library of Congress Catalog Card Number: 2002072845
ISBN: set: 0-275-97771-4
        v.I: 0-275-97865-6
        v.II: 0-275-97866-4
        v.III: 0-275-97867-2
        v.IV: 0-275-97868-0
ISSN: 1540-5265

First published in 2002

Praeger Publishers, 88 Post Road West, Westport, CT 06881
An imprint of Greenwood Publishing Group, Inc.
www.praeger.com

Printed in the United States of America

The paper used in this book complies with the
Permanent Paper Standard issued by the National
Information Standards Organization (Z39.48-1984).

10 9 8 7 6 5 4 3 2 1

To my parents, Carlos L. and Helen E. (Simmons) Stout,
to my wife and soulmate, Dr. Karen Beckstrand, and
to my children and heroes, Grayson Beckstrand Stout and
Annika Beckstrand Stout.

You all have taught and continue to teach me so very much.

Contents

Foreword

First of all, I want to note the impressive collection of academics, thinkers, activists, and clinicians congregated in this set of volumes. Through their active engagement, the result is a series of works that crosscut an immense range of related factors—historical contexts; group dynamics; social psychological aspects; behavioral, forensic, psychopathological, evolutionary theory, peace-building, and conflict resolution perspectives; as well as the political, clinical, and social aspects of prevention, intervention, and security issues. Global perspectives vis-à-vis understanding, empathy, bias, prejudice, racism, and hate are also represented.

This group of authors offers a unique combination of talents and viewpoints rarely seen in the worlds of academia or activism. Their work and voices move knowledge and understanding forward in a way that will serve as a framework and catalyst for readers to consider ways in which to respond to terrorism in its various displays. Dr. Stout has fostered a self-organizing environment that has enabled this work to be a collaboration of ideas that goes beyond the traditional and almost complacent; instead it is realistically erudite and even provocative in some instances.

I suspect that the readership will likewise be broad and crosscutting—including academics and departments of psychology, political science, religious studies, military sciences, law enforcement, public health, sociology, anthropology, social work, and law, as well as the lay public and the media, policy makers, elected government officials, leaders of nongovernmental organizations, ambassadors and diplomats, military leaders, law enforcement professionals, the intelligence community, and members of think tanks and private and public policy institutes and centers.

Such integration of diversity in thought and perspective parallels our "Forum Plus" strategy at the World Economic Forum. This strategy aims to advance critical issues on the global agenda through the creation of task forces and initiatives that integrate business, governments, international organizations, civil society, academics, and technical experts.

Similarly, Dr. Stout has been successful in gathering some of the greatest thinkers on this topic from around the world, including Fulbright scholars, a Kellogg International fellow, a Pulitzer Prize winner, a Beale fellow (Harvard), a *boursier de la Confédération Suisse*, a Medical Research Council fellow, American Psychological Association fellows, a Royal College of Physicians fellow, an American College of Psychiatrists fellow, American Psychiatric Association fellows, and a Regents scholar. Authors represent a wide array of academic institutions: the University of Pennsylvania; Harvard Medical School; Rutgers University; Princeton University; Northwestern University Medical School; Mount Sinai School of Medicine; Nelson Mandela School of Medicine, University of Natal, South Africa; George Mason University; University of Massachusetts; University of Michigan; Civitan International Research Center at the University of Alabama; Institute for Mental Health Initiatives at George Washington University; Marylhurst University; Portland State University; Southwest Texas State University; Al Aksa University in Gaza; University of Lagos, Akoka-Yaba, Lagos, Nigeria; University of Wisconsin; Northern Arizona University; Bryn Mawr College; Randolph-Macon College; Illinois State University; University of South Florida; Elmhurst College; Howard University; University of Texas Health Science Center; Texas A&M College of Medicine; University of California; Saybrook Graduate School and Research Center; New School University; and New York University. Authors also represent the United Nations (a Humanitarian Affairs Officer, an Assistant to the Under-Secretary-General for Peacekeeping, and an Assistant to the Special Representative of the Secretary-General to the former Yugoslavia and to NATO), the Disaster Mental Health Institute; the Comprehensive Medical Center in Dubai, United Arab Emirates; GGZ Den Bosch/Outpatient and Daytreatment Centre for Refugees in the Netherlands; the Human Sciences Research Council in South Africa; Delta Psychiatric Teaching Hospital in Poortugaal, the Netherlands; Maagalim–Institute of Psychotherapy and Counseling in Tel Aviv; the United Nations Development Program for Women; the USAID Rwanda Rule of Law Project; and the Christian Children's Fund.

Many of the authors are also current or past officers of a wide variety of professional associations and other organizations: the World Psychiatric Association on Urban Mental Health; the Commission on Global Psychiatry of the American Psychiatric Association; the South African Institute for Traumatic Stress; Solomon Asch's Center for Ethno-Political Conflict at the University of Pennsylvania; the American Psychological Association Committee on Global Violence and Security within Division 48; the Society for the Study of Peace, Conflict, and Violence; the Association for Humanistic Psychology; the Non Governmental Organizations Executive Committee on Mental Health—UN; Psychologists for Social Responsibility; the Conflict Resolution Action Committee; the Conflict Resolution Working Group (of Division 48 of the American Psychological Association); the Philadelphia Project for Global Security; the American Academy of Psychiatry and the Law; the National Council of State Medical Directors; the Board of Presidents of the Socialist Countries' Psychiatric Associations in Sofia, Bulgaria; the Society for the Study of Peace, Conflict and Violence: Peace Psychology Division of the American Psychological Association (APA); the International Society for Political Psychology; the Committee for International Liaisons for the Division of International Psychology (APA); and the Common Bond Institute.

Dr. Stout has also assembled some of the best and the brightest to serve as his Editorial Advisory Board: Terrance Koller, Dana Royce Baerger, Malini Patel, Ron Levant, and Stephen Kouris.

The rapid growth of global communications, information technology, and international business in the second half of the twentieth century increased the need for a common platform where the stakeholders of society could be brought together to consider and advance the key issues on the global agenda. The World Economic Forum's goal is to provide that platform, asking a mix of individuals to articulate the major problems facing the world and to find solutions. Works like this are catalytic to our thinking and dialogue.

It is our hope at the Forum to support the global public interest and to improve the state of the world. I believe this series adds to such a mission by its integration of thinking and facilitation of dialogue among different stakeholders and across different regions and intellectual disciplines. This series promotes progress by expanding common ground and developing new approaches.

Klaus Schwab
Founder and President
World Economic Forum

Acknowledgments

A project such as this one—with authors from all over the world covering a breadth and depth of examination of such a complex topic—can only happen as the result of a team effort. As such, I would like first of all to thank my family. Annika, Grayson, and I have sacrificed many a weekend of playing together; and I have also missed time with my very supportive partner and wife, Dr. Karen Beckstrand. Debora Carvalko, our editor at Greenwood, has been the crucial link in this project. She has worked with herculean effort to keep things organized and working. In fact, it is thanks to her that this project was even undertaken. The Editorial Advisory Board worked diligently, reading and commenting on many more manuscripts than those seen herein. The work of Terrence Koller, Malini Patel, Dana Royce Baerger, Steven P. Kouris, and Ronald F. Levant was impeccable and key to ensuring the quality of the chapters. I am also indebted to the council of Hedwin Naimark for invaluable help and thinking.

Professor Klaus Schwab has been a valued resource to me over the years and he was kind enough to provide the foreword. Harvey Langholtz has been an ongoing source of inspiration and mentorship to me. He is without a doubt the most diplomatic of all psychologists I know (it must have been all those years at the United Nations). And, this project would have been no more than an idea without the intellectual productivity of the contributing authors. We were fortunate to have more submissions than we could use in the end, but even those whose works were not used surely had an impact on my thinking and perspective, and I am very grateful. Finally, behind-the-scenes thanks to Ralph Musicant, Lawrence W. Osborn, Phillip Zimbardo, Patrick DeLeon, and Michael Horowitz.

I am markedly indebted to you all at a level that I shall never be able to repay. My sincere thanks to each of you.

Introduction

In thinking about the words to write here, I am struck with the vast array of ironies.

I had been writing and presenting talks on issues of terrorism for a while before September 11, 2001. In June 2001, I had submitted a proposal dealing with issues of terrorism for a clinical practice conference in November 2001, and I cannot help but suspect that the proposal could easily have been rejected because of a busy agenda and other competing topics that would have been considered more important to attendees. Instead, the proposal was accepted and it was the largest crowd I have ever addressed. Standing room only, and the only presentation over the course of a three-day conference that was videotaped. Sad, indeed, how some things change. I now often find myself reminding audiences that terrorism existed before September 11, 2001. In fact, that was what my talk was about. Terrorism in Japan, in Lebanon, in Ireland. In the world. In our world. For many of us who are U.S. citizens, the term "our world" now has a new and different meaning.

I have presented and written a fair amount on terrorism, and war, and trauma, and civilian casualties. I've worked with children who have been tortured, talked with traumatized refugees, broken bread with former political prisoners, and worked with a center offering pro bono clinical services to refugees who are victims of torture. I've seen the aftermath of atrocities—exhumed corpses, mass graves, and murdered infants. I have gone on medical missions to far-off places around the world. I have slides and statistics, bar graphs and citations; I can quote numerous facts and figures. But prior to September 11, 2001, all of that was done with a certain degree of clinical detachment. I would go somewhere else, and then come home. I have not ever been in an active war zone, nor have I been a victim of a terrorist attack. After September 11, I feel a bit different.

More people now know what is meant by a "dirty bomb," or what anthrax and Cipro are, than knew before September 11. I'm not sure if that is a good thing or not. I work in Chicago, the city that again has title to the tallest building in the United States. Who could have ever imagined such an odd occurrence? The reclaiming of such a title as the result of a kiloton of destructive force toppling the towers of the World Trade Center, all for the price of a plane ticket and a box cutter. Unbelievable.

I cannot help but wonder what might have been different if the West/North had dealt before September 11 with brewing, yet largely ignored, issues—from an intelligence perspective, a psychological perspective (in all its varieties, forms, and flavors), a diplomacy and foreign policy perspective. I wonder what might have been achieved in tackling the larger dynamics of both the good and the bad that accompany globalization. All of this juxtaposed with issues of religious fundamentalism and politics. I'd like to believe things would have been better, but perhaps they would not.

Terrorism is a complex issue that does not respond well to reductionism. I apologize in advance if somehow this project looks as if it tries to simplify the complexities. My objective is not to teach the reader everything he or she ever wanted to know about terrorism in four easy lessons, but rather to offer a sampling of diverse and rich thought. Perhaps this can be the spark that starts a dialogue or a debate. That is OK by me. I have been amazed at the diversity, if not downright division, of some of the opinions and resultant debates following September 11. There are arguments regarding violent and aggressive responses versus forgiveness and passivism, evil versus good, behavioral reinforcement versus social psychology theories, isolationism versus globalism, "we are victims" versus "we brought this on ourselves," and my favorite dichotomy—"this is a start of the end" versus "this is the start of a new beginning." I think back to the horrible nature of the Oklahoma City bombing. That event was not at the same level as the New York and D.C. attacks in terms of the loss of life, damage, destruction and, frankly, vast media coverage. But the horror may also be mitigated by the fact that it was done by a McVeigh, not a bin Laden.

Everything is a political act, it simply cannot be escaped. A lack of political participation (such as not voting) or a lack of political activism (such as not supporting a cause) is still a political act (as in support of a status quo). As you will see, some of our authors are academics, some are clinicians, and some are activists. Try as we all do to check our political biases at the door, they surely squeak in, and most likely in ways that are difficult to see. I hope that an Editorial Advisory Board makes it more difficult to miss these biases, but I still suggest that readers, like all good academics, seek to understand by questioning assumptions and looking for empirical evidence wherever possible. Certainly this topic may often not comply with such methods, but we have all tried our best to present good scholarship herein.

This project started out as one book. It quickly grew to four volumes. Many more chapters went unused due to space limitations, duplication, or other technical reasons. There simply is no singular psychology of terrorism, no unified field theory if you will. None of the chapters is a stand-alone work; they are best understood in the greater context of the book, and then likewise in the wider context of the series. In some instances, the reader may see differences of perspectives or tensions between viewpoints. None of the books is a homogenized or sterile rendition of information. Personally, I find it difficult to talk about terrorism without also talking about war. And it's hard to discuss war without getting into issues of torture. Similarly, it's difficult to discuss torture without also discussing violence, and so forth. Thus, in this project on terrorism, readers will see discussions concerning such various related issues, because none of these issues can easily or correctly be dis-integrated from terrorism. Thus these four books emanated from an organic, self-organizing developmental process, resulting in:

I.   The Psychology of Terrorism: A Public Understanding
II.   The Psychology of Terrorism: Clinical Aspects and Responses
III.   The Psychology of Terrorism: Theoretical Understandings and Perspectives (with a special section on the Roles and Impacts of Religions)
IV.   The Psychology of Terrorism: Programs and Practices in Response and Prevention

While there is no unifying perspective per se, I hope that these books may act as a unified source of perspectives. Also, they are incomplete. Individuals representing even more perspectives had hoped to contribute, but the realities prevented them from doing so. Certainly there will be continued interest, and I hope to see much more on these issues as we all become more aware and wise.

Volume I—A Public Understanding—provides an overview of issues in a way to help the public, in general, better understand the various issues involved. Volume II—Clinical Aspects and Responses—is an adequately telling title and offers much in the way of dealing with the emotional impacts of such traumas. Volume III—Theoretical Understandings and Perspectives—offers various perspectives of psychological understanding and theory intertwined with culture, context, politics, globalization, and social injustice as well as diplomatic processes. This volume also has a special section on the roles and impacts of religions that covers apocalyptic dreams, cults, religious archetypes, Islamic fundamentalism, and religious fanaticism.

Volume IV—Programs and Practices in Response and Prevention—provides a mix of preventative ideas and methods for youth and communities, as well as therapeutic aspects for those in trouble. For example, it includes articles on ethnopolitical warfare, family traumatic stress and refugee children; children's responses to traumatic events; aggression in adolescents; peace building; cooperative learning communities; antiviolence programming in school settings; and raising inclusively caring children. Granted, not all of these programs can be applied to a global set of venues, but they may offer much to those interested in developing their own variations on the theme.

What is my goal with this project? As noted earlier, I hope it provides readers with a mix of opinion and perspectives from which further thought and dialogue may occur. As you read these volumes, I would like you to keep in mind that through the work you do, no matter who you are, you can have an impact upon others that affects not only the individuals you encounter today, but potentially generations thereafter.

Part I:
Terrorism in Context

1

Psychological Issues in Understanding Terrorism and the Response to Terrorism

Clark McCauley

This chapter begins with a brief effort to put modern terrorism in context. Thereafter, the chapter is divided into two main sections. The first section deals with psychological issues involved in understanding the perpetrators of terrorism, including their motivations and strategies. The second section deals with the U.S. response to terrorism, including issues of fear and identity shift in reaction to the events of September 11, 2001. I cannot offer a full review of the literature related to even one of these issues, and for some issues there is so little relevant literature that I can only point in the general directions that research might take. In using a very broad brush, I need to apologize in advance to scholars whose knowledge and contributions are not adequately represented here. A little theory can be a dangerous thing, especially in the hands of a nonspecialist in the relevant area of theory. But the events of September 11 warrant some additional risk-taking in connecting psychological research to understanding of the origins and effects of terrorism.

TERRORISM AS A CATEGORY OF VIOLENCE

Violence and the threat of violence to control people is an idea older than history, but the use of the word *terror* to refer to political violence goes back only to the French Revolution of the 1790s. The revolutionaries, threatened by resistance within France and foreign armies at its borders, undertook a Reign of Terror to suppress the enemy within. This first violence to be called terrorism had the power of the state behind it. Terrorism today is usually associated with political violence perpetrated by groups without the power of the state. Few of these nonstate groups have referred to themselves as terrorists, although prominent exceptions include the Russian Narodnaya Volya in the late 1800s and the Zionist Stern Gang of the late 1940s. Most nonstate terrorists see themselves as revolutionaries or freedom fighters.

State terrorism was not only first, it continues to be more dangerous. Rummel (1996) estimates 170 million people were killed by government in the twentieth century, not including 34 million dead in battle. Most of the victims were killed by their own government, or, more precisely, by the government controlling the area in which the victims were living. Stalin, Mao, and Hitler were the biggest killers (42 million, 37 million, 20 million killed, respectively), with Pol Pot's killing of 2 million Cambodians coming in only seventh in the pantheon of killers. By comparison, killing by nonstate groups is minuscule. Rummel estimates 500,000 killed in the twentieth century by terrorists, guerrillas, and other nonstate groups. State terrorism is thus greater by a ratio of about 260 to 1. Worldwide, Myers (2001) counts 2,527 deaths from terrorism in all of the 1990s. Three thousand terrorist victims on September 11 is thus a big increment in the killing done by terrorists, but does not change the scale of the comparison: State terrorism is by far the greater danger.

Despite the origin of the term *terrorism* in reference to state terror, and despite the pre-eminence of state terror in relation to nonstate terror, terrorism today is usually understood to mean nonstate terrorism. Nonstate terrorism includes both anti-state terror and vigilante terror, but it is usually anti-state terrorism that is the focus of attention—violence against recognized states by small groups without the power of a state. Most definitions of anti-state terrorism also include the idea of violence against noncombatants, especially women and children, although the suicide bombing of the U.S. Marine barracks in Beirut in 1984 is often referred to as terrorism, as is the September 11 attack on the Pentagon.

Anti-state terrorism cannot be understood outside the context of state terrorism. Compared with the nineteenth century, the twentieth century saw massive increases in state power. The modern state reaches deeper into the lives of citizens than ever before. It collects more in taxes, and its regulations, rewards, and punishments push further into work, school, and neighborhood. The state culture is thus ever harder to resist; any culture group that does not control a state is likely to feel in danger of extinction. But resistance to state culture faces state power that continues to grow. It is in the context of growing state power that anti-state terrorists can feel increasingly desperate.

Much has been written about how to define anti-state terrorism, but I generally agree with those who say the difference between a terrorist and a freedom fighter is mostly in the politics of the beholder (see McCauley, 1991, and McCauley, in press-b, for more on this issue). The psychological question is how members of a small group without the power of a state become capable of political violence that includes violence against noncombatants. In the remainder of this chapter, I follow common usage in referring to anti-state terrorism simply as "terrorism."

TERRORIST MOTIVATIONS

Individuals become terrorists in many different ways and for many different reasons. Here I will simplify to consider three kinds of explanation of the September 11 attacks: they are crazy, they are crazed by hatred and anger, or they are rational within their own perspective. My argument is that terrorism is not to be understood as pathology, and that terrorists emerge out of a normal psychology of emotional commitment to cause and comrades.

Terrorism as Individual Pathology

A common suggestion is that there must be something wrong with terrorists. Terrorists must be crazy, or suicidal, or psychopaths without moral feelings. Only someone with something wrong with him could do the cold-blooded killing that a terrorist does.

The Search for Pathology

Thirty years ago, this suggestion was taken very seriously, but thirty years of research has found little evidence that terrorists are suffering from psychopathology. This research has profited by what now amount to hundreds of interviews with terrorists. Some terrorists are captured and interviewed in prison. Some active terrorists can be found in their home neighborhoods, if the interviewer knows where to look. And some retired terrorists are willing to talk about their earlier activities, particularly if these activities were successful. Itzhak Shamir and Menachem Begin, for instance, moved from anti-Arab and anti-British terrorism to leadership of the state of Israel. Interviews with terrorists rarely find any disorder listed in the American Psychiatric Association's *Diagnostic and Statistical Manual of Mental Disorders.*

More systematic research confirms the interview results. Particularly thorough were the German studies of the Baader-Meinhof Gang. Although the terrorists had gone underground and their locations were unknown, their identities were known. Excellent German records provided a great deal of information about each individual. Prenatal records, perinatal records, pediatric records, preschool records, lower-school records, grade school records, high school records, university records (most had had some university education)—all of these were combed for clues to understanding these individuals. Family, neighbors, schoolmates—all those who had known an individual before the leap to terrorism—were interviewed. A comparison sample of individuals from the same neighborhoods, matched for gender, age, and socioeconomic status, was similarly studied. The results of these investigations take several feet of shelf space, but are easy to summarize. The terrorists did not differ from the comparison group of nonterrorists in any substantial way; in particular, the terrorists did not show higher rates of any kind of psychopathology.

Terrorists as Psychopaths

Some have suggested that terrorists are antisocial personalities or psychopaths. Psychopaths can be intelligent and very much in contact with reality; their problem is that they are socially and morally deficient. They are law-breakers, deceitful, aggressive, and reckless in disregarding the safety of self and others. They do not feel remorse for hurting others. As some individuals cannot see color, psychopaths cannot feel empathy or affection for others.

Explaining terrorism as the work of psychopaths brings a new difficulty, however. The September 11 attackers were willing to give their lives in the attack. So far as I am aware, no one has ever suggested that a psychopath's moral blindness can take the form of self-sacrifice. In addition, psychopaths are notably impulsive and irresponsible. The mutual commitment and trust evident within each of the four groups of attackers, and in the cooperation between groups, are radically inconsistent with the psychopathic personality.

It is possible that a terrorist group might recruit a psychopath for a particular mission, if the mission requires inflicting pain or death without the distraction of sympathy for the victims, but the mission would have to be a one-person job, something that requires little or no coordination and trust. And the mission would have to offer a reasonable chance of success without suicide.

The Case Against Pathology

Of course there are occasional lone bombers or lone gunmen who kill for political causes, and such individuals may indeed suffer from some form of psychopathology. A loner like Theodore Kaczynski, the "Unabomber," sending out letter bombs in occasional forays from his wilderness cabin, may suffer from psychopathology. But terrorists operating in groups, especially groups that can organize attacks that are successful, are very unlikely to suffer from serious psychopathology.

Indeed, terrorism would be a trivial problem if only those with some kind of psychopathology could be terrorists. Rather, we have to face the fact that normal people can be terrorists, that we are ourselves capable of terrorist acts under some circumstances. This fact is already implied in recognizing that military and police forces involved in state terrorism are all too capable of killing noncombatants. Few would suggest that the broad range of soldiers and policemen involved in such killing must all be suffering some kind of psychopathology.

Terrorism as Emotional Expression

When asked at a press conference on October 11, 2001, why people in the Muslim world hate the United States, President Bush expressed amazement and replied, "That's because they don't know us."

President Bush is not the only one to accept the idea that the September 11 attacks were an expression of hatred. "Why do they hate us?" has been the headline of numerous stories and editorials in newspapers and magazines. Despite the headlines, there has been little analysis of what hatred means or where it may come from.

Hatred and Anger

The surprising fact is that, although a few psychoanalysts have discussed hatred, there is very little psychological research focused on hate or hatred. Gordon Allport (1954) offered brief mention of hatred in writing about *The Nature of Prejudice*, and more recently Marilyn Brewer (2001) has asked "When does ingroup love become outgroup hate?" But empirical research on hatred, particularly research that distinguishes hatred from anger, is notably absent. In contrast, there is a large and well-developed research literature on the emotion of anger. Does hatred mean anything more than strong anger? An example suggests that hatred may be different. A parent can be angry with a misbehaving child, angry to the point of striking the child. But even caught up in that violence, the parent would not hate the child.

A few differences between anger and hatred show up in the way these words are used in everyday speech. Anger is hot, hatred can be cold. Anger is a response to a particular incident or offense; hatred expresses a longer-term relation of antipathy. We sometimes talk about hatred when we mean only strong dislike, as in "I hate broccoli," but even in this usage there is the sense of a long-term unwavering dislike, a dislike without exceptions, and perhaps even the wish that broccoli should be wiped from every menu.

In *The Deadly Ethnic Riot*, Donald Horowitz offers a distinction between anger and hatred that is consistent with the language just considered. Horowitz (2001, p. 543) quotes Aristotle as follows: "The angry man wants the object of his anger to suffer in return; hatred wishes its object not to exist." This distinction begs for a parallel distinction in offenders or offenses, a distinction that can predict when an offense leads to anger and when to hatred. One possibility (see also Brewer, 2001) is that an offense that includes long-term threat is more likely to elicit the desire to eliminate the offender. The emotional reaction to threat is fear. Thus hatred may be a compound of anger and fear, such that anger alone aims to punish whereas hatred aims to obliterate the threat. If hatred is related to anger, then research on anger may be able to help us understand the behavior of terrorists.

The Psychology of Anger

Explanation of terrorism as the work of people blinded by anger is at least generally consistent with what is known about the emotion of anger. In particular, there is reason to believe that anger does get in the way of judgment. In *Passions Within Reason*, Robert Frank (1988) argues that blindness to self-interest is the evolutionary key to anger. If each individual acted rationally on self-interest, the strong could do anything they wanted to the weak. Both would realize that the weaker cannot win and the weaker would always defer to the stronger. But anger can lead the weaker to attack the stronger despite the objective balance of forces. The stronger will win, but he will suffer some costs along the way and the possibility of these costs restrains the demands of the stronger.

This perspective suggests an evolutionary advantage for individuals for whom anger can conquer fear. The result should be a gradual increase in the proportion of individuals who are capable of anger. Everyday experience suggests that most people are capable of anger under the right circumstances. What are those circumstances—that is, what are the elicitors of anger?

There are basically two theories of anger (Sabini, 1995, pp. 411–428). The first, which comes to us from Aristotle, says that anger is the emotional reaction to insult—an offense in which the respect or status due to an individual is violated. The second, which emerged from experimental research with animals, says that anger is the emotional reaction to pain, especially the pain of frustration. Frustration is understood as the failure to receive an expected reward. These theories obviously have a great deal in common. Respect expected but not forthcoming is a painful frustration. For our purposes, the two theories differ chiefly in their emphasis on material welfare. Insult is subjective, asocial, whereas at least some interpretations of frustration include objective poverty and powerlessness as frustrations that can lead to anger. This interpretation of frustration–aggression theory was popular at the 2002 World Economic Forum, at which many luminaries cited material deprivation as the cause or at least an important cause of violence aimed at the West (Friedman, 2002a).

Individual Frustration and Insult

The immediate difficulty of seeing the September 11 terrorists as crazed with anger is the fact, much cited by journalists and pundits, that the September 11 terrorists were not obviously suffering from frustration or insult. Mohammed Atta came from a middle-class family in Egypt, studied architecture in Cairo, traveled to Hamburg, Germany, for further studies in architecture, and had a part-time job doing architectural drawings for a German firm. His German thesis, on the ancient architecture of Aleppo, was well received. According to Thomas Friedman's (2002b) inquiries, several others of the September 11 pilot-leaders came from similar middle-class backgrounds, with similar threads of personal success.

The origins of the September 11 terrorist-leaders are thus strikingly different from the origins of the Palestinian suicide terrorists that Ariel Merari has been studying for decades in Israel (Lelyveld, 2001). The Palestinian terrorists are young, male, poor, and uneducated. Their motivations are manifold but notably include the several thousand dollars awarded to the family of a Palestinian martyr. The amount is small by Western standards but enough to lift a Palestinian family out of abject poverty, including support for parents and aged relatives and a dowry for the martyr's sisters. It is easy to characterize these suicide terrorists as frustrated by poverty and hopelessness, with frustration leading to anger against Israel as the perceived source of their problems.

But this explanation does not fit at least the leaders of the September 11 terrorists. Whence their anger, if anger is the explanation of their attacks? Perhaps they are angry, not about their own personal experience of frustration and insult, but about the frustrations and insults experienced by their group.

Group Frustration and Insult

In the *Handbook of Social Psychology*, Kinder (1998) summarizes the accumulated evidence that political opinions are only weakly predicted by narrow self-interest and more strongly predicted by group interest. The poor do not support welfare policies more than others, young males are not less in favor of war than others, parents of school-age children are not more opposed than others to busing for desegregation. Rather it is group interest that is the useful predictor. Sympathy for the poor predicts favoring increased welfare. Sympathy for African Americans predicts support for busing and other desegregation policies. Unless individual self-interest is exceptionally large and clear cut, voters' opinions are not self-centered but group-centered.

Similarly, Kinder recounts evidence that political action, including protest and confrontation, is motivated more by identification with group interest than by self-interest.

> Thus participation of black college students in the civil rights movement in the American South in the 1960s was predicted better by their anger over society's treatment of black Americans in general than by any discontent they felt about their own lives. . . . Thus white working-class participants in the Boston antibusing movement were motivated especially by their resentments about the gains of blacks and professionals, and less by their own personal troubles. (Kinder, 1998, p. 831)

Group identification makes sense of sacrifice from individuals who are not personally frustrated or insulted. The mistake is to imagine that self-sacrifice must come from personal problems, rather than identification with group problems. This mistake rests in ignorance of the fact that many post-World War II terrorists have been individuals of middle-class origins, people with options. The Baader-Meinhof Gang in Germany, the Red Brigade in Italy, the Weather Underground in the United States—these and many other post-WWII terrorist groups are made up mostly of individuals with middle-class origins and middle-class skills honed by at least some university education (McCauley & Segal, 1987). Explaining self-sacrifice as a result of personal problems is no more persuasive for terrorists than for Mother Teresa or U.S. Medal of Honor winners.

The power of group identification is thus the foundation of intergroup conflict, especially for large groups where individual self-interest is probably maximized by free-riding, that is, by letting other group members pay the costs of advancing group welfare that the individual will profit from. Here I am asserting briefly what I elsewhere argue for in more detail (McCauley, 2001; McCauley, in press-a).

The explanation of terrorist sacrifice as a fit of anger overcoming self-interest can now be reformulated in terms of anger over group insult and group frustration. The potential origins of such anger are not difficult to discern.

Insult and Frustration as Seen by Muslims (and Others)

From Morocco to Pakistan lies a belt of Muslim states in which governments have police and military power but little public support. The gulf between rich and poor is deep and wide in these countries, and government is associated with Western-leaning elites for whom government, not private enterprise, is the source of wealth. Political threat to the state is not tolerated; imprisonment, torture, and death are the tools of the state against political opposition. As the Catholic Church in Poland under communism came to be the principal refuge of political opposition, so fundamentalist Muslim mosques are the principal refuge of political opposition to government in these states.

In this conflict between Muslim governments and Muslim peoples, the United States and other Western countries have supported the governments. When the Algerian government was about to lose an election to the Islamic Salvation Front in 1992, the government annulled the election and Europeans and Americans were glad to accept the lesser of two evils. Western countries have supported authoritarian governments of Egypt, Jordan, and Pakistan with credits and military assistance. U.S. support for Israel against the Palestinians is only one part of this pattern of supporting power against people.

Al-Qaeda is an association of exiles and refugees from the political violence going on in Muslim countries. Long before declaring *jihad* against the United States, bin Laden was attacking the house of Saud for letting U.S. troops remain in the holy land of Mecca and Medina after the Gulf War. Fifteen of the September 11 terrorists came originally from Saudi Arabia, although most seem to have been recruited from the Muslim diaspora in Europe. The United States has become a target because it is seen as supporting the governments that created the diaspora. The United States is in the position of someone who has stumbled into a family feud. If this scenario seems strained, consider the parallel between Muslims declaring *jihad* on the United States for supporting state terrorism in Muslim countries, and the United States declaring war on any country that supports terrorism against the United States.

It is important to recognize that it is not only Arab and Muslim countries in which U.S. policies are seen as responsible for terrorist attacks against the United States In an IHT/Pew poll of 275 "opinion-makers" in twenty-four countries, respondents were asked how many ordinary people think that U.S. policies and actions in the world were a major cause of the September 11 attack (Knowlton, 2001). In the United States, only 18 percent of respondents said many people think this; in twenty-three other countries, an average of 58 percent said most or many people think this. In Islamic countries, 76 percent said most or many think this, and even in Western European countries, 36 percent said most or many think this. Americans do not have to accept the judgments of other countries, but will have to deal with them.

Anger or Love?

If group identification can lead to anger for frustrations and insults suffered by the group, it yet remains to be determined if there is any evidence of such emotions in the September 11 terrorists. Our best guide to the motives of those who carried out the attacks of September 11 is the document found in the luggage of several of the attackers. Four of the five pages of this document have been released by the FBI and these pages have been translated and interpreted by Makiya and Mneimneh (2002). I am indebted to Hassan Mneimneh for his assistance in understanding this document.

The four pages are surprising for what they do not contain. There is no list of group frustrations and insults, no litany of injustice to justify violence. "The sense throughout is that the would-be martyr is engaged in his action solely to please God. There is no mention of any communal purpose behind his behavior. In all of the four pages available to us there is not a word or an implication about any wrongs that are to be redressed through martyrdom, whether in Palestine or Iraq or in 'the land of Muhammad,' the phrase bin Laden used in the al-Jazeera video that was shown after September 11" (Makiya & Mneimneh, 2002, p. 21). Indeed, the text cites approvingly a story from the Koran about Ali ibn Talib, cousin and son-in-law of the Prophet, who is spat upon by an infidel in combat. The Muslim holds his sword until he can master the impulse for vengeance—an individual and human motive—and strikes only when he can strike for the sake of God.

Rather than anger or hatred, the dominant message of the text is a focus on the eternal. There are many references to the Koran, and the vocabulary departs from seventh-century Arabic only for a few references to modern concepts such as airport and plane (and these modern words are reduced to one-letter abbreviations). To feel connection with God and the work of God, to feel the peace of submission to God's will—these are the imperatives and the promises of the text. Invocations and prayers are to be offered at every stage of the journey: the last night, the journey to the airport, boarding the plane, takeoff, taking the plane, welcoming death. The reader is reminded that fear is an act of worship due only to God. If killing is necessary, the language of the text makes the killing a ritual slaughter with vocabulary that refers to animal sacrifice, including the sacrifice of Isaac that Abraham was prepared to offer.

Judging from this text, the psychology of the September 11 terrorists is not a psychology of anger, or hatred, or vengeance. The terrorists are not righting human wrongs but acting with God and for God against evil. In most general terms, it is a psychology of attachment to the good rather than a psychology of hatred for evil. Research with U.S. soldiers in World War II found something similar; hatred of the enemy was a minor motive in combat performance, whereas attachment to buddies and not wanting to let them down was a major motive (Stouffer et al.,

1949). This resonance with the psychology of combat—a psychology usually treated as normal psychology—again suggests the possibility that terrorism and terrorists may be more normal than is usually recognized.

Terrorism as Normal Psychology

The trajectory by which normal people become capable of doing terrible things is usually gradual, perhaps imperceptible to the individual. This is among other things a moral trajectory, such as Sprinzak (1991) and Horowitz (2001) have described. In too-simple terms, terrorists kill for the same reasons that groups have killed other groups for centuries. They kill for cause and comrades, that is, with a combination of ideology and intense small-group dynamics. The cause that is worth killing for and dying for is not abstract but personal—a view of the world that makes sense of life and death and links the individual to some form of immortality.

The Psychology of Cause

Every normal person believes in something more important than life. We have to, because, unlike other animals, we know that we are going to die. We need something that makes sense of our life and our death, something that makes our death different from the death of a squirrel lying by the side of the road as we drive to work. The closer and more immediate death is, the more we need the group values that give meaning to life and death. These include the values of family, religion, ethnicity, and nationality—the values of our culture. Dozens of experiments have shown that thinking about death, their own death, leads people to embrace more strongly the values of their culture (Pyszcznski, Greenberg, & Solomon, 1997).

These values do not have to be explicitly religious. Many of the terrorist groups since World War II have been radical-socialist groups with purely secular roots: the Red Brigade in Italy, the Baader-Meinhof Gang in Germany, the Shining Path in Peru. Animal rights and saving the environment can be causes that justify terrorism. For much of the twentieth century, atheistic communism was such a cause. Thus there is no special relation between religion and violence; religion is only one kind of cause in which individuals can find an answer to mortality.

What is essential is that the cause should have the promise of a long and glorious future. History is important in supporting this promise. A cause invented yesterday cannot easily be seen to have a glorious and indefinite future. The history must be a group history. No one ever seems to have had the idea that she or he alone will achieve some kind of immortality. Immortality comes as part of a group: family group, cultural group, religious group, or ideological group. A good participant in the group, one who lives up to the norms of the group and contributes to the group, will to that extent live on after death as part of the group. The meaning of the individual's life is the future of the cause, embodied in the group that goes on into the future after the individual is dead.

The Psychology of Comrades

The group's values are focused to a personal intensity in the small group of like-minded people who perpetrate terrorist violence. Most individuals belong to many groups—family, co-workers, neighborhood, religion, country—and each of these groups has some influence on individual beliefs and behavior. Different groups have different values, and the competition of values reduces the power of any one group over its members. But members of an underground terrorist group have put this group first in their lives, dropping or reducing every other connection. The power of this one group is now enormous, and extends to every kind of personal and moral judgment. This is the power that can make violence against the enemy not just acceptable but necessary.

Every army aims to do what the terrorist group does: to link a larger group cause with the small-group dynamics that can deliver individuals to sacrifice. Every army cuts trainees off from their previous lives so that the combat unit can become their family; their fellow-soldiers become their brothers and their fear of letting down their comrades becomes greater than their fear of dying. The power of an isolating group over its members is not limited to justifying violence. Many nonviolent groups also gain power by separating individuals from groups that might offer competing values. Groups using this tactic include religious cults, drug treatment centers, and residential schools and colleges. In brief, the psychology behind terrorist violence is normal psychology, abnormal only in the intensity of the group dynamics that link cause with comrades.

Some commentators have noted that the September 11 terrorists, at least the pilot-leaders, spent long periods of time dispersed in the United States. How could the intense group dynamics that are typical of underground groups be maintained in dispersal? There are two possible answers. The first is that physical dispersal is not the same as developing new group connections. It seems that the dispersed terrorists lived without close connections to others outside the terrorist group. They did not take interesting jobs, become close to co-workers, or develop romantic relationships. Although living apart, they remained connected to and anchored in only one group, their terrorist group.

The second possibility is that group dynamics can be less important to the extent that the cause—the ideology of the cause—is more important. As noted earlier, the pilot-leaders of the September 11 terrorists were not poor or untalented; they were men with a middle-class background and education. For educated men, the power of ideas may substitute to some degree for the everyday reinforcement of a like-minded group. Indeed, the terrorist document referred to above is a kind of manual for using control of attention to control behavior, and this kind of manual should work better for individuals familiar with the attractions of ideas. Probably both possibilities—a social world reduced to one group despite physical dispersal, and a group of individuals for whom the ideology of cause is unusually important and powerful—contributed to the cohesion of the September 11 perpetrators.

The Psychology of Cult Recruiting

Studies of recruiting for the Unification Church provide some insight into individual differences in vulnerability to the call of cause and comrades (McCauley & Segal, 1987). Galanter (1980) surveyed participants in Unification Church recruiting workshops in southern California, and found that the best predictor of who becomes a member was the answer to a question about how close the individual feels to people outside the Unification Church. Those with outside attachments were more likely to leave, whereas those without outside connections are more likely to join. This is the power of comrades. Barker (1984) surveyed participants in Unification Church recruiting workshops in London, and found that the best predictor of who becomes a member was the answer to a question about goals. Those who said "something but I don't know what" were more likely to join. This is the power of cause, a group cause that can give meaning to an individual's life. Terrorist groups, like cult groups, cut the individual off from other contacts and are particularly attractive to individuals without close connections and the meaning that comes with group anchoring. Only those who have never had the experience of feeling cut off from family, friends, and work will want to see this kind of vulnerability as a kind of pathology. The rest of us will feel fortunate that we did not at this point in our lives encounter someone recruiting for a cult or terrorist group.

The Psychology of Crisis

The psychology of cause and comrades is multiplied by a sense of crisis. Many observers have noted an apocalyptic quality in the worldview of terrorists. Terrorists see the world precariously balanced between good and evil, at a point where action can bring about the triumph of the good. The "end times" or the millennium or the triumph of the working class is near, or can be made near by the right action. Action, extreme action, is required immediately, for the triumph of the good and the defeat of evil. This "ten minutes to midnight" feeling is part of what makes it possible for normal people to risk their lives in violence.

Consider the passengers of the hijacked flight that crashed in western Pennsylvania. The passengers found out from their cell phones that hijacked planes had crashed into the World Trade Center. They had every reason to believe that their plane was on its way to a similar end. Unarmed, they decided to attack the hijackers, and sacrificed their lives in bringing the plane down before it could impact its intended target, which was probably the Pentagon or the White House. When it is ten minutes to midnight, there is little to lose and everything to gain.

The sense of crisis is usually associated with an overwhelming threat. In the case of the September 11 terrorists, the threat seems to be a fear that fundamentalist Muslim culture is in danger of being overwhelmed by Western culture. The military and economic power of the West, and the relative feebleness of once-great Muslim nations in the modern era, are submerging Muslims in a tidal wave of individualism and irreligion. Note that it is attachment to a view of what Muslims should be and fear for the future of Muslims that are the emotional foundations of the terrorists. They do not begin from hatred of the West, but from love of their own group and culture that they see in danger of extinction from the power of the West.

Similarly, the United States, mobilized by President Bush for a war against terrorism, does not begin from hatred of al-Qaeda but from love of country. Mobilization includes a rhetoric of crisis, of impending threat from an evil enemy or, more recently, an "axis of evil." Americans' anger toward al-Qaeda, and perhaps more broadly toward Arabs and Muslims, is not an independent emotion but a product of patriotism combined with a crisis of threat.

The Psychology of the Slippery Slope

The sense of crisis does not spring full-blown upon an individual. It is the end of a long trajectory to terrorism, a trajectory in which the individual moves slowly toward an apocalyptic view of the world and a correspondingly extreme behavioral commitment. Sprinzak (1991) has distinguished three stages in this trajectory: a *crisis of confidence*, in which a group protests and demonstrates against the prevailing political system with a criticism that yet accepts the system's values; a *conflict of legitimacy*, in which the group loses confidence in reform and advances a competing ideological and cultural system while moving to angry protest and small-scale violence; and a *crisis of legitimacy*, in which the group embraces terrorist violence against the government and everyone who supports the government. Whether as an individual joining an extreme group, or as a member of a group that becomes more extreme over time, the individual becomes more extreme in a series of steps so small as to be near invisible. The result is a terrorist who may look back at the transition to terrorism with no sense of having ever made an explicit choice.

Psychology offers several models of this kind of slippery slope (see McCauley & Segal, 1987, for more detail). One is Milgram's obedience experiment, in which 60 percent of subjects are willing to deliver the maximum shock level ("450 volts XXX Danger Strong Shock") to a supposed fellow subject in a supposed learning experiment. In one variation of the experiment, Milgram had the experimenter called away on a pretext and another supposed subject came up with the idea of raising the shock one level with each mistake from the "learner." In this variation, 20 percent went on to deliver maximum shock. The 20 percent yielding cannot be attributed to the authority of the experimenter and is most naturally understood as the power of self-justification acting on the small increments in shock level. Each shock delivered becomes a reason for giving the next higher shock, because the small increments in shock mean that the subject has to see something at least a little wrong with the last shock if there is something wrong with the next one. A clear choice between good and evil would be a shock generator with only two levels, 15 volts and 450 volts, but the 20 percent who go all the way never see a clear choice between good and evil.

Another model of the terrorist trajectory is more explicitly social-psychological. Group extremity shift, the tendency for group opinion to become more extreme in the direction initially favored by most individuals, is currently understood in terms of two mechanisms: relevant arguments and social comparison (Brown, 1986, pp.

200–244). Relevant arguments explains the shift as a result of individuals hearing new arguments in discussion that are biased in the initially favored direction. Social comparison explains the shift as a competition for status in which no one wants to fall behind in supporting the group-favored direction. In the trajectory to terrorism, initial beliefs and commitments favor action against injustice, and group discussion and ingroup status competition move the group toward more extreme views and more extreme violence.

The slippery slope is not something that happens only in psychology experiments and foreign countries. Since September 11, there have already been suggestions from reputable people that U.S. security forces may need to use torture to get information from suspected terrorists. This is the edge of a slope that leads down and away from the rule of law and the presumption of innocence.

Terrorism as Strategy

Psychologists recognize two kinds of aggression, emotional and instrumental. Emotional aggression is associated with anger and does not calculate long-term consequences. The reward of emotional aggression is hurting someone who has hurt you. Instrumental aggression is more calculating—the use of aggression as a means to other ends. The balance between these two in the behavior of individual terrorists is usually not clear and might usefully be studied more explicitly in the future. The balance may be important in determining how to respond to terrorism: As argued above, emotional aggression should be less sensitive to objective rewards and punishments, while instrumental aggression should be more sensitive.

Of course, the balance may be very different in those who perpetrate the violence than in those who plan it. The planners are probably more instrumental; they are usually thinking about what they want to accomplish. They aim to inflict long-term costs on their enemy and to gain long-term advantage for themselves.

Material Damage to the Enemy

Terrorism inflicts immediate damage in destroying lives and property, but terrorists hope that the long-term costs will be much greater. They want to create fear and uncertainty far beyond the victims and those close to them. They want their enemy to spend time and money on security. In effect, the terrorists aim to lay an enormous tax on every aspect of the enemy's society, a tax that transfers resources from productive purposes to anti-productive security measures. The costs of increased security are likely to be particularly high for a country like the United States, where an open society is the foundation of economic success and a high-tech military.

The United States is already paying enormous taxes of this kind. Billions more dollars are going to the FBI, the CIA, the Pentagon, the National Security Agency, and a new bureaucracy for the director of homeland security. Billions are going to bail out the airlines, to increase the number and quality of airport security personnel, to pay the National Guard stationed at airports. The costs to business activity are perhaps even greater. Long lines at airport security and fear of air travel cut business travel and holiday travel. Hotel bookings are down, urban restaurant business is down, all kinds of tourist businesses are down. Long lines of trucks at the Canadian and Mexican borders are slowed for more intensive searches, and the delays necessarily contribute to the cost of goods transported. The Coast Guard and the Immigration and Naturalization Service focus on terrorism and decrease attention to the drug trade. I venture to guess that the costs of increased security and the war on terrorism will far outrun the costs of losses at the World Trade Center and the reparations to survivors of those who died there.

Political Damage to the Enemy

In the longer term, the damage terrorism does to civil society may be greater than any dollar costs (see McCauley, in press-b). The response to terrorism inevitably builds the power of the state at the expense of the civil society. The adage that "war is the health of the state" is evident to anyone who tracks the growth of the federal government in the United States. With every war—the Civil War, World War I, World War II, the Korean War, the Vietnam War, the Gulf War, and now the war against terrorism—the power of the government has grown in directions and degrees that are not relinquished after the war has ended. During World War II, for example, the income tax, which previously had applied only to high-income people, was imposed even on low-income people. The federal government also introduced withholding to make it easier to collect tax money. After the war, income taxes and tax withholding remained as a normal part of American life (Higgs, 1987).

Polls taken in years preceding the terrorist attack on September 11 indicate that about half of adult Americans saw the federal government as a threat to the rights and freedoms of ordinary Americans. No doubt fewer would say so in the aftermath of the recent attacks, a shift consistent with the adage that "war is the health of the state." But if more security could ensure the safety of the nation, the Soviet Union would still be with us. It is possible that bin Laden had the Soviet Union in mind in an interview broadcast by CNN. "Osama bin Laden told a reporter with the Al Jazeera network in October that 'freedom and human rights in America are doomed' and that the U.S. government would lead its people and the West 'into an unbearable hell and a choking life'" (Kurtz, 2002).

Mobilizing the Ingroup

Terrorists particularly hope to elicit a violent response that will assist them in mobilizing their own people. A terrorist group is the apex of a pyramid of supporters and sympathizers. The base of the pyramid is composed of all those who sympathize with the terrorist cause even though they may disagree with the violent means that the terrorists use. In Northern Ireland, for instance, the base of the pyramid is all who agree with "Brits Out." In the Islamic world, the base of the pyramid is all those who agree that the United States has been hurting and humiliating Muslims for fifty years. The pyramid is essential to the terrorists for cover and for recruits. The terrorists hope that a clumsy and overgeneralized strike against them will hit some of those in the pyramid below them. The blow will enlarge their base of sympathy, turn the sympathetic but unmobilized to action and sacrifice, and strengthen their own status as leaders at the apex of this pyramid.

Al-Qaeda had reason to be hopeful that U.S. strength could help them. In 1986, for instance, the United States attempted to reply to Libyan-supported terrorism by bombing Libya's leader, Muammar Qaddafi. The bombs missed Qaddafi's residence but hit a nearby apartment building and killed a number of women and children. This mistake was downplayed in the United States but it was a public relations success for anti-U.S. groups across North Africa. In 1998, the United States attempted to reply to al-Qaeda attacks on U.S. embassies in Africa by sending cruise missiles against terrorist camps in Afghanistan and against a supposed bomb factory in Khartoum, Sudan. It appears now that the "bomb factory" was in fact producing only medical supplies.

A violent response to terrorism that is not well aimed is a success for the terrorists. The Taliban did their best to play up U.S. bombing mistakes in Afghanistan, but were largely disappointed. It appears that civilian casualties resulting from U.S. attacks in Afghanistan had by February 2002 added up to somewhere between 1,000 and 3,700 deaths, depending on who is estimating (Bearak, 2002). Although Afghan civilian losses may thus approach the 3,000 U.S. victims of September 11, it is clear that U.S. accuracy has been outstanding by the standards of modern warfare. Al-Qaeda might still hope to profit by perceptions of a crusade against Muslims if the United States extends the war on terrorism to Iraq, Iran, or Somalia.

U.S. REACTION TO SEPTEMBER 11: SOME ISSUES OF MASS PSYCHOLOGY

In this section I consider several psychological issues raised by the U.S. reaction to the terrorist attacks of September 11. Has the United States been terrorized? What kinds of identity shifts may have occurred after September 11?

Fear After September 11

There seems little doubt that the events of September 11, soon followed by another plane crash at Rockaway Beach, did make Americans less willing to fly. In early 2002, air travel and hotel bookings were still significantly below levels recorded in the months before the attacks. Beyond fear of flying, there is evidence that Americans became generally more anxious and insecure. Some law firms specializing in preparation of wills and trusts saw a big increase in business after September 11. Gun sales were up in some places after September 11, suggesting a search for increased security broader than against the threat of terrorism. Owning a gun may not be much help against terrorists, but, at least for some individuals, a gun can be a symbol and reassurance of control and personal safety. Pet sales were also reported up in some places. Again, a pet is not likely to be much help against terrorists, but, at least for some individuals, a pet may be an antidote to uncertainty and fear. A pet offers both an experience of control and the reassurance of unconditional positive regard (Beck & Katcher, 1996).

It is tempting to interpret a big decrease in air travel as evidence of a big increase in fear, but it may be that even a small increase in fear can produce a large decrease in willingness to fly. When the stakes are high, a small change in risk perception can trigger a large decrease in willingness to bet. Indeed, decreased willingness to fly need not imply any increase in fear. Some may have already been afraid of flying, and found September 11 not a stimulus to increased fear but a justification for fears—or for acting on fears—that had been previously ridiculed and suppressed. Thus there may be only a minority with increased fear of flying after September 11. Myers (2001) offered four research generalizations about perceived risk that can help explain increased fear of flying after September 11. We are biologically prepared to fear heights, we fear particularly what we cannot control, we fear immediate more than long-term and cumulative dangers, and we exaggerate dangers represented in vivid and memorable images. All of these influences can help explain fear of flying, but only the last can explain why fear of flying increased after September 11. Fear of heights preceded September 11, every passenger gives up control on entering a plane, and the immediate risk of climbing onto a plane is little affected by four or five crashes in a brief period of time.

Myers notes, however, that the risks of air travel are largely concentrated in the minutes of takeoff and landing. This is a framing issue: Do air travelers see their risk in terms of deaths per passenger mile—which makes air travel much safer than driving—or do they see the risk as deaths per minute of takeoff and landing? With the latter framing, air travel may be objectively more risky than driving.

Still, Myers may be correct in focusing on the importance of television images of planes slicing into the World Trade Center, but the importance of these images may have more to do with control of fear and norms about expressing fear than with the level of fear. Myers reports a Gallup poll indicating that, even before September 11, 44 percent of those willing to fly were willing to admit they felt fearful about flying. It is possible that this fear is controlled by a cognitive appraisal that flying is safe, and the images of planes crashing interfere with this appraisal. This interpretation is similar to the "safety frame" explanation of how people can enjoy the fear arousal associated with riding a roller coaster or watching a horror film (McCauley, 1998a).

If the safety frame is disturbed, the fear controls behavior and, in the case of air travel, people are less willing to fly. One implication of this interpretation is that, for at least some individuals, government warnings of additional terrorist attacks in the near future would make no difference in the level of fear experienced—vivid crash images may release the latent fear no matter what the objective likelihood of additional crashes.

Acting on the fear experienced is a separate issue. It is possible that warnings of future terrorist attacks affect the norms of acting on fear of flying, that is, the warnings reduce social pressure to carry on business as usual and reduce ridicule for those who are fearful about flying. Fear of flying is an attitude, and there is no doubt that social norms have much to do with determining when attitudes are expressed in behavior (Ajzen & Fishbein, 1980).

Indeed, the impact of government warnings and increased airport security are very much in need of investigation. President Bush was in the position of trying to tell Americans that they should resume flying and that new airport security made flying safe again, even as security agencies issued multiple warnings of new terrorist attacks. These warnings had the peculiar quality of being completely unspecific about the nature of the threat or what to do about it. The possible downside of such warnings is suggested by research indicating that threat appeals are likely to be repressed or ignored if the appeal does not include specific and effective action to avoid the threat (Sabini, 1995, pp. 565–566). Even the additional airport security may be of dubious value. It is true that many Americans seemed reassured to see Army personnel with weapons stationed in airports, although the objective security value of troops with no training in security screening is by no means obvious. But if there is any value to the framing interpretation of increased fear offered above, then adding military security at airports may actually increase fear. Vivid images of armed troops at airports may be more likely to undermine than to augment the safety frame that controls fear of flying.

Differences in security procedures from one airport to another can also contribute to increased fear. A journalist from Pittsburgh called me not long after new security procedures were introduced at U.S. airports. His paper had received a letter to the editor written by a visitor from Florida, a letter excoriating the Pittsburgh airport for inadequate security. The writer had been frightened because she was asked for identification only once on her way to boarding her return flight from Pittsburgh, whereas she had been stopped for identification five times in boarding the Florida flight to Pittsburgh.

Fear of flying is not the only fear to emerge from September 11. Survivors of the attacks on the World Trade Center (WTC), those who fled for their lives on September 11, may be fearful of working in a high-rise building and afraid even of all the parts of lower Manhattan that were associated with commuting to and from the WTC. Many corporate employees who escaped the WTC returned to work in new office buildings in northern New Jersey. In these new settings, some may have been retraumatized by frequent fire and evacuation drills that associated their new offices and stairwells with the uncertainties and fears of the offices and stairwells of the WTC. For these people, the horror of the WTC may have been a kind of one-trial traumatic conditioning experiment, with follow-up training in associating their new workplace with the old one. Their experience and their fears deserve research attention.

A small step in this direction was a December conference at the University of Pennsylvania's Solomon Asch Center for Study of Ethnopolitical Conflict. The conference brought together eight trauma counselors from around the United States who had been brought in to assist WTC corporate employees returning to work in new office spaces. A report of lessons learned from this conference is in preparation, but a few issues can already be discerned. Perhaps most important is that the counselors were selected and directed by corporate Employee Assistance Programs with more experience of physical health problems than of mental health problems. Thus the counselors were all contracted to use Critical Incident Stress Debriefing techniques with every individual and every group seen; at least officially, no room was left for a counselor to exercise independent judgment about what approach might best suit a particular situation.

Similarly, the counselors were understood as interchangeable resources, so that a counselor might be sent to one corporation on one day and a different corporation the next day, even as another counselor experienced the reverse transfer. The importance of learning a particular corporate culture and setting, the personal connection between individual counselor and the managers that control that setting, the trust developed between an individual counselor and individuals needing assistance and referral in that setting—these were given little attention in the organization of counseling assistance. It appears that the experience of counselors working with WTC survivors has not yet been integrated with the experience of those working with survivors of the Oklahoma City bombing (Pfefferbaum, Flynn, Brandt, & Lensgraf, 1999). There is a long way to go to develop anything like a consensus on "best practice" for assisting survivors of such attacks.

In sum, fear after September 11 includes a range of fear reactions, including fear of flying by those with no personal connection to the WTC, more general fears and anxieties associated with death from uncontrollable and unpredictable terrorist attacks, and specific workplace fears among those who escaped the WTC attacks. These reactions offer theoretical challenges that can be of interest to those interested in understanding the relation between risk appraisal and fear (Lazarus, 1991), as well as to those interested in the commercial implications of public fears.

Cohesion After September 11: Patriotism

All over the United States, vehicles and homes were decorated with the U.S. flag after September 11. Walls, fences, billboards, and e-mails were emblazoned with "God Bless America." It is clear that the immediate response to the attacks was a sudden increase in patriotic expression. The distribution of this increase across the United States could be a matter of some interest. Was the new patriotism greater in New York City and declining in concentric circles of distance from New York? Was it greater among blue-collar than white-collar families? Was it greater for some ethnic groups than for others? Was it greater in cities, possibly perceived as more threatened by future terrorist attacks, than in suburbs and small towns?

The attacks of September 11 represent a natural experiment relevant to two prominent approaches to conceptualizing and measuring patriotism. In the first approach, Kosterman and Feshbach (1989) distinguish between patriotism and nationalism. Patriotism is love of country and is generally accounted a good thing; nationalism is a feeling of national superiority that is accounted a source of intergroup hostility and conflict. In the second approach, Schatz, Staub, and Lavine (1999) offer a distinction between *constructive* and *blind* patriotism. *Constructive* patriotism refers to love of country expressed as willingness to criticize its policies and its leaders when these go wrong; *blind* patriotism refers to love of country coupled with norms against criticism—"my country right or wrong." Constructive patriotism is here accounted the good thing and blind patriotism the danger.

Thus, both approaches distinguish between good and bad forms of patriotism, and both offer separate measures of the good and bad forms. That is, there is a scale of patriotism and a scale of nationalism, and a scale of constructive patriotism and a scale of blind patriotism. In both approaches, there is some evidence that the two scales are relatively independent. Some individuals score high on patriotism, for instance, but low on nationalism. Similarly, some individuals score high on constructive patriotism but also score high on blind patriotism (an inconsistency that seems to bother those answering questions less than it bothers theorists).

What happened to these different aspects of patriotism among Americans after September 11? As increased cohesion is known to increase conformity and pressure on deviates, one might expect that patriotism, blind patriotism, and nationalism increased, whereas constructive patriotism decreased. Another possibility is that scores on these measures were unchanged after September 11, but identification with the country increased in relation to other directions of group identification. That is, Americans rating the importance of each of a number of groups—country, ethnic group, religious group, family, school—might rate country higher in relation to other groups.

It seems likely that both kinds of patriotism increased, both scores on the patriotism scales and ratings of the relative importance of country. If so, additional questions can be raised. Did nationalism and blind patriotism increase more or less than the "good" forms of patriotism? Was the pattern of change different by geography, education, or ethnicity?

Cohesion After September 11: Relations in Public

News reports immediately after September 11 suggested a new interpersonal tone in New York City. Along with shock and fear was a new tone in public interactions of strangers, a tone of increased politeness, helpfulness, and personal warmth. Several reports suggested a notable drop in crime, especially violent crime, in the days after the attacks.

It would be interesting to know if these reports can be substantiated with more objective measures of social behavior in public places (McCauley, Coleman, & DeFusco, 1978). Did the pace of life in New York slow after the attacks? That is, did people walk slower on the streets? Did eye contact between strangers increase? Did commercial transactions (e.g., with bus drivers, postal clerks, supermarket cashiers) include more personal exchange? Did interpersonal distance in interactions of strangers decrease? This research will be hampered by the absence of relevant measures from New York in the months before September 11, but it may not be too late to chart a decline from levels of public sociability and politeness that may still have been elevated in early 2002.

Cohesion After September 11: Minority Identity Shifts

A few reports have suggested that minority groups experienced major changes of group identity after September 11. Group identity is composed of two parts: private and public identity. Private identity is how the individual thinks of him- or herself in relation to groups to which the individual belongs. Public identity is how the individual thinks others perceive him.

Public Identity Shift for Muslims and Arabs

The attacks of September 11 produced an immediate effect on the public identity of Arabs, Muslims, and those, like Sikhs, who can be mistaken by Americans for Arab or Muslim. Actual violence against members of these groups seems mercifully to have been rare, with thirty-nine hate crimes reported to the New York City Police Department in the week ending September 22 but only one a week by the end of December (Fries, 2001). Much more frequent has been the experience of dirty looks, muttered suggestions of "go home," physical distancing, and discrimination at work and school (Sengupta, 2001). Many Arab Americans and Muslims say they have afraid to report this kind of bias.

American reactions to Muslims and Arabs after September 11 pose a striking theoretical challenge. How is it that the actions of nineteen Arab Muslims can affect American perceptions of the Arabs and Muslims that they encounter? The ease with which the nineteen were generalized to an impression of millions should leave us amazed; "the law of small numbers" (Tversky & Kahneman, 1971), in which small and unrepresentative samples are accepted as representative of large populations, has not been observed in research on stereotypes. Indeed, the difficulty of changing stereotypes has often been advanced as one of their principal dangers.

Of course, not every American accepted the idea that all Arabs are terrorists, but even those who intellectually avoided this generalization sometimes found themselves fighting a new unease and suspicion toward people who looked Arab. Whether on the street or boarding a plane, Americans seem to have had difficulty controlling their emotional response to this newly salient category. It seems unlikely that an attack by nineteen Congolese terrorists would have the same impact on perceptions of African Americans. Why not?

One possible explanation of the speed and power of the group generalization of the September 11 terrorists is that humans are biologically prepared to essentialize cultural differences of members of unfamiliar groups. Gil-White (2001) has suggested that there was an evolutionary advantage for individuals who recognized and generalized cultural differences so as to avoid the extra costs of interacting with those whose norms did not mesh with local norms. This perspective suggests that we may have a kind of default schema for group perception that makes it easy to essentialize the characteristics of a few individuals encountered from a new group. To essentialize means to see the unusual characteristics of the new individuals as the product of an unchangeable group nature or essence. Previous familiarity with the group, a pre-existing essence for the group, could interfere with this default, such that African terrorists would not easily lead to a generalization about African Americans.

It would be useful to know more about the experience of Muslims and Arabs in the United States after September 11, not least because those experiencing bias may become more likely to sympathize with terrorism directed against the United States, Interviews and polls might inquire not only about the respondent's personal experience of bias, but about the respondent's perception of what most in his or her group experienced. As elaborated above, the motivation for violence may have more to do with group experience than with personal problems.

Public Identity Shift for African Americans

The attacks of September 11 may also have produced an effect on the public identity of African Americans. Their sharing in the costs and threats of terrorist attack may have strengthened their public status as Americans. Several African Americans have suggested that the distancing and unease they often feel from whites with whom they interact was markedly diminished after September 11. The extent and distribution of this feeling of increased acceptance by white Americans could be investigated in interviews with African Americans. Again, the distinction between personal experience and perception of group experience could be important in estimating the political impact of September 11 on African Americans.

Finally, there is an issue of great practical importance in understanding the public identity of Muslim African Americans as a minority within a minority. This group is likely to have faced conflicting changes after September 11, with increased acceptance as African Americans opposed by decreased acceptance as Muslims. The distinctive attire of African American Muslims, particularly the attire of women of this community, makes them readily identifiable in public settings. With the attire goes a community lifestyle that also sets this minority apart from other African Americans. Thus public reactions to Muslim African Americans should be very salient in their experience, and this experience could be determined by researchers with entrée to their community. Again, the distinction between personal experience of the respondent and perceived group experience may be important.

One way of learning about shifts in the public identities of minorities is to study changes in the mutual stereotyping of majority and minority. Stereotypes are today generally understood as perceptions of probabilistic differences between groups, differences that may include personality traits, abilities, occupations, physique, clothing, and preferences (McCauley, Jussim, & Lee, 1995). Thus, researchers might ask both minority and majority group members about whether and how September 11 changed their perceptions of the differences between majority and minority.

Perhaps even more important for understanding the public identity of minorities would be research that asks about *metastereotypes*. Metastereotypes are perceptions of what "most people" believe about group differences. Although they are little studied, there is some evidence that metastereotypes are more extreme than personal stereotypes, that is, that individuals believe that most people see stronger ingroup–outgroup differences than they do (Rettew, Billman, & Davis, 1993). The public identity of the minority might thus be measured as the average minority individual's perception of what "most people" in the majority group see as the differences between minority and majority. Related metastereotypes might also be of interest: the average minority individual's perception of what most minority members believe about majority–minority differences, the average majority member's perception of what most majority members believe about these differences, and the average majority member's perception of what most minority members believe about these differences.

The attacks of September 11 and their aftermath offer a natural experiment in conflicting pressures on public identity. Research on public identities of minorities could enliven theoretical development even as the research contributes to gauging the potential for terrorist recruitment in groups—Muslim Arabs in the United States, Muslim African Americans—that security services are likely to see as being at risk for terrorist sympathies. In particular, public identity shifts for Muslim African Americans will be better understood by comparison with whatever shifts may obtain for African Americans who are not Muslim.

Private Identity Shifts

Private identity concerns the beliefs and feelings of the individual about a group to which the individual belongs. The most obvious shifts in private identity are those already discussed as shifts in patriotism. Patriotism is a particular kind of group identification, that is, identification with country or nation, and increases in patriotism are a kind of private identity shift. This obvious connection between national identification and patriotism has only recently become a focus of empirical research (Citrin, Wong, & Duff, 2001; Sidanius & Petrocik, 2001).

Here I want to focus on shifts in private identities of minorities. As with public identity shifts, the three minority groups of special interest are Muslim Arabs living in the United States, African Americans, and Muslim African Americans. For each group, research can ask about changes since September 11 in their feelings toward the United States and feelings toward their minority group. What is the relation between changes in these two private identities? It is by no means obvious that more attachment to one identity means less attachment to others, but in terms of behavior there may be something of a conservation principle at work. Time and energy are limited, and more behavior controlled by one identity may mean less behavior controlled by others. There is much yet to be learned about the relation between more particularistic identities, including ethnic and religious identities, and overarching national identity.

Group Dynamics Theory and Political Identity

Public reaction to terrorist attacks is strikingly consistent with results found in research with small face-to-face groups. In the group dynamics literature that began with Festinger's (1950) theory of informal social influence, cohesion is attachment to the group that comes from two kinds of interdependence. The obvious kind of interdependence arises from common goals of material interest, status, and congeniality. The hidden interdependence arises from the need for certainty that can only be obtained from the consensus of others. Agreement with those around us is the only source of certainty about questions of value, including questions about good and evil and about what is worth living for, working for, and dying for.

It seems possible that identification with large and faceless groups is analogous to cohesion in small face-to-face groups (McCauley, 2001; McCauley, in press-a). A scaled-up theory of cohesion leads immediately to the implication that group identification is not one thing but a number of related things. Research has shown that different sources of cohesion lead to different kinds of behavior. Cohesion based on congeniality, for instance, leads to groupthink, whereas cohesion based on group status or material interest does not lead to groupthink (McCauley, 1998b).

Similarly, different sources of ethnic identification may lead to different behaviors. Individuals who care about their ethnic group for status or material interest may be less likely to sacrifice for the group than individuals who care about their group for its social reality value—for the moral culture that makes sense of the world and the individual's place in it. Research on the effects of September 11 on group identities might try to link different measures of group identification with different behaviors after September 11: giving blood or money, community volunteer work, revising a will, changing travel plans, spending more time with family. The distinctions between patriotism and nationalism, and between constructive and blind patriotism, as cited above, are steps in this direction.

Group dynamics research has shown that shared threat is a particularly potent source of group cohesion; similarly, as discussed above, the threat represented by the September 11 attacks seems to have raised U.S. patriotism and national identification. Research also shows that high cohesion leads to accepting group norms, respect for group leaders, and pressure on deviates (Duckitt, 1989). Similarly, U.S. response to the September 11 attacks seems to have included new respect for group norms (less crime, more politeness), new respect for group leaders (President Bush, Mayor Giuliani), and new willingness to sanction deviates (hostility toward those who sympathize with Arabs and Muslims; see Knowlton, 2002).

CONCLUSION

In the first part of this paper, group dynamics theory was the perspective brought to bear in understanding the power of cause and comrades in moving normal people to terrorism. In particular I suggested that the power of a group to elicit sacrifice depends upon its terror-management value, which is another way of talking about the social reality value of the group.

Group dynamics research and the psychology of cohesion also provide a useful starting point for theorizing about the origins and consequences of group identification, including many aspects of public reaction to terrorism. Terrorism is a threat to all who identify with the group targeted, and at least the initial result of an attack is always increased identification—increased cohesion—in the group attacked. The non-obvious quality of this idea is conveyed by the many unsuccessful attempts to use air power to demoralize an enemy by bombing its civilian population (Pape, 1996).

In sum, I have argued that both origins and effects of terrorist acts are anchored in group dynamics. Along the way I have tried to suggest how the response to terrorism can be more dangerous than the terrorists.

REFERENCES

Ajzen, I., & Fishbein, M. (1980). *Understanding attitudes and predicting behavior.* New York: Prentice Hall.

Allport, G. W. (1954). *The nature of prejudice.* Cambridge, MA: Addison Wesley.

Barker, E. (1984). *The making of a Moonie: Choice or brainwashing.* London: Basil Blackwell.

Bearak, B. (2002, February 11). Afghan toll of civilians is lost in the fog of war. *International Herald Tribune*, pp. 1, 8.

Beck, A., & Katcher, A. (1996). *Between pets and people: The importance of animal companionship.* West Lafayette, IN: Purdue University Press.

Brewer, M. (2001). Ingroup identification and intergroup conflict: When does ingroup love become outgroup hate? In R. D. Ashmore, L. Jussim, & D. Wilder (Eds.), *Social identity, intergroup conflict, and conflict reduction* (pp. 17–41). New York: Oxford University Press.

Brown, R. (1986). *Social psychology, the second edition.* New York: Free Press.

Citrin, J., Wong, C., & Duff, B. (2001). The meaning of American national identity: Patterns of ethnic conflict and consensus. In R. D. Ashmore, L. Jussim, & D. Wilder (Eds.), *Social identity, intergroup conflict, and conflict reduction* (pp. 71–100). New York: Oxford University Press.

Duckitt, J. (1989). Authoritarianism and group identification: A new view of an old construct. *Political Psychology, 10,* 63–84.

Festinger, L. (1950). Informal social communication. *Psychological Review, 57,* 271–282.

Frank, R. L. (1988). *Passions within reason: The strategic role of the emotions.* New York: Norton.

Friedman, A. (2002a, February 5). Forum focuses on "wrath" born of poverty. *International Herald Tribune*, p. 11.

Friedman, T. (2002b, January 28). The pain behind Al Qaeda's Europe connection. *International Herald Tribune*, p. 6.

Fries, J. H. (2001, December 22). Complaints of anti-Arab bias crimes dip, but concerns linger. *New York Times*, p. B8.

Galanter, M. (1980). Psychological induction into the large group: Findings from a modern religious sect. *American Journal of Psychiatry, 137,* 1574–1579.

Gil-White, F. (2001). Are ethnic groups biological "species" to the human brain? *Current Anthropology, 42,* 515–554.

Higgs, R. (1987). *Crisis and leviathan: Critical episodes in the growth of American government.* New York: Oxford University Press.

Horowitz, D. L. (2001). *The deadly ethnic riot.* Berkeley, CA: University of California Press.

Kinder, D. (1998). Opinion and action in the realm of politics. In D. T. Gilbert, S. Fiske, & G. Lindzey (Eds.), *The handbook of social psychology* (Vol. II, pp. 778–867). New York: McGraw-Hill.

Knowlton, B. (2001, December 20). How the world sees the United States and Sept. 11. *International Herald Tribune,* pp. 1, 6.

Knowlton, B. (2002, February 12). On U.S. campuses, intolerance grows. *International Herald Tribune,* pp. I, IV.

Kosterman, R., & Feshbach, S. (1989). Towards a measure of patriotic and nationalistic attitudes. *Political Psychology, 10,* 257–274.

Kurtz, H. (2002, February 2–3). America is 'doomed,' Bin Laden says on tape. *International Herald Tribune,* p. 5.

Lazarus, R. S. (1991). Cognition and motivation in emotion. *American Psychologist, 46,* 352–367.

Lelyveld, J. (2001, October 28). All suicide bombers are not alike. *New York Times Magazine,* pp. 48–53, 62, 78–79.

Makiya, K., & Mneimneh, H. (2002, January 17). Manual for a "raid." *New York Review of Books, XLIX,* pp. 18–21.

McCauley, C. (1991). Terrorism research and public policy: An overview. In C. McCauley (Ed.), *Terrorism research and public policy* (pp. 126–144). London: Frank Cass.

McCauley, C. (1998a). When screen violence is not attractive. In J. Goldstein (Ed.), *Why we watch: The attractions of violent entertainment* (pp. 144–162). New York: Oxford University Press.

McCauley, C. (1998b). Group dynamics in Janis's theory of groupthink: Backward and forward. *Organizational Behavior and Human Decision Processes, 73,* 142–162.

McCauley, C. (2001). The psychology of group identification and the power of ethnic nationalism. In D. Chirot & M. Seligman (Eds.), *Ethnopolitical warfare: Causes, consequences, and possible solutions* (pp. 343–362). Washington, DC: APA Books.

McCauley, C. (in press-a). The psychology of ethnic group conflict. In W. Licht (Ed.), *The challenge of ethnopolitical conflict: Can the world cope?* Philadelphia: University of Pennsylvania Press.

McCauley, C. (in press-b). Making sense of terrorism after 9/11. In R. Moser (Ed.), *Shocking violence II: Violent disaster, war and terrorism affecting our youth.* New York: Charles C. Thomas.

McCauley, C., & Segal, M. (1987). Social psychology of terrorist groups. In C. Hendrick (Ed.), *Review of Personality and Social Psychology, Vol. 9* (pp. 231–256). Beverly Hills, CA: Sage.

McCauley, C., Coleman, G., & DeFusco, P. (1978). Commuters' eye-contact with strangers in city and suburban train stations: Evidence of short-term adaptation to interpersonal overload in the city. *Environmental Psychology and Nonverbal Behavior, 2,* 215–255.

McCauley, C., Jussim, L., & Lee, Y.-T. (1995). Stereotype accuracy: Toward appreciating group differences. In Y.-T. Lee, L. J. Jussim, & C. R. McCauley (Eds.), *Stereotype accuracy: Toward appreciating group differences* (pp. 293–312). Washington, DC: APA Books.

Myers, D. G. (2001). Do we fear the right things? *American Psychological Society Observer, 14,* 3, 31.

Pape, R. A. (1996). *Bombing to win: Air power and coercion in war.* Ithaca: Cornell University Press.

Pfefferbaum, B., Flynn, B. W., Brandt, E. N., & Lensgraf, S. J. (1999). Organizing the mental health response to human-caused community disasters with reference to the Oklahoma City bombing. *Psychiatric Annals, 29,* 109–113.

Pyszcznski, T., Greenberg, J., & Solomon, S. (1997). Why do we need what we need? A terror management perspective on the roots of human social motivation. *Psychological Inquiry, 8,* 1–20.

Rettew, D. C., Billman, D., & Davis, R. A. (1993). Inaccurate perceptions of the amount others stereotype: Estimates about stereotypes of one's own group and other groups. *Basic and Applied Social Psychology, 14,* 121–142.

Rummel, R. J. (1996). *Death by government.* New Brunswick, NJ: Transaction Publishers.

Sabini, J. (1995). *Social psychology* (2nd ed.). New York, Norton.

Schatz, R. T., Staub, E., & Lavine, H. (1999). On the varieties of national attachment: Blind versus constructive patriotism. *Political Psychology, 20,* 151–174.

Sengupta, S. (2001, October 10). Sept. 11 attack narrows the racial divide. *New York Times,* p. B1.

Sidanius, J., & Petrocik, J. R. (2001). Communal and national identity in a multiethnic state: A comparison of three perspectives. In R. D. Ashmore, L. Jussim, & D. Wilder (Eds.), *Social identity, intergroup conflict, and conflict reduction* (pp. 101–129). New York: Oxford University Press.

Sprinzak, E. (1991). The process of delegitimization: Towards a linkage theory of political terrorism. In C. McCauley (Ed.), *Terrorism research and public policy* (pp. 50–68). London: Frank Cass.

Stouffer, S. A., Lumsdaine, A. A., Lumsdaine, M. H., et al. (1949). *The American soldier, volume 2: Combat and its aftermath.* Princeton, NJ: Princeton University Press.

Tversky, A., & Kahneman, D. (1971). Belief in the law of small numbers. *Psychological Bulletin, 2,* 105–110.

2

The Unanticipated Consequences of Globalization: Contextualizing Terrorism

Michael J. Stevens

Some scholars have forecast a decline in terrorism due to international efforts toward prevention and, ironically, as I will show, due to the global expansion of free markets and democracy (Johnson, 2001). However, they acknowledge that the 1990s witnessed a significant increase in casualties due to terrorism (Johnson, 2001; Merari, 2000). Others argue that emerging ethnic and religious sensibilities, the widening gap between rich and poor, the status of the United States as the only superpower, links to organized crime, access to the Internet, and the availability of weapons of mass destruction will increase the incidence of terrorism (Crenshaw, 2000; Jensen, 2001; Medd & Goldstein, 1997; Merari, 2000). Given the unprecedented attacks on the World Trade Center and Pentagon, and evidence of an active network of terrorist groups worldwide (e.g., al-Qaeda), there is an urgency to understand and respond to the threat posed by such groups and their members.

In this chapter, I argue that globalization contributes to the creation of sociocultural and psychosocial conditions from which terrorism may emerge. I first review the definition of terrorism and trace its recent history and future course. I then highlight how positivistic psychological theories have rooted terrorism in individual pathology or small-group processes, thereby perpetuating decontextualized, cause-effect accounts of terrorism that have useful, but narrow, meaning. I go on to describe globalization and provide examples of the sociocultural dislocation and psychosocial dysfunction it has reaped. I then articulate how constitutive, relational approaches offer meaningful frameworks for understanding terrorism in the context of the dramatic transformations produced by globalization. I outline three perspectives that are useful in conceptualizing terrorism as resistance to globalization: social identity theory, social reducton theory, and Vygotsky's sociocultural theory, and I apply these perspectives to instances of domestic, foreign, and international terrorism. I conclude with a call to integrate positivistic and constitutive paradigms in order to stimulate more comprehensive and compelling research on terrorism.

TERRORISM

Terrorism Defined

When asked to define terrorism, Lenin supposedly replied that the purpose of terrorism was to terrorize. Although a gross oversimplification, the statement underscores the power of terror as an instrument of social influence. Regrettably, experts have yet to forge a universally agreed upon definition of terrorism (Brannan, Esler, & Strindberg, 2001; Cooper, 2001; Medd & Goldstein, 1997), owing to political debate. In addition, terrorism is not easily distinguished from communal violence or guerrilla warfare, partly because the practice of terrorism is so diverse (e.g., assassination, kidnappings, high-tech sabotage) (Byman, 1998). As a result, scholars continue to investigate a phenomenon about which they disagree, adding to a scattered literature.

The most oft-cited definition of terrorism is the one adopted by the U.S. State Department, Department of Defense, and Central Intelligence Agency: "The term 'terrorism' means premeditated, politically motivated violence perpetrated against noncombatant targets by subnational groups or clandestine agents, usually intended to influence an audience. The term 'international terrorism' means terrorism involving citizens or territory of more than one country. The term 'terrorist' group means any group practicing, or that has any significant subgroups that practice, international terrorism" (Office of the Coordinator for Counterterrorism, 1994, p. 19). Terrorism, then, is systematic violence directed by a few toward the intimidation of a captive population. Although most definitions of terrorism fail to clarify its motive, focusing instead on its target and its relationship to conventional warfare, it is ordinarily prompted by resistance to economic, political, and religious oppression (Byman, 1998; Cooper, 2001; Crenshaw, 2000).

History of Terrorism

Early forms of terrorism (e.g., assassination) were used by Shi'ite Muslims to repel Christian Crusaders during the Middle Ages. One of the first instances of state-sponsored terror occurred during the French Revolution, when Maximillian Robespierre abused the organs of power to eliminate enemies of the state and pacify the populace. In late nineteenth-century Russia, the People's Will targeted key figures in the royal family and government ministries whom they deemed responsible for economic and political oppression, hoping to ignite revolution. After the failed Easter uprising of 1916, Michael Collins and other Irish Republican Army leaders began a campaign of terrorism that targeted military personnel and administrative centers that supported the British occupation. In the 1950s, the Algerian Armed Islamic Group attacked French military posts, bars and bistros, and vacationers at resorts and, with popular support, wore down a French occupation force and gained Algerian independence in 1962. Similarly, the Mau Mau of Kenya, undaunted by British forces, liberated themselves in 1963 from colonial rule by dismembering and mutilating collaborators and slaughtering families of the governing elite.

In the 1960s, a more intense and protracted form of terrorism emerged in the Middle East as radical Palestinians sought to redress their political and social conditions by targeting Israelis and Israeli institutions (Medd & Goldstein, 1997). Because of Israel's readiness to take swift and harsh counterterrorism measures, the military branch of the Palestine Liberation Organization and related terrorist organizations (e.g., Hamas) escalated their methods to include skyjacking, in part because of media attention given to their cause.

Since the late 1960s, terrorism has been used to coerce social change by a rapidly growing number of organizations (Medd & Goldstein, 1997). In the 1970s, terrorism was mostly politically inspired and linked to national-separatist (e.g., Palestinian) or social-revolutionary (e.g., Marxist) movements (Byman, 1998; Crenshaw, 2000; Medd & Goldstein, 1997). The political terrorism of this era typically involved seizing hostages, hijacking airplanes, car bombs, and assassination. Political terrorists often targeted prominent government and industry leaders.

Although their methods remained much the same (Merari, 2000), terrorists in the 1980s became less discriminating and more lethal in pursuing their goals (Crenshaw, 2000; Jensen, 2001; Medd & Goldstein, 1997). More importantly, terrorism evolved to include economic and religious objectives in addition to political ones. Blaming them for much of society's ills, terrorists targeted Western symbols, including centers of industry and government as well as key political leaders. Mutually beneficial relationships emerged in the Middle East between Palestinian and Islamic movements and in Latin America between leftist guerrillas and drug cartels. For example, the term "narcoterrorism" was created to acknowledge the partnership between organized crime and terrorism in the struggle for power and profit. In Colombia, four presidential candidates, sixty judges, seventy journalists, and one thousand police have been killed by narcoterrorists. Moreover, during the 1980s, terrorists adopted chemical methods for economic blackmail. In 1989, fruit exported by Chile was reportedly laced with cyanide. Although only two poisoned grapes were ever found, the Chilean fruit industry lost $333 million.

While the 1990s heralded a new era of peace, owing to the end of the Cold War and to the expansion of interdependent free-market democracies, the partnership between terrorism and organized crime grew stronger (Medd & Goldstein, 1997). Furthermore, various nations have discovered the strategic value of terrorism in advancing their regional economic and political agendas (e.g., Iran, North Korea). Most disturbing has been the globalization of targets by terrorists to include highly visible Western symbols on U.S. and foreign soil. The World Trade Center bombing in 1993 killed eight (Medd & Goldstein, 1997) and injured one thousand. Also in 1993, several CIA employees were shot in front of their national headquarters. Investigators of these events discovered that additional terrorist acts on U.S. soil had been planned, including the bombing of the United Nations. Regardless of whether their motivation is economic, political, or religious, terrorists have realized that commerce is the Achilles' heel of the West. Hence, financial centers, transportation and energy infrastructures, and the media have become tantalizing targets.

Future of Terrorism

The twenty-first century may have inaugurated a new era of terrorism, featuring the interlaced elements of religious zealotry, globalization, and the United States' superpower status (Weinberg & Eubank, 2000). First, twenty-first-century terrorism is predicated on a struggle to transform the world, with accountability only to God or a transcendental idea and a desire for martyrdom (Crenshaw, 2000). Data on terrorism point to the Muslim world as especially inclined toward violent conflict with other civilizations, most notably—but not exclusively (take, for example, the Hindu–Muslim conflict in Kashmir)—with Western civilization, owing to the latter's destabilizing effect on nations and culture and the backlash that such unchecked power engenders (Aram, 1997; Weinberg & Eubank, 2000). Placing economic, political, and cultural grievances in the framework of religious doctrine provides a compelling meaning structure that can be exploited to mobilize widespread support not merely for national sovereignty or pan-Arabism, but for the restoration of Islamic civilization worldwide (Crenshaw, 2000).

Second, globalization has weakened state boundaries by making them less relevant (Barber, 1995; Jensen, 2001). Globally interdependent economies have shifted identities from those tied to a nation to ones that involve ethnicity and religion, providing fertile soil for violent xenophobic and fundamentalist antipathy toward Western political and cultural hegemony. Relative economic disparity also contributes to discontent. Although globalization has raised the absolute standard of living worldwide (Friedman, 2000), it has widened the gap between rich and poor (Byman, 1998; Jensen, 2001). Anti-globalization rhetoric motivates violence because it rests on envy and indignation; terrorism holds the promise of relief from exploitation and deprivation (Barber, 1995; Byman, 1998).

Finally, as the world's only superpower, the United States has increasingly intervened in foreign affairs, whether through peacekeeping missions, through overtly and covertly influencing both democracies and dictatorships perceived as friendly to American interests (e.g., the autocratic Islam Karimov, president of Uzbekistan and ally in the war against terrorism), or through establishing international partnerships to access foreign markets and cheap labor (Jensen, 2001). As a consequence, terrorists are likely to target U.S. interests, gaining media coverage of their struggle against Western hegemony (Byman, 1998). By targeting a sovereign nation's interests, terrorists also hope to provoke a forceful response. Such a response will either intimidate or radicalize moderates who compose the main obstacle to terrorists' political aspirations. In either case, as greater numbers of insurgents emerge, the possibility for conflict resolution becomes more remote, with retaliatory strikes by terrorists couched as expressions of a righteous revolt against oppression (Byman, 1998).

The methods that terrorists of the twenty-first century might adopt will reflect the growing dependency of the economy, military, and infrastructure of the West on information technology. Lethal chemical and biological material may also be used to blackmail Western nations into making concessions or as a way to repel foreign influence. Experts concede that terrorists will have the resources and inclination to inflict fear, havoc, and death on an unprecedented scale (Crenshaw, 2000; Jensen, 2001; Medd & Goldstein 1997; Merari, 2000). Several terrorist organizations have dedicated themselves to eradicating Western influence by whatever means from parts of the world where that influence has threatened national sovereignty, economic stability, cultural identity, and religious morality (e.g., al-Qaeda) (Crenshaw, 2000; Medd & Goldstein, 1997).

Psychological Study of Terrorism

To understand terrorism and terrorists, it is essential to avoid outgroup stereotyping (Brannan et al., 2001; Euben, 1995). This problem is nowhere better illustrated than in a recent statement by Philip Zimbardo (2001), president of the American Psychological Association, on the September 11, 2001, terrorist strike. Notwithstanding an explicit exhortation to avoid calling terrorism and terrorists insane, Zimbardo repeatedly referred to terrorism and terrorists as *evil*. A universal basis for moral indignation does not exist, and such judgments are clearly anchored in history and culture (Gergen, 2001). Rather than prejudge terrorism as immoral or being trapped by the pejorative connotation of the word itself, terrorism must be understood through an examination of its underlying rationale, however unconventional, and the worldview from which it obtains (Byman, 1998; Crenshaw, 2000).

Although the systematic study of terrorism was launched in the 1970s, it faces persistent problems. Beyond the lack of a universally accepted definition of terrorism, enmeshment between academic researchers and government agencies dedicated to counterterrorism has compromised the psychological study of terrorism (Brannan et al., 2001; Crenshaw, 2000). Because models of terrorism often obtain from a hermeneutic of crisis management (Brannan et al., 2001), the literature perpetuates a received view of terrorism rather than charting new frameworks that explain the dynamics of terrorists' identity formation and behavior within historical and cultural contexts (Brannan et al., 2001). Policy makers have demanded unambiguous psychological profiles with which to identify actual or potential terrorists. This expectation has prompted researchers to isolate specific psychopathologies and personality characteristics that might describe terrorists and explain terrorism.

For example, Ulrike Meinhof, founding member of the German Red Army Faction, allegedly suffered from narcissism rooted in early trauma to self-esteem inflicted by a domineering father and exacerbated by an unavailable mother. Other formulations emphasize the causal primacy of fantasies of cleanliness, inconsistent mothering, and unresolved Oedipal issues (Brannan et al., 2001; Levine, 1999). Less psychodynamic though still pathological characteristics include alienation, suspiciousness, intellectualization of emotions, internalized hostility transferred onto institutionalized authority, low frustration tolerance, cognitive rigidity, and violence-proneness (Hoffman, 1999; Levine, 1999). Qualities that are free of pathology include deference to authority, forthrightness, idealism, intelligence, love of mankind, naiveté, need for validation, seriousness of purpose, and social responsibility (Slote, 1996). Although these diagnoses and descriptors humanize terrorists by configuring what is known about their psychological history and functioning within a coherent canonical template, they minimize the interpersonal and small-group contexts that generate terrorism. Moreover, most of these diagnoses and descriptors obtain from case studies of terrorists that have been rightly criticized for drawing heavily from secondary sources (e.g., reports by government task forces) (Brannan et al., 2001; Byman, 1998; Crenshaw, 2000).

Alternative conceptualizations have been proposed that articulate the small-group processes believed to cultivate terrorism (Brannan et al., 2001). These approaches typically link psychological history to political, religious, and social movements that provide the context within which a person develops into a terrorist. That is, terrorism affords individuals with unmet needs and violent proclivities opportunities to bolster their self-esteem through identification with the cause, leader, and members of a group. Delineating ideologies and adversaries, sharing destiny and risks, and relating to other terrorists are opportunities for identity development and socialization that are available in terrorist groups. For example, members of the Aum Shinrikyo cult, which in 1995 gassed Tokyo subway commuters, found opportunities for identity development and need fulfillment through an apocalyptic worldview, obedience to a charismatic leader, and solidarity with similar group members (Merari, 2000). Additional features of groups that nurture the identity development and socialization of terrorists include a manifesto that reveals the source of ideological truth, rules governing dress and conduct, and ceremonial rituals (Levine, 1999). Thus, terrorism can emerge when individuals who have been exposed to violence meet their needs for belonging, esteem, meaning, and justice in an environment of zealotry (Levine, 1999). Although explanations of terrorism that center on the interaction between individual needs and small-group processes are useful in articulating the identity development and socialization of terrorists, they are wanting. They isolate the terrorist from his or her history and culture and, consequently, fail to provide a meaningful context for the ongoing discourse between terrorist groups and the global milieu in which they are constituted (Brannan et al., 2001; Byman, 1998; Crenshaw, 2000).

Challenges to Studying Terrorism

In addition to the lack of a universally recognized definition of terrorism, the influence of government policy on independent scholarship, and the tendency to render "diagnoses at a distance" (Crenshaw, 2000, p. 407), psychological investigations of terrorism are hindered by the fact that terrorism and the actions of terrorists are constantly adapting to an evolving, interdependent world. It remains unclear whether valid generalizations can be made from earlier analyses of more conventional forms of terrorism. Even if a common purpose is assumed, which is arguable given how terrorism has changed over the years (Crenshaw, 2000; Jensen, 2001; Medd & Goldstein, 1997; Merari, 200; Weinberg & Eubank, 2000), terrorism unfolds within different organizational structures and social contexts. For example, if terrorist organizations have become more decentralized and scattered due to their exploitation of the Internet, what is the role, if any, of a charismatic leader? Can ignorance, oppression, and poverty, as well as psychological conflict and trauma, be manipulated in the service of terrorism without an identified leader?

Because of its nascent status, the study of terrorism lacks a sufficiently developed common knowledge base from which to account for the diversity of terrorism and terrorist groups, let alone address the historical, religious, and social contexts that define them. Under these circumstances, researchers may be susceptible to introducing ethnocentric biases into their scholarship. Ethnocentrism neglects "the unique collection of social roles, institutions, values, ideas, and symbols operative in every group, which radically conditions the way in which its members see the world and respond to its challenges" (Brannan et al., 2001, p. 15). Researchers on terrorism can avoid ethnocentrism in three ways. First, researchers must recognize that terrorism and terrorists are found in a wide array of cultures. Therefore, they should deliberately place manifestations and perpetrators of terrorism within specific cultural contexts in order to minimize stereotyped representations. Second, researchers must acknowledge cultural differences between themselves and the phenomena that they study. They should intentionally organize and process information so as to avoid prejudicing the impartiality of their observations and validity of their inferences. Finally, researchers must confront the limitations of mainstream psychological theories in explaining and studying terrorism. They should consider alternative conceptual frameworks and investigative methodologies that underscore the neglected global circumstances in which terrorists are constituted and how these contribute to the emergence of terrorism.

GLOBALIZATION

Globalization Defined

Globalization has been the watchword of developed nations since the fall of communism in the early 1990s. Friedman (2000) defines globalization as "the inexorable integration of markets, nation-states and technologies to a degree never witnessed before—in a way that is enabling individuals, corporations and nation-states to reach around the world farther, faster, deeper and cheaper than ever before, and in a way that is enabling the world to reach into individuals, corporations and nation-states farther, faster, deeper, cheaper than ever before" (p. 9). Globalization is characterized by worldwide integration through an ongoing, dynamic process that involves the interplay of free enterprise, democratic principles and human rights, the high-tech exchange of information, and movement of large numbers of people.

Western powers have been unchallenged in their quest to mold worldwide economic and political conditions. Unlike traditional conquerors, the West is not content to subdue others. Rather, the West insists that others embrace free markets, democracy, and technology for their own good (Barber, 1995; Friedman, 2000). To this end, the West has exported its economy, political institutions, technologies, and culture with little regard to how they might be received. Many nations and peoples view the West as arrogant because of its claim to values that are either universal or superior to those of other cultures (Wheeler, 1998). While the juggernaut of free enterprise, democracy, and technology offers the best chance of wealth creation, which is a prerequisite for improving the human condition (Aram, 1997; Friedman, 2000), it has produced economic inequality, indifference to the status of women and children, threats to language and community, and support for oppressive regimes (Barber, 1995; Nikelly, 2000). By prioritizing individualism, consumerism, and pragmatism, the traditional values and customs of many cultures have become endangered. Simply put, economic measures of well-being overlook the sociocultural and psychosocial costs of globalization (Aram, 1997; Barber, 1995; Wheeler, 1998). These unanticipated costs have triggered a backlash by those brutalized, humiliated, or left behind by the new world order. This backlash was also unanticipated because of Western assumptions that indigenous cultures would be unable to resist economic, political, and social homogenization (Barber, 1995; Friedman, 2000; Wheeler, 1998).

Although the benefits of globalization to peoples of the developing world are manifest (e.g., improved health, higher income, greater literacy), the West has been unwilling to acknowledge globalization's downside. Globalization per se does not cause terrorism nor does it explain all forms of terrorism. However, the extent to which globalization foments sufficient resistance to hearten some individuals and groups to pursue terrorism merits investigation. Below, I examine the sequelae of globalization more closely, particularly those that might offer a milieu that generates terrorism.

Sociocultural Dislocation as an Outcome of Globalization

The worldwide march toward economic growth and democratic ideals is welcome in the framework of a Western perspective of limitless self-realization, but can trigger political and social instability elsewhere (Aram, 1997; Barber, 1995; Nikelly, 2000). As noted earlier, globalization is pinned to an individualistic, impersonal, competitive, privatistic, and mobile worldview. This worldview strongly contradicts the parameters of communitarian cultures (Euben, 1995; Nikelly, 2000; Wheeler, 1998). Within such cultures, individuals are linked through common interests, shared resources, and mutual respect. Intimacy and support are valued. Personal goals are subordinated to cooperation and obligation. Globalization weakens collectivist values by exporting a highly divergent liberal worldview (Nikelly, 2000). Globalization also pools enormous affluence and power within a few while the vast majority toil to enhance others' wealth and status. Such outcomes disrupt the fabric of society and create psychological distress for millions. That globalization has been resisted is not surprising given the fact that 70 percent of the world's population belongs to non-Western cultures (Nikelly, 2000).

Globalization undermines social cohesion in three ways. First, nations are weakened due to challenges to centralized economies and the pursuit of private wealth as well as the growing standardization of experience via telecommunications (Aram, 1997; Barber, 1995; Friedman, 2000). The weakening of nations yields a political vacuum that is often filled by xenophobic and aggressive reactionary forces, some international in scope, that, paradoxically, strengthen either a malignant form of nationalism that globalization was expected to supplant or a parochialism that might fuel international conflict and support terrorism (Aram, 1997; Barber, 1995; Friedman, 2000; Weinberg & Eubank, 2000).

Second, globalization places civil society in jeopardy (Aram, 1997; Barber, 1995). The traditional functions of such cohesive social units as family, clan, and voluntary association are enfeebled by the relentless pursuit of material gain and personal freedom. The self-absorption of consumerism, the alienation of technologically based living, and the mobility of large segments of the population have undercut the social capacity for institutional regulation (Aram, 1997). For communitarian societies, keyed to historical continuity, group coherence and security, personal rootedness, and the affirmation of moral righteousness, empowering the individual is equated with rending society asunder (Euben, 1995; Friedman, 2000; Wheeler, 1998). Globalization has strained the relationship between the individual and community so that many social institutions appear to be disintegrating (Friedman, 2000). The withering of civil society can precipitate violent compensatory reactions intended to reclaim and fortify cultural institutions that are threatened by globalization (Barber, 1995).

Finally, longstanding multicultural tensions in different parts of the world prevent recently imported democratic institutions from transcending class, ethnicity, and religion (Aram, 1997). The tenets of democracy, most notably equality and self-determination, overlook the concerns of culturally diverse groups, which often find themselves in conflict with the symbols and values of the dominant culture. The democratic principle of consensus is often experienced as cultural homogenization in that the special needs and issues of some constituencies fall second to the interests of the majority. Because globalization necessitates the mingling of different ethnic, racial, and religious groups, it poses a challenge for democracy. Paradoxically, then, globalization's economic and political agenda, having sought to realize social equality and individual rights by fiat, may exacerbate intergroup conflict due to forced contact and competition between cultures, as well as between indigenous cultures and the West (Barber, 1995). Such conflict may become violent when governments apply coercive measures to suppress the expression of disempowered groups, especially during turbulent macro-social change (Aram, 1997).

Psychosocial Dysfunction as an Outcome of Globalization

The weakening of national sovereignty, erosion of civil society, and expression of intergroup conflict are indicators of the sociocultural dislocation associated with globalization. It is plausible that various manifestations of psychosocial dysfunction co-vary with these macro-social symptom indicators (Kleinman, 2001). There is growing consensus that, although the benefits of globalization accrue over time, globalization produces psychosocial dysfunction rapidly, especially for those vulnerable to the transition to a free market (Barber, 1995; Friedman, 2000). For example, Bandura (2001) hypothesized that globalization challenges people to find control over their destinies because daily life is increasingly shaped by events in distant places. Globalization affects social systems by reducing opportunities for agentic transactions through which efficacy expectancies develop. With weaker efficacy expectancies, people are more vulnerable to psychosocial dysfunction. Considerable research must be done, however, to establish that globalization threatens psychosocial well-being and to determine which aspects of globalization impair psychosocial functioning (Kleinman, 2001). Nevertheless, there is suggestive evidence that globalization adversely affects individuals living in non-Western, communitarian societies. Four examples follow.

- Clinically defined, addiction refers to a progressive, chronic pattern of behavior that involves features such as a compulsion to use substances, loss of control over substance use, and continued substance use in spite of adverse consequences. Addictive behavior is endemic to free-market democracies because such societies often disenfranchise people from traditional sources of psychological, social, and spiritual support (Alexander, 2000). Disenfranchised people struggle to restore their lost integration, pursuing substitute lifestyles that often center on the maladaptive use of substances. When substitute lifestyles are the best adaptation that people can achieve, they cling to them. Not only is there a historical and contemporary correlation between dislocation and addictive behavior (e.g., the epidemic of alcoholism in the United States during the free-market expansion of the 1800s, the adaptational function of the "crack economy" for African Americans), but, because the free market is the bulwark of globalization, the prevalence of addictive behavior is increasing worldwide (Alexander, 2000).

- Compulsive dieting and debilitating eating disorders are widespread among young women in Western societies. The claim that eating disorders are culture-bound has been challenged by studies of young women in several non-Western nations. Lee and Lee (1996) found that body dissatisfaction and eating disorders among Chinese adolescent females in Hong Kong were predicted by family conflict and the lack of family cohesion. A plausible argument for these results is the heightened exposure of these women to Western culture. The findings suggest that eating disorders may be mediated by traditional social structures weakened by globalization.

• Young South African Indian women have a relatively high rate of suicide. Investigations have sought to place the suicidal tendencies of these women in the context of cultural dislocation engendered by globalization (Wassenaar, van der Veen, & Pillay, 1998). Tension between traditional Indian culture and globalization in South Africa have challenged longstanding patriarchal power relations between Indian men and women. For example, globalization in South Africa has exposed women to images of emancipation in the media and offered them educational and vocational opportunities for aspiring to social roles of their own choosing. These challenges may produce conflict that has psychological and interpersonal implications. The consequent deterioration of psychological functioning, marital relations, and overall fabric of life appears to be a precursor of suicidal behavior for these women. Similar gender-linked tensions are associated with suicidal behavior worldwide, particularly in Asian nations where women have low social standing (Wassenaar et al., 1998).

• Evidence exists showing that globalization has interfered with the traditional child-rearing practices of the Maori of New Zealand (Sachdev, 1990). Maori child rearing is characterized by an indulgent infancy, the substitution during childhood of peer involvement for parental succorance, and reintegration into adult society during adolescence (Sachdev, 1990). The imposition of Western culture, notwithstanding government initiatives that formalize a commitment to respect Maori customs (Gergen, Gulerce, Lock, & Misra, 1996), appears to have disrupted the personality development of Maori children. Globalization, with its emphasis on self-sufficiency and independence from family, has been hypothesized to explain the high rates of incarceration in prisons and utilization of psychiatric facilities among the Maori (Gergen et al., 1996).

Terrorism as an Outcome of Globalization

The challenge for the twenty-first century is to achieve a balance between the global movement toward free markets and democratic institutions and the preservation of indigenous culture and collective identity (Friedman, 2000). When such a balance cannot be found, dislocation and dysfunction tend to ensue, followed by active resistance that can destabilize governments and societies (Barber, 1995; Friedman, 2000). The current resistance to globalization is broad, is fueled by many issues, and is manifested in various ways. For example, many nations have witnessed a rise in individual and organized crime (e.g., East Europe), with individuals or groups seeking their own security without regard for community or morality (Stevens, 2002). Fundamentalism represents another manifestation of resistance to globalization (Barber, 1995; Euben, 1995; Friedman, 2000; Wheeler, 1998). Fundamentalists detest the homogenization of culture and uprooting of traditional values and customs that anchor people to their world. Resistance to globalization may escalate into violence when economic, political, religious, and cultural forms of resistance coalesce.

Because globalization grants individuals more opportunities and capabilities to shape the world, extreme reactionaries may be emboldened and empowered to wage war on globalization. They are able to do so by exploiting globalization against itself, using telecommunications, financial networks, and weapons of mass destruction to inflict fear, damage, injury, and death. Regardless of whether they have a coherent and viable ideological alternative to globalization, they vent against the West for the turmoil and suffering it has visited upon their world. Targeting the West is sensible from the standpoint that it is the identifiable force behind globalization, with its financial centers, military might, and advanced infrastructure mobilized to export globalization. Although it is unclear whether terrorists genuinely believe they can transform the world, it is plain that they have a potentially achievable goal: to arrest the encroachment of globalization onto the values and traditions that form their worldview.

Psychology's Capacity to Construe Globalization

As American psychology prepares for the challenges of the twenty-first century, it is striving to become more inclusive by globalizing its base of scientific knowledge and applied skills. This effort reflects the cultural and ethnic diversity of populations worldwide, global economic and political interdependence, and sophisticated telecommunications (Mays, Rubin, Sabourin, & Walker, 1996). The globalization of psychology also rests on the premise that the science and practice of psychology must become less parochial and more responsive if it is to help solve problems of living that have no borders (e.g., crime, pollution, poverty, racism) (Mays et al., 1996).

However, "psychologists have been notorious for their absence from the major debates of the past 20 years" (Gergen, 2001, p. 811), including those on terrorism. Much of this neglect is because psychology's traditional focus on individual behavior and small-group processes is ill-suited for addressing societal, national, and global problems. For example, in summarizing the literature related to terrorism, Zimbardo (2001) cited decontextualized research by Milgram on obedience and his own prison-simulation study. It is not only ethnocentric but also bad science and practice to assume that conceptual models and investigative methodologies for small-group phenomena developed by Western psychologists can be applied successfully in larger and different cultures. Moreover, it is not easy to separate psychology from other disciplines, especially when addressing an overdetermined topic such as terrorism. For example, the collective identity and political activism of disempowered groups are essentially inseparable (Gergen, 1996; Gergen et al., 1996). Because terrorism, like intergroup conflict, is rooted in a complex matrix of economics, history, politics, psychology, and religion, a comprehensive understanding of terrorism and terrorists can only be achieved in a contextually sensitive and multidisciplinary manner.

As stated before, the primary reason for psychology's neglect of the adverse sociocultural and psychosocial impact of globalization is the absence in most theories of constructs that explain the process of macro-social change and resistance to such change. The positivistic basis for most psychological theory and research does not identify mechanisms by which economic, political, religious, and cultural variables mediate and moderate both change and stability. Psychological positivism favors the observation of regularities and tends not to cast people as constituted, interactive, and agentic (Stevens, 2002).

The psychological vision of the modern, industrial world called for the separation of individuals from communities that, in pre-modern terms, had shaped and defined them. Psychology endeavored to understand this isolated individual whose actions and interactions were hypothesized to fashion the structure and dynamics of larger social formations (e.g., community, society, nation) (Sampson, 1989). Positivistic psychology also makes claim to an objectivity that supersedes cultural limits and a universally applicable investigative methodology (Gergen, 2001; Gergen et al., 1996). However, assumptions of a rational, materialistic, functionalist, and self-contained individual often fail to capture the "local truth" about individuals who are constituted in non-Western cultures (Gergen et al., 1996).

Growing awareness that the world is becoming a globally interdependent network of individuals, communities, and nations, coupled with a recognition of the dangers of ethnocentric science and practice, has fostered a transformation in psychology. Theories of the person and about unusual events have become more sensitive to the sociocultural world in which people function and events occur (Gergen, 1996, 2001; Sampson, 1989). The modernist tradition of individualism is slowly evolving into a postmodern framework (e.g., deconstructionism, feminism). Postmodernism aims to understand the nature of individuals and groups in the context of a globally linked world (Sampson, 1989). Within this paradigm, the conception of the individual has been reconstructed as relational and constituted by his or her sociocultural milieu (Gergen, 1996, 2001; Gergen et al., 1996). Hence, the study of the individual adopts nonreductionistic approaches that preserve the unity of the person and the context in which he or she is embedded. This reformulation has not yet been applied to the dramatic manifestations of the new world order, namely a constitutive, relational interpretation of globalization and terrorism.

PSYCHOLOGICAL THEORIES THAT LINK TERRORISM TO GLOBALIZATION

Psychological explanations of how the adverse effects of globalization contribute to terrorism must draw on paradigms that link the individual to economics, history, politics, religion, and culture (Crenshaw, 2000; Pynchon & Borum, 1999). As already discussed, modern psychology rests on a positivistic or decontextualized approach to discovering the causes of behavior; with respect to terrorism, positivistic psychology has yielded useful but incomplete accounts of terrorism by focusing mainly on intra- and interpersonal causal factors. I believe that behavior generally and terrorism specifically can be more fully explained when causal perspectives are complemented by normative ones. Normative frameworks stipulate that behavior is constituted in social relations. That is, behavior is generated by meaning systems that are collectively constructed and contextually sensitive (Moghaddam & Lvina, 2002). Normative frameworks offer powerful ways to understand the phenomenon of terrorism and terrorists and extend what can be gleaned from positivistic models (Pynchon & Borum, 1999). I draw on three normative theories to provide a contextualized understanding of terrorism as an unanticipated consequence of globalization: social identity theory (Tajfel & Turner, 1979, 1986; Turner, Hogg, Oakes, Reicher, & Wetherell, 1987), social reducton theory (Moghaddam & Harré, 1996), and Vygotsky's (1978) sociocultural theory.

Social Identity Theory

Social identity theory is concerned with the relations between groups, especially groups that have unequal power (Hewstone & Greenland, 2000; Pynchon & Borum, 1999; Taylor & Moghaddam, 1994). The theory predicts the circumstances in which people are motivated to maintain or change their group membership and intergroup situation. It construes group relations as fluid and intergroup conflict as determined by normal psychological processes operating in unusual circumstances.

The major assumption underlying social identity theory is that individuals are motivated to maintain or achieve a positive, more inclusive self-definition (Tajfel & Turner, 1979, 1986; Turner et al., 1987). In a group context, this implies a preference to belong to groups that have prestige and value. According to the theory, individuals define themselves partly by their group membership, which fulfills several basic psychological needs, including belongingness, distinctiveness, respect, understanding, and agency. Social identity per se consists of elements of self-concept that derive from groups to which a person belongs, the status ascribed to group membership, and the emotional consequences of membership in positively or negatively valenced groups. Simply put, being a member of a group contributes to self-concept and the valence of that group influences self-worth.

In addition to categorizing the social environment into groups and identifying themselves by groups to which they belong (i.e., ingroups), individuals make social comparisons between groups (Tajfel & Turner, 1979, 1986; Turner et al., 1987). Specifically, they compare characteristics of the ingroup to other groups in order to determine the extent to which the ingroup offers them a distinct and positive identity. When group members evaluate the ingroup more favorably, they make positive attributions about the ingroup and experience satisfaction. Less favorable evaluations relative to another group contribute to the formation of a negative social identity and dissatisfaction.

An inferior ingroup evaluation prompts efforts to improve the relative status of the ingroup. The choice of restorative strategies depends on the ingroup's perception of its status vis-à-vis the outgroup. These perceptions are determined by three parameters: the legitimacy and stability of the social-comparison outcome and the permeability of group boundaries (Tajfel & Turner, 1979, 1986; Turner et al., 1987). The outcome of a social comparison may be viewed as legitimate or illegitimate (i.e., just vs. unjust) or as stable or unstable (i.e., open to change vs. exempt from change); the boundaries between groups may also perceived as permeable or impermeable (i.e., integration vs. segregation). Unfavorable group comparisons experienced by the ingroup as illegitimate and stable and that occur in circumstances in which group boundaries are impermeable result in a profound state of relative deprivation for the ingroup, sowing the seeds of terrorism. Negative social-comparison outcomes perceived as illegitimate and stable deprive the ingroup of alternatives to its negative status; perceptions of group impermeability further deprive ingroup members of mobility.

The parameters that influence ingroup perceptions of its relative status also affect the breadth of cognitive alternatives that mediate the choice of strategies for improving social identity (Tajfel & Turner, 1979, 1986; Turner et al., 1987). Members may redefine ingroup characteristics more positively (e.g., "Black is beautiful"), create or find new dimensions for making more favorable comparisons (e.g., "Palestinians are defenders of the Holy Land"), or find an alternative group against which to make a social comparison (e.g., by comparing themselves to Jewish *untermenschen*, Nazis resurrected German identity following World War I). Depending on the level of illegitimacy, stability, and impermeability, ingroup members may confront the reference group directly, even violently, in order to redress perceived inequalities in status. Feeling aggrieved as a group is necessary in order for people to engage in violent struggle on behalf of their group.

Social identity theory also proposes that group membership becomes particularly salient during intergroup conflict because of heightened awareness of shared grievances (Tajfel & Turner, 1979; 1986; Turner et al., 1987). Under these conditions, social components of self-concept become more prominent than individual components. Concern with the ingroup replaces self-interest, self-perceptions and conduct conform to ingroup stereotypes (e.g., *my* experiences become *our* experiences), and the ingroup is viewed as coherent and homogeneous. Moreover, studies have shown that when they are in conflict groups become more prejudiced attitudinally and aggressive behaviorally than do individuals (e.g., Mummendey, Kessler, Klink, & Mielke, 1999), perhaps because of a tendency toward outgroup stereotyping (Simon & Klandermans, 2001). Intergroup violence can be further intensified if a group with a negative social identity is isolated and its members rely on a leader for information about current events. In such cases, ingroup members' perceptions of outgroups and relevant external events may become distorted, causing them to view the outgroup as an enemy. Consequently, ingroups may be willing to inflict costly harm on their adversaries via terrorism (Simon & Klandermans, 2001).

Social identity theory has been applied to Hindu–Muslim conflict in India, revealing the degree to which individuals and groups will defend cherished social identities (Ghosh & Kumar, (1991). The illustration below will clarify how the theory can explain growing international tensions resulting from globalization and the expression of such tensions through terrorism.

The militia movement in the United States is not a mere extension of America's long fascination with right-wing extremism (Pitcavage, 2001). The militia movement, with its distinctive ideology, arose from a series of events that occurred in the 1990s, including the Brady Law and ban on assault weapons and the tragedies at Ruby Ridge and Waco. However, the event that most clearly links globalization to the militia movement was the passage of the North American Free Trade Agreement (NAFTA). NAFTA formalized a more open, unified market for the exchange of goods and services. With its passage, Americans with access to this market and the wherewithal to sell their goods and services became extremely successful. However, NAFTA also widened the income gap after decades of relative stability. This disparity could be traced to increased immigration, which drove down wages, the shift in manufacturing from high- to low-wage countries (e.g., from the United States to Mexico), and technological advances in production (e.g., robots that replaced human workers) (Barber, 1995; Friedman, 2000).

Those who did not benefit from NAFTA found themselves as members of a downwardly mobile ingroup. Whereas they had once identified themselves as belonging to an internationally competitive labor group whose prestige augmented their self-worth, the downwardly mobile now compared themselves to other groups in the workforce that seemed to thrive in the robust economy of the 1990s. Such comparisons yielded a decidedly inferior ingroup evaluation that contributed to the formation of a new, negative social identity and subjective dissatisfaction. The downwardly mobile interpreted their loss of economic viability and prestige as unjust since NAFTA, the source of their social displacement, was never ratified by popular vote. In addition, they considered their inferior group status as permanent because regional trade relations were unlikely to change once ratified. Finally, they viewed themselves as losers in the winner-take-all arena of free trade because of their belief that the government is in league with an international cabal to establish a new world order whose aims are the elimination of sovereign nation-states, the dilution of traditional Western values, and the mongrelization of the races. Thus, the downwardly mobile perceived their devalued group status as illegitimate and stable, with access denied to membership in more economically viable outgroups. As a consequence, the downwardly mobile experienced considerable frustration as there were no perceived avenues to improve their negative group status and identity.

Given the limited means at their disposal to restore self-worth, many of these downwardly mobile may have turned to the militia movement and its anti-globalization ideology of gun ownership, malevolent government, Christian identity, white supremacy, and global conspiracy. The social structure and ideology of militias provided these downwardly mobile with new opportunities to meet their blocked needs for meaning, purposive action, and self-worth. Compelled to distort their inferior ingroup identity due to perceptions that their ingroup membership was unjust, stable, and impermeable, the downwardly mobile who joined militias began to compare themselves favorably with selected outgroups, such as Hispanics and Jews who, through affirmative action and worldwide financial artifice, respectively, are responsible for their adverse social predicament. The militia movement also encourages the invention of new standards against which the downwardly mobile can reevaluate their ingroup status more favorably. For example, militia members' uncompromising stance on firearm ownership is intimately tied to the belief that they are defenders of American sovereignty and values against a tyrannical government in partnership with a usurping global order. That is, they attempt to reestablish their legitimacy by cloaking their agenda and actions in the mantle of law (Pitcavage, 2001). Finally, militia members may make various other distorted comparisons in order to bolster their social standing. David Kuehn, writing for the New Jersey Militia, suggested that "the worst terrorists are centralized governments run amok . . . horrific events like Ruby Ridge and Waco rank alongside the . . . Oklahoma City bombing . . ." (as cited in Pitcavage, 2001, p. 964).

Cognitive distortion and social control increase the potential for violence by militia members. Members' sense of having been wronged by globalization is intensified by rhetoric in which it is claimed that their grievances are shared by a majority of less vocal white, Christian Americans. The desire to protect other perceived victims from mistreatment and suffering focuses militia members on their collective identity and common concerns about globalization to the exclusion of real differences in the strength of ingroup identity and commitment to the movement's anti-globalization agenda. Perceived homogeneity in group identity encourages attitudinal and behavioral conformity, often precursors to violence toward outgroups (e.g., non-white, non-Christian). In addition, conflict between the militias and various government agencies not only radicalizes elements of the militia movement, but also mobilizes people from the political mainstream to join (Pitcavage, 2001). After Ruby Ridge and Waco, there were more frequent splits between extremist cells and their parent militias (e.g., the Bradley Glover group, which seceded from the Third Continental Congress in 1997 for not being sufficiently violent in its struggle against the global order). Finally, militia leaders have learned to inflame members' prejudices toward outgroups and forces perceived as connected to globalization by exploiting communications technology, including computer bulletin boards, satellite radio shows, and fax networks (Pitcavage, 2001). Members' attitudes and actions become even more extreme when militias are physically isolated, like those in remote areas of the United States, since they are insulated from competing perspectives on globalization. There is no better example of the extremes to which militias can go in enacting an ideology created to restore their ingroup status than Timothy McVeigh's bombing of the Murrah Federal Building in Oklahoma City in 1995.

Social Reducton Theory

Social reducton theory (Moghaddam & Harré, 1996) examines the flip-side of macro-social change, namely social continuity and stability, and can be applied to various manifestations of resistance to globalization, including terrorism. Social reducton theory is grounded in the observation that local identity and cultural differences in behavior are surprisingly resilient in the face of imposed change (e.g., economic policies and legislative initiatives) and, when such changes actually occur, they are modest (Wheeler, 1998). A social reducton is a basic unit of analysis that subsumes small-scale patterns of social interaction that take place in daily life (e.g., indigenous customs). Stable social orders that are resistant to "top-down" change are found where social reductons have long been established, specifically, where local meaning structures and derivative actions are so entrenched they are taken for granted.

Social reducton theory (Moghaddam & Harré, 1996) attempts to explain the apparent paradox that globalization, which promises to improve people's material existence and expand individual rights, is met with profound, sometimes violent resistance (Wheeler, 1998). The theory rests on four propositions that articulate resistance to change. First, the rate of macro-social change, involving institutional transformations, occurs more rapidly than change that takes place at the micro-social level of everyday interaction. Second, micro-social change occurs within social reducton systems or "inter-connected networks of locally valid practices, implemented through implicit norms and related social skills that realize social relationships in particular domains" (Moghaddam & Harré, 1996, p. 231). Social reducton systems include family, village, and, in the case of globalization, culture. Third, social reducton systems consist of interlaced units of interaction (i.e., reductons), each expressed in a way that is congruent with local norms and impacts social relationships. Finally, social reducton systems are maintained by carriers (e.g., myths, traditions) that are embedded in culture and influence members of a culture through socialization. Because some carriers have been strengthened by their survival over many generations, they are able to resist macro-social change (Moghaddam & Lvina, 2002).

Carriers have three important characteristics. First, carriers serve as anchors, limiting the amount of change by seeking homeostasis. Second, carriers vary in the importance of the meaning attached to them. Finally, carriers are flexible in how they are called upon to rally support for resistance to imposed change. Carriers represent valued features of culture and include such symbols as flags. Carriers also include cognitive constructions, such as stereotypes about individuals based on their group membership (e.g., all Americans are seen by some Muslims as infidels). Social reducton theory has been applied to France, Iran, Japan, and Russia with the consistent finding that macro-social change is limited when it is imposed, due to the resilience of elementary normative practices (Moghaddam et al., 1999; Moghaddam & Harré, 1996; Moghaddam & Lvina, in press). I will now apply social reducton theory to explain emerging Islamic resistance to globalization, including the use of terrorism.

The Iranian revolution of 1978–1979 installed a regime that aimed to establish an Islamic state by transforming everyday social relations (Moghaddam & Harré, 1996). Comprehensive efforts were undertaken to compel a major shift in two fundamental social reductons: gender relations (i.e., women's role in society) and power hierarchies (e.g., mechanisms for becoming an authority figure). To accomplish this, Iran's ayatollahs drew upon a well-articulated set of normative standards from the Koran that govern daily conduct. Although Westernization had rendered these Islamic social ordinances less salient, most Iranians were familiar with them, and it was relatively easy for the government to institute them as a culturally congruent means of resisting the encroachment of Westernization.

Islamic revolution is not limited to Iran. In his will, Ayatollah Khomeini summoned Muslims to perpetuate divine revolution against "world-devouring America" (Foreign Broadcast Information Services, 1989). Islamic fundamentalism has spread to many parts of the Muslim world (Euben, 1995; Friedman, 2000; Jensen, 2001; Weinberg & Eubank, 2000). The surfacing of intensely felt and violently expressed conflict reflects vast differences in the rational-actor worldview of Western civilization and the divine-sovereignty worldview of Islamic civilization, as well as powerful resentment of the hegemonic and homogenizing influence of globalization (Wheeler, 1998). Ideologically, fundamentalists decry that the world is dominated by humanly conceived economic and political systems that deny or corrupt divine authority (Euben, 1995; Jensen, 2001). More tangibly, globalization has eroded Islamic institutions and practices that maintain social cohesion and individual well-being (Aram, 1997; Friedman, 2000; Nikelly, 2000). By placing economic, political, and cultural grievances into a religious framework, Islamic fundamentalists offer a familiar and compelling meaning structure to mobilize widespread resistance to globalization (Crenshaw, 2000; Euben, 1995; Friedman, 2000; Tessler & Nachtwey, 1998). In terms specific to social reducton theory, Islamic meaning structures involve the explicit identification and strengthening of Muslim formulas of social understanding and interaction that predate globalization and serve to resist the macro-social changes that obtain from it (Tessler & Nachtwey, 1998; Wheeler, 1998).

The fact that globalization continues to advance in spite of Islamic resistance may explain the emergence of a more extreme, twenty-first-century form of terrorism. Technology (e.g., cell phones, the Internet) decays traditional social reducton systems and the cultural norms that they express by exposing isolated societies to Western information and values. Beyond technology, the economic and political policies associated with globalization accelerate the disintegration of indigenous culture (Moghaddam et al., 1999; Nikelly, 2000). These policies vastly expand entitlements and capabilities, creating unprecedented opportunities for individual choice. Orthodox Islamic societies find the explosion of information and opportunities for individual choice extremely threatening because they are not readily accommodated by social reducton systems. Thus, globalization tends to undermine social reducton systems (Euben, 1995; Wheeler, 1998).

There are several carriers in the Muslim world that function to resist globalization. The veil, and more conservative apparel such as the chador and burqa, is a meaningful carrier that symbolizes an implicit set of normative rules that anchor the role of women in relation to men and to society, generally (Moghaddam & Harré, 1996; Mule & Barthel, 1992). Specifically, the veil reminds women to think and behave modestly, to honor family, and to model culturally valued forms of social conduct (e.g., eye contact and touch are prohibited because they may arouse desire). The veil also symbolizes social reductons that define women's public roles. In conservative Muslim countries, women are segregated in public places, such as schools and mosques. Recently, young, educated, middle-class women from various Muslim countries have returned to the veil (Mule & Barthel, 1992). They reject the negative image of women's liberation associated with globalization. For many Muslim women, globalization imposed an ideology of freedom from social constraints that can lead to exploitation by men and a consequent decline in status and respect. Through the veil, they rediscover a powerful source of cultural identity and esteem sanctioned by Islam. The veil, then, is a nonviolent carrier of Muslim women's protest against globalized feminism that threatens to alienate them from their family and heritage; it advertises cultural loyalty in a milieu where such loyalty is equated with national, ethnic, and religious honor, dignity, and purity (Mule & Barthel, 1992).

As described earlier, carriers can also include cognitive representations, such as stereotypes. A frequently expressed stereotype in radicalized parts of the Muslim world identifies America as "The Great Satan." This negative stereotype of an entire nation has political implications as well as obvious religious significance. It not only has a stabilizing function by offering a simple, normative explanation for concerns about globalization but also can incite violent reactionary responses against entities identified as responsible for current and anticipated grievances linked to globalization. The message of this particular carrier is that globalization is morally illegitimate because it deviates from Islamic law, and, hence, demands a profound response (Tessler & Nachtwey, 1998). Consequently, it activates a variety of social reductons that implement the tenets and preserve the integrity of Islamic culture: the unity of political and moral realms (i.e., Islam provides the basis for governance in law, not secular knowledge), divine authority over earthly matters (i.e., realization of a global world must be premised on morality, not self-interest), and the redemptive role of collective action that expresses divine will (i.e., righteous Muslims must sacrifice themselves to restore God's sovereignty, not base their actions on a rational evaluation of risk) (Euben, 1995).

Last, there are carriers that are not traditionally Islamic, but which have been expropriated or invented to engender radical resistance to globalization. Fundamentalists of all stripes have become adept at weaving economic, political, and cultural grievances against globalization into symbols of militant backlash. Televised demonstrations in Pakistan against the allied incursion into Afghanistan have shown protesters carrying posters of Osama bin Laden, now a human carrier who represents ultraviolent resistance to globalization. Likewise, the image of a raised fist holding a Kalashnikov rifle is a flexible carrier used to promote armed resistance to globalization. Both carriers represent an Islamic social reducton, albeit distorted, that mandates prescribed behavior by Muslims (i.e., *jihad*) to solve problems created by Western ignorance and arrogant disrespect for divine law (Euben, 1995).

Vygotsky's Sociocultural Theory

Vygotsky's sociocultural theory centers on how the beliefs, customs, skills, and values of a culture are transmitted (Vygotsky, 1978). Vygotsky believed that individuals are active and constructive and that learning is socially mediated and life-long. He proposed that dialogues with experienced members of the community are necessary for the acquisition of a cultural worldview. The essential features of culture transmitted through such interaction are internalized and used to guide effective action and further the development of life skills. Vygotsky essentially conceptualized development as learning via interaction, followed by internationalization, and culminating in the transformation of meaning. The ability and opportunity to communicate with others is critical to an evolution in understanding and behavior necessary for adaptation to a changing world.

The significance of Vygotsky's (1978) work owes much to its displacement of psychology's emphasis on autonomous, self-contained individuals with a more relational conception of the person. Although much of Vygotsky's research focused on cognitive development and the use of language by children, by extension, his perspective offers a framework for conceptualizing cultural resistance to globalization. The notion of culture as a regulatory system that provides rules and recipes for effective behavior dovetails with Vygotsky's theory of how such regulation becomes internalized as a sign system that, in turn, mediates attitudes and behavior.

As noted, globalization involves economic, political, and social change. It short-circuits existing sign systems that govern daily life. Globalization creates a gap between existing sign systems that regulate behavior and new controls that have yet to be learned and internalized, but which are essential for negotiating a social order in flux. People in non-Western cultures who have been impacted by globalization experience psychological disequilibrium because formulas for successful living based on established patterns of social interaction no longer work. Disequilibrium motivates efforts to regain control by mastering and internalizing a new set of cultural interactions with which to understand and adjust to the dislocations wrought by globalization. It is this sort of adaptation, motivated by a need to understand macro-social change via interaction, that Vygotsky (1978) termed the zone of proximal development, or locus of individual change. Cultural guides assume a critical role in mediating the cognitive gap created by globalization because they provide opportunities for interpersonal engagement, learning, internationalization, and adjustment. The lack of formative experiences and opportunities to internalize interpersonal interactions produces adaptational failure (i.e., living without cultural guidelines) and maladjustment. Likewise, the closing of cognitive gaps through interaction with cultural guides who advocate ideology and action aimed at obliterating the sources of disequilibrium can lead to the acquisition of an internal sign system that produces a violent, terroristic worldview as a way to master the world. Vygotsky's sociocultural theory has been used to describe the sociocultural and psychosocial consequences of Westernization among rural Africans (Gilbert, 1989). I now apply Vygotsky's sociocultural theory to the Marxist revolutionary movement against modernization in Venezuela and extrapolate it to emerging terrorist resistance to globalization.

Following the discovery of oil, Venezuela entered into a turbulent period of transition. National values and customs were challenged by international economic, political, and social forces that propelled Venezuela into the industrialized world. As with nations undergoing rapid macro-social change as a result of today's globalization, Venezuela was host to many contrasts that were difficult to reconcile psychologically (e.g., steel and glass apartment buildings adjacent to tin shacks) and that yielded social unrest. When confronted by the poverty and oppression under which many lived, coupled with the lack of opportunity and means to share in the prosperity enjoyed by the few, a small group of Venezuelans, many of whom were deeply committed to the betterment of humanity, became radicalized by Marxism. Prior to their revolutionary indoctrination, these individuals were in a state of psychological disequilibrium because they did not possess the understanding and mastery of the social interactions necessary to render their existing humanitarian sign system compatible with the demands of a free-market, multinational world. However, they were able to acquire an alternative sign system through their exposure to Marxism, for which there is a cultural affinity in Latin America. Their exposure was interpersonal in that they learned about Marxism by interacting with seasoned revolutionary guides, many from Cuba. Discussing and living Marxism provided these dislocated and disaffected individuals with a zone of proximal development that yielded an new internalized sign system with which to engage a changing Venezuela. Thus, they succeeded in adjusting by internalizing a doctrine that was centered on equality, sharing, and responsibility for others and that directed them purposively toward violent confrontation with the oppressive institutions and unjust policies of the government.

The role of *madrasahs* (religious schools) in Pakistan that spawned the Taliban can also be analyzed from Vygotsky's (1978) sociocultural theory. Thousands of graduates of these schools have returned not only to Afghanistan, but also to central Asian nations as well as Indonesia, Malaysia, Thailand, and the Philippines, where they promote a militant Islam in mosques, schools, and charitable organizations. The mullahs who serve as instructors are cultural mentors for disenfranchised and traumatized young men. They facilitate the replacement of obsolete sign systems that are not capable of negotiating the globalized world by engaging their students in a zone of proximal development that mediates the acquisition and internalization of new learning. In turn, the graduates of these schools are cultural mentors to many more who learn and incorporate new regulatory formulas for dealing with globalization. They close the cognitive chasm by reconstructing their shattered cultural worldview with a violent ideology, transmitted to them via social discourse, that fosters terrorist action directed toward the source of their discontinuity and distress.

CONCLUSION

Globalization per se does not cause terrorism nor does it explain all forms of terrorism. However, the extent to which globalization dislocates individuals from their sociocultural roots and creates psychosocial distress is revealed in the magnitude and intensity of resistance to globalization. Because a strong connection exists between the effects of globalization and conditions that nurture terrorism, I urge scholars to consider the benefits of investigating terrorism from conceptual and methodological perspectives that have a constitutive, relational orientation. Such perspectives are particularly well-suited for addressing the social, transnational, and global realities of contemporary terrorism. Social identity theory, social reducton theory, and Vygotsky's sociocultural theory can complement and extend what has been discovered through positivistic psychological approaches. These theories have generated a large body of cross-cultural and transnational research. They have testable hypotheses that can be applied to a wide range of groups and intergroup phenomena, including groups engaged in violence and terrorism. Finally, they examine issues relevant to the study of terrorism, such as the effects of inferior group status on individual and collective action, the role of cultural carriers in resisting globalization, and the interpersonal learning of radical ideologies. By melding the complex economic, historical, political, religious, and cultural contexts in which terrorism unfolds with accounts of the psychological history and functioning of terrorists and the small-group processes that mediate the identity formation and socialization of terrorists, terrorism can be more coherently and fully understood. It is for future researchers to evaluate empirically the explanatory power and predictive utility of the relationship between globalization and terrorism provided by social identity theory, social reducton theory, and Vygotsky's sociocultural theory, specifically, and by the integration positivistic and constitutive paradigms, generally.

I am optimistic that future research that incorporates innovative models and methodologies will advance the nascent field of terrorism studies. I also believe that such efforts will contribute to policies and interventions that are more effective in preventing terrorism and improving discourse among different cultures. There is no *a priori* reason why a balance cannot be struck between the global movement toward free enterprise and democracy and the preservation of indigenous culture and collective identity. While recent events and human history suggest that our linguistic and cognitive capacities are not adequate to the task of overcoming hard-wired tendencies to solve problems through violence, Gaddis (2001) reminds us that implementation of a strategic vision can remedy many of the grievances that fuel terrorism. Pointing to Cold War precedents, Gaddis notes how the West succeeded in fashioning a much more congenial second half of the twentieth century through multilateralism, cultivating great-power relationships, pursuing regional justice in a consistent manner while preserving geopolitical order, and balancing free-market forces against a social safety net.

Given these lessons, we must dedicate ourselves to realizing a kinder, gentler globalization, one that invites genuine partnership, shows respect for cultural differences, nurtures democratic institutions, and offers more sensitive methods for its inevitable implementation. Such a globalization stands to benefit rather than harm developing nations and the world generally.

REFERENCES

Alexander, B. K. (2000). The globalization of addiction. *Addiction Research, 8,* 501–526.

Aram, J. D. (1997). Challenges to the social foundations of capitalism in an age of global economics. *Human Relations, 50,* 967–986.

Bandura, A. (2001). The changing face of psychology at the dawning of a globalization era. *Canadian Psychology, 42,* 12–24.

Barber, B. R. (1995). *Jihad vs. McWorld.* New York: Times Books.

Brannan, D. W., Esler, P. F., & Strindberg, N. T. A. (2001). Talking to "terrorists": Towards an independent analytical framework for the study of violent substate activism. *Studies in Conflict and Terrorism, 24,* 3–24.

Byman, D. (1998). The logic of ethnic terrorism. *Studies in Conflict and Terrorism, 21,* 149–169.

Cooper, H. H. A. (2001). Terrorism: The problem of definition revisited. *American Behavioral Scientist, 44,* 881–893.

Crenshaw, M. (2000). The psychology of terrorism: An agenda for the 21st century. *Political Psychology, 21,* 405–420.

Euben, R. (1995). When worldviews collide: Conflicting assumptions about human behavior held by rational actor theory and Islamic fundamentalism. *Political Psychology, 16,* 157–178.

Foreign Broadcast Information Services. (1989, June 5). *Part I of will and testament* [radio broadcast]. Tehran, Iran: Tehran Radio.

Friedman, T. L. (2000). *The Lexus and the olive tree* (2nd ed.). New York: Anchor Books.

Gaddis, J. L. (2001). And now this: Lessons from the old era for the new one. In S. Talbott & N. Chanda (Eds.), *The age of terror: America and the world after September 11.* New York: Basic Books.

Gergen, K. J. (1996). Theory under threat: Social construction and identity politics. In C. Tolman, F. Cherry, R. Van Hezewijk, & I. Lubeck (Eds.), *Problems of theoretical psychology* (pp. 13–23). North York, ON, Canada: Captus Press.

Gergen, K. J. (2001). Psychological science in a postmodern context. *American Psychologist, 56,* 803–813.

Gergen, K. J., Gulerce, A., Lock, A., & Misra, G. (1996). Psychological science in cultural context. *American Psychologist, 51,* 496–503.

Gilbert, A. (1989). Things fall apart? Psychological theory in the context of rapid social change. *South African Journal of Psychology, 19,* 91–100.

Ghosh, E. S., & Kumar, R. (1991). Hindu–Muslim intergroup relations in India: Applying socio-psychological perspectives. *Psychology and Developing Societies, 3,* 93–112.

Hewstone, M., & Greenland, K. (2000). Intergroup conflict. *International Journal of Psychology, 35,* 136–144.

Hoffman, B. (1999). The mind of the terrorist: Perspectives from social psychology. *Psychiatric Annals, 6,* 337–340.

Jensen, C. J., III. (2001). Beyond the tea leaves: Futures research and terrorism. *American Behavioral Scientist, 44,* 914–936.

Johnson, L. C. (2001). The future of terrorism. *American Behavioral Scientist, 44,* 894–913.

Kleinman, A. (2001). A psychiatric perspective on global change. *Harvard Review of Psychiatry, 9,* 46–47.

Lee, A. M., & Lee, S. (1996). Distorted eating and its psychosocial correlates among Chinese adolescent females. *International Journal of Eating Disorders, 20*, 177–183.

Levine, S. (1999). Youth in terroristic groups, gangs, and cults: The allure, the animus, and the alienation. *Psychiatric Annals, 6*, 342–349.

Mays, V. M., Rubin, J., Sabourin, M., & Walker, L. (1996). Moving toward a global psychology: Changing theories and practice to meet the needs of a changing world. *American Psychologist, 51*, 485–487.

Medd, R., & Goldstein, F. (1997). International terrorism on the eve of a new millennium. *Studies in Conflict and Terrorism, 20*, 281–316.

Merari, A. (2000). Terrorism as a strategy of struggle: Past and future. In M. Taylor & J. Horgan (Eds.), *The future of terrorism* (pp. 52–65). Portland, OR: Frank Cass.

Moghaddam, F. M., Bianchi, C., Daniels, K., & Apter, M. J. (1999). Psychology and national development. *Psychology and Developing Societies, 11*, 119–141.

Moghaddam, F. M., & Harré, R. (1996). Psychological limits to political revolutions: An application of social reducton theory. In E. Hasselberg, L. Martienssen, & F. Radtke (Eds.), *Der dialogbegriff am ende des 20 jahrhunderts* [The concept of dialogue at the end of the 20th century] (pp. 230–240). Berlin: Hegel Institute.

Moghaddam, F. M., & Lvina, E. (2002). Toward a psychology of societal change and stability: The case of human rights and duties. *International Journal of Group Tensions, 31*, 31–51.

Mule, P., & Barthel, D. (1992). The return to the veil: Individual autonomy vs. social esteem. *Sociological Forum, 7*, 323–332.

Mummendey, A., Kessler, T., Klink, A., & Mielke, R. (1999). Strategies to cope with negative social identity: Predictions by social identity theory and relative deprivation theory. *Journal of Personality and Social Psychology, 76*, 229–245.

Nikelly, A. G. (2000). Globalization and community feelings: Are they compatible? *Journal of Individual Psychology, 56*, 435–447.

Office of the Coordinator for Counterterrorism. (1994). *Patterns of global terrorism: 1994* (U.S. Department of State Publication No. 10136). Washington, DC: U.S. Department of State.

Pitcavage, M. (2001). Camouflage and conspiracy: The militia movement from Ruby Ridge to Y2K. *American Behavioral Scientist, 44*, 957–981.

Pynchon, M. R., & Borum, R. (1999). Assessing threats of targeted group violence: Contributions from social psychology. *Behavioral Sciences and the Law, 17*, 339–355.

Sachdev, P. S. (1990). Personality development in traditional Maori society and the impact of modernization. *Psychiatry: Journal for the Study of Interpersonal Processes, 53*, 289–303.

Sampson, E. E. (1989). The challenge of social change for psychology: Globalization and psychology's theory of the person. *American Psychologist, 44*, 914–921.

Simon, B., & Klandermans, B. (2001). Politicized collective identity: A social psychological analysis. *American Psychologist, 56*, 319–331.

Slote, W. H. (1996). Conflict in action: A psychosocial study of a Venezuelan revolutionary. *Political Psychology, 17*, 229–251.

Stevens, M. J. (2002). The interplay of psychology and societal transformation. *International Journal of Group Tensions, 31*, 5–30.

Tajfel, H., & Turner, J. C. (1979). An integrative theory of intergroup conflict. In W. G. Austin & S. Worchel (Eds.), *The social psychology of intergroup relations* (pp. 33–47). Monterey, CA: Brooks/Cole.

Tajfel, H., & Turner, J. C. (1986). The social identity theory of intergroup behavior. In S. Worchel & W. G. Austin (Eds.), *Psychology of intergroup relations* (pp. 7–24). Chicago: Nelson-Hall.

Taylor, D. M., & Moghaddam, F. M. (1994). *Theories of intergroup relations: International social psychological perspectives* (2nd ed.). Westport, CT: Praeger.

Tessler, M., & Nachtwey, J. (1998). Islam and attitudes toward international conflict. *Journal of Conflict Resolution, 42*, 619–636.

Turner, J. C., Hogg, M. A., Oakes, P. J., Reicher, S. D., & Wetherell, M. S. (1987). *Rediscovering the social group: A self-categorization theory*. Oxford, England: Blackwell.

Vygotsky, L. S. (1978). *Mind in society: The development of higher psychological processes*. Cambridge, MA: Harvard University Press.

Wassenaar, D. R., van der Veen, M. B. W., & Pillay, A. L. (1998). Women in cultural transition: Suicidal behavior in South African Indian women. *Suicide and Life-threatening Behavior, 28*, 82–93.

Weinberg, L., & Eubank, W. (2000). Terrorism and the shape of things to come. In M. Taylor & J. Horgan (Eds.), *The future of terrorism* (pp. 94–105). Portland, OR: Frank Cass.

Wheeler, D. L. (1998). Global culture or culture clash. New information technologies in the Islamic World: A view from Kuwait. *Communication Research, 25*, 359–376.

Zimbardo, P. G. (2001, November). Opposing terrorism by understanding the human capacity for evil. *Monitor on Psychology, 32*, 48–50.

3

Cultural and Contextual Aspects of Terrorism

Giovanni Caracci

INTRODUCTION

Terrorism, in all its various forms, has leapt to the foreground as one of the greatest challenges for mental health in the twenty-first century. No longer a distant phenomenon limited to local warring factions, it is increasingly viewed as having a global reach with international ramifications affecting the everyday lives of countless civilians throughout the world. Greatly facilitated by faster and less expensive communication and other technological advances, terrorists are carrying out bold and destructive acts once believed to be beyond the grasp of a rational mind. In an attempt to explain what appears so unexplainable, mental health professionals are often asked to provide an opinion on the genesis of such brutal acts of destruction. While psychological factors may have significance in many terrorist acts, they do not exist in a vacuum; rather, they are inextricably woven with cultural and contextual factors (Caracci, 2000). This chapter argues for a theoretical reframing of the subject of terrorism along cultural and contextual lines, with the purpose of complementing psychological factors to achieve a comprehensive conceptual theory. To this end, examples of cultural/contextual issues underlying terrorist activities will be provided for each domain explored.

The chapter will end with a brief summary of the cultural and contextual aspects of the al-Qaeda group.

CULTURAL AND CONTEXTUAL

The National Institute of Mental Health's Group on Culture and Diagnosis gave the following definition of culture: "Culture refers to meanings, values and behavioral norms that are learned and transmitted in the dominant society and within its social groups. Culture powerfully influences cognition, feelings, and the self concept as well as the diagnostic process and treatment decisions" (Mezzich et al., 1993).

Context is defined by Webster's dictionary as "the interrelated conditions under which something exists or occurs." Though overlapping with culture, context appears to represent a more dynamic concept, based on relations occurring as necessary but not sufficient conditions, a medium for a phenomenon that may require many variables to occur at the same time. Conditions, in other words, are not always prerequisites; rather they should be considered as modifiers or restrictors of terrorism.

Context is used to broaden the view of a complex phenomenon that has backgrounds including other realms, such as the socioeconomic, political, and historic, and media and communications. A discussion of the contextual aspect is meant to complement the cultural aspects rather than excluding them, although there may be a great deal of overlap between the two.

STUDYING TERRORISM

The study of terrorism has gained impetus over the past two decades. From a methodological viewpoint, however, there is little consensus on how to approach the problem. How do we study terrorism when the subjects being studied are clandestine, in hiding, and not available for interview? Seeing interviewers/researchers as agents of governments, institutions, or counterterrorist organizations, terrorists expectedly reject offers for interviews unless it is to promote their agenda through the media. Arrests after failed attempts usually do not shake their deeply rooted convictions, and cases of repentant terrorists willing to provide a glimpse into their inner world are rare. The process of studying terrorism therefore remains by necessity inductive, with all the concomitant limitations and pitfalls. The ideal goal of formulating a comprehensive theory of terrorism often clashes with the complex peculiarity of each terrorist group, a fact that accounts for the reason why many pieces of the puzzle often do not fit.

THE ISSUE OF MOTIVATION

Most of the literature on terrorism relevant to mental health concerns itself with motivation. Who are the terrorists and why do they engage in those behaviors? In this area, the focus is more on purpose than on the background. For example, in her book *The Ultimate Terrorist*, Jessica Stern mentions a few possible reasons why terrorists use weapons of mass destruction, such as attracting attention, emulating God, attacking the economic establishment, or destabilizing governments. She adds that to be successful at killing a large number of people, however, motivation is not enough, as the terrorists would need to be "technically proficient, capable of overcoming moral constraints, organized to avoid detection and willing to use these weapons despite formidable political costs" (Stern, 1999). Regarding subjective reporting, a notable effort in the literature is the one by Cordes, who analyzed the content of terrorists' statements and written documents. Her interesting analysis is based on groups' dynamics as a theoretical framework (Cordes, 1987).

One interesting study, perhaps the largest sample of its kind, comes from West Germany, where social scientists analytically reviewed the life course of 250 West German terrorists, most of them from the Red Army Faction and the June 2nd Movement. The author gathered developmental information pointing to important disruptions in the terrorists' upbringing, such as the loss of one or both parents in about 25 percent of the sample and a conflictual relationship with a hostile father in 75 percent. Moreover, they had a pattern of educational and vocational failures in their lives (Ministry of Interior, Federal Republic of Germany, 1981).

Yet motivation cannot be fully explained without placing the terrorist act in its cultural contextual milieu. Terrorist acts carried out by West European groups such as the Red Army from Germany differ significantly in motivational as well as cultural/contextual factors from others such as the Montoneros in Argentina or the Shining Path in Peru. The same could be said if we compare nationalistic movements such as the Basques to religious fundamentalists such as the Islamic fundamentalist movements. And although groups share beliefs, strategies, and values, cultural/contextual intragroup differences are common. For example, recruits in some of the religious fundamentalist groups include individuals from low, middle, and high social classes, a finding that highlights the wide appeal of these groups among people of different socioeconomic means. In the current literature, individual motivation is often seen as the result of psychological forces, while cultural and contextual factors are viewed as social determinants. In reality, motivational/psychological factors closely articulate with cultural/contextual factors, in the process shaping belief systems and behaviors. As Marta Crenshaw aptly indicated: "Psychological variables must be integrated with environmental factors in order to reach a comprehensive theory" (Crenshaw, 1990b).

LITERATURE ON CULTURAL AND CONTEXTUAL ASPECTS

The literature on cultural issues in terrorism is limited. Cultural factors may be mentioned as important but are usually not the main focus of inquiry. It stands to reason that the cultural matrix of terrorism differs from case to case. The terrorism cultural background of the Basque Nation and Liberty (ETA) is different from that of the Tamil Tigers of Malaysia. Nevertheless, there is no clear-cut systematic study on cultural aspects of terrorism. Typically, researchers have attempted to find common ground among different cultures, rather than focusing on differences and the uniqueness of each group. Noting that when studying terrorism it is easy to over-generalize and engage in reductionism, Walter Reich has stated: "Researchers should take special care to identify the individual and the groups whose behavior they are studying and limit their explanations to those individuals and groups, define the circumstances under which those explanations are valid, and not to suggest more than they do" (Reich, 1990).

Contextual factors are discussed on an individual basis (for example, historical) rather than comprehensively, with rare exceptions (Crenshaw, 1995). We contend that placing terrorist groups in their cultural/contextual perspective may help add focus to this often-problematic field of research.

INDIVIDUAL VERSUS GROUP

Although terrorism can be studied on an individual basis by studying individual terrorists and their cultural contextual milieus, terrorists belong to groups that share their views and shape their beliefs as well as behaviors. Understanding the group's perspective is therefore essential for studying terrorism (Post, 1986). Group leaders provide their followers with both the ideological core and the rules on whose basis the morality of the terrorist action is founded. Group pressure to conform, a process of indoctrination, and the repression of any challenge to the basic principles of the group's ideology are constantly practiced and monitored by the group adherents themselves. The enemy is seen as evil and ready to destroy the group, which, however, is permeated with an aura of invincibility and shares a belief that it will ultimately prevail. Individuals enter groups with a certain cognitive make-up, which was shaped by cultural and contextual factors. These beliefs are then molded within the group, along the lines of its own cultural and contextual factors. Drawing a cognitive map of the group's dominant beliefs may greatly help in understanding and even anticipating its terrorist behavior. Beliefs can be gleaned from a variety of sources, such as scripts, documents, proclamations, historical references, and symbols. The purpose is to create a blueprint for each terrorist group, so that appropriate counterterrorist measures can be tailored with a reasonable degree of predictability.

CULTURAL AND CONTEXTUAL FRAMEWORK OUTLINE

To better understand the impact of cultural and contextual factors on terrorism, we propose the Cultural and Contextual Framework Outline, a tool based on systematically assembling and recording information along cultural and contextual lines.

By articulating culturally relevant material with other sources of inquiry, such as the psychological one, the outline intends to deepen the scope of inquiry on terrorism, and to provide a narrative portrait of the terrorist group free of traditional research constraints. The outline should be seen as a mutable databank, a reservoir of information that may change over time or with additional information.

The provisional and flexible nature of this approach takes into consideration two important facts: first, information we have often falls into gray zones of uncertainty. Second, the traditional academic method may take too long to study terrorism. While we do not advocate departing from traditional scientific methods of research, the real and immediate nature of terrorism's threat compels us to use less time-consuming approaches to collect and classify information. Though in this chapter the outline concerns itself with groups, it can also be applied to individuals when enough information is available.

The cultural and contextual framework outline is divided into a cultural and a contextual section. The cultural section includes the following domains: cultural aspects of the group's identity; cultural aspects of the meaning of the terrorist act; cultural aspects of the perceived causes of the terrorist act; cultural aspects related to the group's social stressors, social support, and level of functioning; cultural aspects of the relationship between the group adherents and its leadership; and overall cultural framework formulation. The contextual section may contain as many contexts as are relevant to the group. For this chapter, we will take into consideration only the following contexts: historic, socioeconomic, political, and media- and communication-related.

CULTURAL IDENTITY

The cultural identity of the terrorist group is key to understanding how terrorists think and operate. Some of the questions this section attempts to answer are: How do these groups consider themselves ethnically? Which cultural groups do they identify with, what languages do they speak, and what is the degree of involvement with the host culture and their culture of origin? Evidence of the terrorist identity is often indirect, and is inferred from their behaviors, statements, and interviews with their families or other elements of the group, such as messages to the media. A narrative description of the collective belief systems that coalesce in the group's shared identity, avoiding the pitfalls of generalization, allows one to gain insights into the group's dynamics. A distinction should be drawn between identity expressed through behaviors that reflect the group's cultural meanings, such as certain religious practices, shared values, dietary practices, celebrations, and so forth, and identity expressed through ideological views, more often found in political or religious ideology.

When assembling information about ethnic and cultural influence, it is important to be mindful of possible stereotyping, which would undermine an unbiased and objective perspective on the group. For example, when talking about Islamic fundamentalists, there are major differences in ethnic and cultural identification among Shi'ites, Sunni, and Ismahil groups. Such differences include ethnic identity, cultural values, language used, and degree of involvement with the culture of origin and the host culture. Yet the Shi'ite Hezbollah has united with the mostly Sunni al-Qaeda in its identification with the same radical fanaticism based on a blend of religious principles and anti-American and anti-Israeli objectives. In this case, religious affiliation and common political goals are stronger than ethnic identification.

In countries with a multiethnic composition, identifying the cultural and ethnic identity of a group may not be an easy task. Nevertheless, an effort should be made to draw a map of relevant belief systems that will allow one to link the person to the group and the group to its society. Some groups may believe in independence, while others may believe in the subversion of a political system, and still others believe in a worldwide fight in religious terms. Cultural identity, far from being a rigid concept, is subject to change over time. This is particularly true for ideological identity, which can shift depending upon historic or political changes. At the individual level, defining developmental experiences that determine cultural identity occur in interactions within families, schools, communities, and religious institutions. This can be considered the "soft indoctrination" phase of many terrorists.

Once an individual decides to join a terrorist group, his or her cultural identity is further shaped, reinforced, and strengthened to prepare him or her for a future mission. This process of "hard indoctrination" is often rigorous and lengthy, demanding physical as well as mental strength. The hard indoctrination phase radicalizes the cultural identity of the individual and often significantly changes it within the values, behaviors, and shared meanings of the group. Acquaintances and families of terrorists who return from training often report that they note profound changes in them. Examples of such cultural reframing can be found among groups preparing their adepts for suicide missions by providing mission-oriented persuasion based on a charismatic person's teaching and the promise of a rewarding afterlife.

Whether most of the changes in the person's identity and view of the world actually occurred before the indoctrination phase remains controversial. In fact, another theory postulates that the terrorist's identity is poorly defined prior to joining the group, where he or she finds both a completion of identity and a justification to act out psychological conflicts. According to Dr. Jerrold Post, "the terrorist group represents an attempt to consolidate a fragmented psychological identity and to be at one with oneself and with society, and most important to belong" (Post, 1990). This intriguing theory sees terrorists not as mentally ill but as individuals who are often developmentally lost, psychologically vulnerable, searching for an identity and finally finding it in the group's cause, where their yearning for cultural belonging can be satisfied.

One analysis of terrorism in the Middle East sees the cultural identity of individuals in the region as often challenged by clashing cultural values (Ajami, 2001). This occurs especially in societies that are undergoing a cultural transition, where, often, young people may have to make a choice between appealing Western values that do not seem to fully fit in with their cultures and traditional values that are increasingly anti-Western and more and more radicalized. This conflict may result in an embrace of radical views, a phenomenon often being referred to as indigenization (Huntington, 1998). Psychosocial identity is very much culturally driven and it is often hard to see where cultural identity starts and psychosocial identity ends.

In sum, a discussion of psychosocial vulnerability should always include a narrative on cultural identity, as ethnic and cultural factors influence (rather than determine) how a terrorist group regards itself, shaping the belief systems, affective responses, and behavioral processes of the individuals involved. Moreover, when studying cultural identity, it is paramount to take into consideration the cultural heterogeneity existing within the same culture, which includes differences in gender, age, factions, and personal preferences.

CULTURAL MEANING OF TERRORIST BEHAVIOR

This section discusses the following question: What is the culturally sanctioned meaning of the terrorist's behavior? How is its inevitability/necessity justified? Much has been written about the terrorist's logic. To some it is based on "strategic conceptions deliberately aimed at political gains, a willful choice made by an organization for political and strategic reasons, rather than the unintended outcome of psychological or social factors" (Crenshaw, 1990a). Behind this apparently rational consistency of the terrorist's behaviors, there are layers of cultural meanings collectively shared by the individual terrorist, the terrorist group, and the society in which the group operates.

The suicide missions by some terrorist groups in the Middle East provide a vivid case in point. Young, single, religiously devout males, usually coming from poor backgrounds, often raised and living in refugees' camps, are lured by the mystique of martyrdom. Within their culture they perceive the unequivocal message that martyrdom is a status symbol. The few fortunate ones who are selected are venerated as heroes, and offered major incentives such as an eternally plentiful and happy afterlife and the promise of considerable financial benefits for their families. The overwhelming cultural message is that immolating oneself to destroy other lives is not only acceptable but highly desirable. An entire cultural structure consisting of family, friends, schools, teachers, religious institutions, press, and political establishment shares and propagates a strong belief system concerning martyrdom for the cause.

To the victims of the terrorist attacks, the perpetrators are acting out insane beliefs of perpetual happiness. But to young men who have struggled to find some significance to their bleak existence, the meaning of their action is perfectly clear and they know that everyone in their culture shares an understanding of this meaning. They will be heroes in everyone's eyes, will have helped the cause, and will be rewarded in the afterlife. There is no known effective antidote to this culturally sanctioned meaning of such extreme forms of violence, unless it comes from within the culture itself.

CULTURAL ASPECTS OF THE GROUP'S PERCEIVED CAUSES OF TERRORISM

Understanding the cultural underpinnings of what the group perceives to be the cause of its behavior can help shed light on the terrorist group's inner workings. Some of the questions this section considers are: What is the group's perceived cause for action? What is the intended outcome of the terrorist activity?

It is well known that groups externalize the cause for terrorism. The logic appears linear: They are trying to destroy us; therefore, before they do, we need to destroy them. Whether determined by nationalistic, religious, or political reasons, the perceived cause is an outside force that needs to be eliminated or defeated. Regardless of what the perceived cause, the course of action is seen as inevitable. The group's assessment of such a threat may range from realistic to completely detached from reality.

Studying the perceived causes can help one to understand terrorism's roots. A good example is provided by the group involved in Egyptian President Anwar Sadat's assassination, al-Jihad. The reason that the group provided for its action was that it wanted Egypt to be ruled under sacred Islamic law. The ultimate goal of al-Jihad is that the world will be governed by the *shari'a,* an Islamic government under Islamic rules after the model of the early Prophet. Sadat had promised to move Egypt to a system governed by the *shari'a* and had added an article to that effect in the country's constitution. He failed to implement this move, however. Al-Jihad also used as a justification the argument, which went counter to the Islamists' logic, that Israel was the most important enemy. (Sadat had signed the peace accord with Israel.) Their principle was that to fight an enemy who is near is more important than to fight an enemy who is far.

The "Neglected Duty" (Jansen, 1986), the group's basic manifesto, argues for eliminating the enemy from within. Getting rid of the enemy within is a variation on the theme of displacement of blame used by many groups. In this case, the perception of cause and consequent justification for terrorism is based on a rereading of the Koran along radically rooted cultural lines. The trial that followed the assassination demonstrated how this extreme faction was acting in the background of a radical milieu within the Egyptian society that basically shared the analysis of perceived causes, viewing Sadat as a traitor after his peace agreement with Israel (Hamouda, 1986).

A discussion of perceived causes naturally evolves into a discussion of morals. Moral justification for terrorist acts is sanctioned by culturally held beliefs shared by terrorist groups and often also shared by the societies where these groups are born. The moral righteousness of terrorism is based on a cognitive restructuring of the moral value of killing, freeing the groups from moral restraints (Kelman, 1973). Bandura has written extensively on the mechanisms of moral disengagement to justify acts of aggression. He mentions displacement and diffusion of responsibility, disregard for or distortion of consequences, and dehumanization of the victims as essential cognitive mechanisms that allow aggressive and violent acts to be justified on the basis of a moral imperative (Bandura, 1986).

While the motives of terrorism may be disparate, these mechanisms of cognitive reframing represent a pattern in all radical shifts of destructive behavior. Bandura's analysis, based on the social learning theory of aggression, has deep cultural implications, as cultures differ considerably in how moral disengagement is expressed (Bandura, 1973). A culturally formulated narrative of this cognitive reframing of justification for terrorist acts can provide useful insights into the terrorists' cognitive framework and their behaviors.

CULTURAL ASPECTS OF SOCIAL STRESS

The impact that social stressors have on creating the conditions for terrorism exhibits important cultural variations. Some of the questions this section considers are: What social stressors or events seem to have contributed to the formation of the terrorist group? What is the meaning and significance of these stressors and events in the terrorists' culture? How have these stressors or events impacted on the terrorist groups and their lives?

Poverty often creates the basis for social instability and turmoil, which in turn provides a fertile ground for violence and the origin of terrorist groups. Epidemics, unemployment, and criminality are the breeding ground for organized violence. Social unrest has proven to be particularly prominent in areas where massive migrations occur. These migrants are often displaced people or refugees who have witnessed atrocities, withstood torture, or lived for years in conditions of deprivation. Migratory waves often greatly heighten social tensions. Many terrorist acts in Europe and Southeast Asia have been the consequences of intolerance toward immigrants and refugees.

At a time when almost half of the world population lives in urban areas, swelling cities are bursting with a growing population, unable to provide proper infrastructure or safe environmental conditions, and housing millions in informal settlements or slums. Gangs and urban guerrillas function as terrorist organizations and have control over large urban neighborhoods, where the social gap between the rich and poor keeps getting wider. A narrative of the cultural aspects of these social determinants of terrorism, which vary considerably from culture to culture, may shed light on the dynamics of these culturally specific phenomena and offer valuable material to planners and policy makers (Caracci & Mezzich, 2001).

CULTURAL ASPECTS OF SOCIAL SUPPORT

This section discusses the following questions: What are the main sources of emotional, instrumental, and social support for the groups? Terrorist activities—especially those that are nationalistic, political, or religious—rely on support from local populations. Such support goes beyond economic and logistical backing. It often means tacit assent, propaganda, media incitement, and favorable assistance at various social levels.

Terrorist groups in democracies such as the United States, Puerto Rico, Canada, and Northern Ireland provide an interesting glimpse into how crucial the support of ordinary people is in shaping the political beliefs that encourage and support terrorism. All of these states are democracies where freedom of expression is a given. In totalitarian regimes it would be much more problematic to openly organize an opposition that would have the same ideological basis as that of the terrorist group.

Gurr has identified the support group for terrorist activities as "any social segment, faction, political tendency, or class, whose members seek a particular kind of political change" (Gurr, 1990). He argues that there are two fundamental processes underlying the social support that leads groups to accept terrorist forms of political struggle. The first is radicalization, whereby a group, frustrated with the slowness of advancing its political agenda, begins viewing violence as justifiable and appropriate. Out of this support group itself, individuals may then take the next step to use violent forms of terrorist expressions.

An example is provided by the Front de Libération de Québec (FLQ), a terrorist group that grew out of a strong separatist movement in Quebec in the 1950s and 1960s. This movement, dissatisfied with the central Canadian government, eventually produced an underground faction that committed several antigovernment terrorist acts in the 1960s. In spite of these extreme forms of dissent, the separatist movement in Quebec gave proof of its strength in the 1970 election (Fournier, 1984).

The second mechanism that works for groups supporting violence as means to an end is reaction to a threatened status. An example is the small but vocal neofascist support groups operating in Italy in the 1960s and 1970s, who were nostalgic for the fascist regimes, who never accepted the democratic process, and who were supportive of extreme forms of violence mounted in the form of terrorist acts, such as bombing of trains and squares, that led to large numbers of civilian casualties.

Just as popular support is crucial for the birth and expression of organized violence, it also plays a fundamental role in the terrorist group's decline. In fact, most terrorist groups have had a tendency to contain the seeds of their own demise, as twenty of those groups virtually disappeared after an average of six and a half years of activity (Crenshaw, 1987). Some of those seeds are found in the disintegration of social support due to a public backlash against terrorist acts, and in the fact that some of the issues raised by sympathizers were addressed.

Culturally significant exceptions exist to this rule. In democracies where small but strong nationalistic groups have operated for decades, such as the Irish Republican Army and ETA, there continues to be support among the Catholic and Basque communities for the ideologies and strategies of the most radical wings.

In sum, culturally articulated pressure points may find expression in large or small segments of support for terrorist activities. A narrative description of cultural-ly relevant aspects of such support can significantly contribute to understanding the terrorist group's strengths and weaknesses as well as help to predict the group's course of action.

CULTURAL ASPECTS OF LEVEL OF FUNCTIONING

Questions pertinent to this section are: How do terrorist groups and individuals function within the communities and societies where they operate? How do their activities affect their social relations, work, and families? What is the degree of open-ness versus clandestinity of their activities within the culture where they operate?

The terrorists' range of level of functioning within society varies from group to group. Clandestine status is favored, for example, by nationalistic groups such as the Tamil Tigers in Sri Lanka—a group fighting the Singalese Indians and respon-sible for murdering Prime Minister Rajiv Gandhi. On the other hand, state-sup-ported terrorism is at times acted out openly, as in a series of murders of opposition elements in Iran in the 1980s and early 1990s.

An interesting development regarding expectation of level of functioning is the recent discovery that elements of the al-Qaeda network were "sleepers," completely immersed in the host culture of Germany, Spain, the United States, or Italy, but ready to act when asked to back or carry out terrorist acts. They held jobs, partici-pated actively in the community, and led a normal life, confounding their neigh-bors when they were apprehended or they were involved in the events of Septem-ber 11. Recent arrests carried out in Singapore, a very tightly controlled country of only four million, confirmed the presence of perfectly integrated members of socie-ty who were allegedly part of an al-Qaeda cell that was researching and planning terrorist activities (Mydans, 2001). This modus operandi represents a departure from the clandestine, full-time nature of terrorist groups, a tactical choice that ren-ders the identification and capture of members particularly problematic.

CULTURAL ASPECTS OF THE RELATIONSHIP BETWEEN THE INDIVIDUAL TERRORISTS AND THE GROUP'S LEADERSHIP

The main questions addressed in this section are: What is the group leader's cultur-al reference group? What are the cultural elements of the relationship between ter-rorists and their leaders? What culturally salient themes affect their interactions? How much intercultural difference within a group may affect members' interac-tions and behaviors?

The Aum Shinrikyo (supreme cult) group in Japan, which in 1995 spread the deadly gas sarin in the underground of Tokyo, leaving twelve dead and thousands injured, provides a good example (Bracket, 1996). The group leader at first was the guru of a Buddhist sect working on spreading a message of peace and happiness in the world. At some point, however, the leader started preaching about the end of the world. He also became convinced that the United States was bent on destroying Japan and that to avert this attack the group had to act first.

The group leader could count on his followers' total obedience. He was ruthless with dissenters and he convinced his followers that murdering individuals who were perceived as threats to the cult was perfectly justified, as the victims would gain access to a higher level of understanding. Many of his followers were scientists, chemists, physicists, and virologists who had given up promising academic careers to devote themselves to the development of weapons of mass destruction commissioned by the leader. In spite of much evidence that the movement's followers suffered years of physical, financial, and mental abuse, followers' activities continued unopposed for a long time, mostly due to the reluctance of Japanese authorities to challenge the rigid rules protecting religious freedom in Japan. There is evidence that even after the arrest of its leader, the group was attempting to make a comeback.

In sum, much can be learned about a group by looking at the culturally mediated rules of conduct in the group's hierarchy.

TERRORISM AND HISTORICAL CONTEXT

It is important to place terrorism in its proper historical context, as historical events have at times created the conditions for momentous societal changes that ignite the birth of movements that later organize into terrorist groups. In the past century alone, terrorism has had many different scenarios as historical background.

A good example of the relationship between historic backdrop and terrorism is provided by Russian terrorism in the nineteenth and twentieth centuries. In Russia, at the beginning of the century, anarchists waged a war of terror against Russian authorities with the aim of bringing about a revolution. That was followed by a more organized wave of terrorism by a movement called the People's Will, which was trying to undermine the despotic czarist government and obtain basic freedom rights. The movement that assassinated Czar Alexander II had sympathizers among the intelligentsia, but did not withstand the repressive reaction that followed the assassination. In the early 1900s, following the founding of the Social Revolutionary Party, an armed group called the Fighting Organization, counting on wider support than the previous organization, carried out a massive wave of strikes against leading political figures throughout Russia and beyond. A turning point was the 1905 revolution that led to constitutional reform. As terrorism became less relevant, the czarist government gradually regained the upper hand and brutally eliminated the group. The Bolshevik revolution of 1917 was not preceded by terrorist activities.

These three quite different groups were active in three different historical stages, each of them marked by a process of profound transformation for Russian society. From a historical perspective, Russian terrorism, rather than leading to a revolution, only succeeded in provoking waves of brutal repression by the czarist regime. Instead, the revolution came as a consequence of political action and strikes (Laqueur, 1999).

TERRORISM AND SOCIOECONOMIC CONTEXT

Social conditions have often been linked to terrorism. Material deprivation and socioeconomic struggle are indeed the source of social tensions and resentment among the less privileged. Yet, if this was directly related to terrorism, it would be hard to explain why terrorism is not more widespread since one in five of the world's people lives on less than a dollar a day.

It is difficult on the other hand to ignore the fact that indigent populations can be easily co-opted by radical organizations that are directly or indirectly involved in terrorist activities. These organizations often fill the void created by governments that are unwilling or unable to provide adequate nutrition, shelter, and education. One example is the *madrasahs* in northern Pakistan, where young, socioeconomically deprived students are offered an opportunity to have their basic needs met in exchange for intensive religious studies. Large families often have no choice but to send several of their children there, because they cannot afford to feed them and to pay for their education. In the *madrasahs*, however, students are infused with more than just religious fervor; they are bathed in lessons of hatred and incitement to act against their enemies, the United States and Israel.

In these "schools" (*madrasah* translates as "the University of All Righteous Knowledge") students are "brainwashed in their early teens," a process acknowledged by Human Rights Watches in Pakistan. Well financed by Saudi Arabia, close to a million students are mentally prepared for *jihad*. Not all the *madrasahs* are incubators of hatred; some are devoted to good education and religious guidance. Nevertheless, although it is not known how many of these students actually decide to join terrorist groups, it has been written that nearly all the Taliban leadership had attended such training (Bragg, 2001). Would these needy youngsters still flock to the *madrasahs* if they had other opportunities? It is hard to answer with certainty. Yet, both common sense and experience have proven that investment in social capital increases opportunities, which in turn enhance personal empowerment. Conversely, relying on the socioeconomically deprived to promote a violent agenda through hard indoctrination will only perpetuate the cycle of terror. Moreover, although only a minority of them may actually become terrorists, the intergenerational transmission of hatred is likely to have a long-lasting impact, creating a fertile ground for more followers to join the torrent of violence.

TERRORISM AND POLITICAL CONTEXT

A link between terrorism and the political climate is most commonly seen in certain areas of the world such as Latin America. Nonetheless, when such a link is less obvious, a close analysis of the political context can add considerable perspective to our understanding. Some have argued that nearly all forms of terrorism are political statements, with an internally consistent logic, aimed at delivering a political message with calculated political consequences (Schmid, 1988).

An intriguing example of the complex interaction of political context and terrorism is provided by the terrorist group called the Red Brigades, an Italian left-wing group that drew most of its members from disaffected middle-class Communist and leftist Christian Democrats during Italy's turbulent 1960s and 1970s. At the time, the Christian Democratic Party, long the mainstay of postwar Italian politics, was seeking alliances to the left with the Socialist Party, while the influential Communists were struggling to gain access to power. Restless young Communists and elements of the more extreme Proletarian Party became increasingly radicalized, accusing both the Communist and Christian Democratic parties of forming a "bourgeois dictatorship" that was oppressing the masses and opposing any social reform that would benefit the working class.

At first the movement seemed to have been successful, as judges and politicians seemed to be intimidated by the movement's killing and maiming of law enforcement agents. Neither Communists nor Christian Democrats were able to mobilize a strategy to counteract the thousands of strikes that the Red Brigades, with the financial backing of the former Soviet Union, mounted in the region. The movement's declared goal was to weaken the country's institutions and promote a national insurrection against the ruling parties.

The tide turned for the Red Brigades after the kidnapping and murder of Aldo Moro, a prominent pro-left Christian Democrat. The act traumatized the Italian public, while it strengthened the resolve of Christian Democrats and leftists alike to defeat the group. This was accomplished in the early 1980s, thanks also to repentant elements within the movement who cooperated with the justice system in exchange for leniency (Weinberger & Eubank, 1987). This is a clear example of how a political context provided the conditions for both the birth and demise of a terrorist group. A recently resurrected version of the new Red Brigades has failed to gain support, since the political context of the country is radically different now.

TERRORISM AND MEDIA AND COMMUNICATION CONTEXT

It is practically impossible to gain a good understanding of a terrorist group without addressing its use of media and communication. Terrorists have found a powerful ally in modern technological advances. It is probably not an exaggeration to state that without the recent advances in media and communication technology, some of the recent complex terrorist acts could not have been carried out. Groups seek out adherents with skills in advanced electronics, train others to use such skills, operate sophisticated media departments, and spare no expense in acquiring the latest equipment, knowing the return will be worth the investment. Media and communications are used by terrorists for four main purposes: publicity, dissemination of information, communication among themselves, and cyberterror.

The resonance terrorist acts have in the media has become an essential element. Groups exploit this to spread their propaganda, as well as to achieve the crucial goal of instilling fear in large segments of the population. Terrorist groups have become very adept at bringing their sensationalist message to the media and manipulating it in an attention-gripping display of human suffering. From this point of view, the hostage crisis in Iran during the Carter administration is particularly significant. After weeks and months of parading the hostages with the intent of publicly frustrating the U.S. authorities, it became clear that the terrorists were also holding hostage the media itself and the public, the former in many ways feeling compelled to show these images, the latter feeling compelled to watch them.

The media are often torn between the need to inform and a qualm about helping to publicize the terrorist group. Governments often appeal to the media's sense of responsibility in airing certain images that, as in the case of September 11, are burned into people's memories. A large part of publicity and dissemination of information also takes place over the Internet. Taking advantage of an unregulated cyberspace, especially in the United States, Web sites offer advice on everything from how to build bombs to the assembly of chemical weapons and guerrilla tactics, often complemented by proclamations, manuals, official documents, speeches, and video clips of terrorist leaders.

Moreover, terrorists make extensive use of more or less anonymous electronic mail, as demonstrated by recent activities of religious fundamentalist groups. Besides the Internet, many groups make extensive use of sophisticated communications technology such as satellite phones and banking operations, which are often difficult to track.

Finally, cyberspace is being directly used to destroy electronic capabilities, a phenomenon usually referred to as cyberterrorism. Although most hackers have been individuals with extraordinary knowledge who are highly motivated to create havoc in extremely complex electronic circuits, it is now clear that any respectable terrorist group now has the personnel and capability to inactivate or disable key electronic defenses of their intended enemies.

As a result of such a global and elusive challenge, counterterrorist organizations are now devoting ever-growing resources to this mostly invisible enemy.

Similar considerations regarding context should be made for each group on other domains, such as the religious one and the group's relation to organized crime. Given the vastness of such domains, they would require a separate chapter.

OVERALL CULTURAL AND CONTEXTUAL FRAMEWORK

The overall framework provided below is a summary of the key cultural findings relevant to the identity of the al-Qaeda group, its view of the meaning and causes of its acts, the cultural aspects of social stress, support, and level of functioning, and the relationship between group members and their leaders. In addition, this section contains a brief synopsis of the most relevant contextual aspects that impact on the group's ideology and behavior.

Cultural and Contextual Framework Outline of al-Qaeda

In time, rigorous academic inquiry will deal with the motives, beliefs, and modus operandi of the terrorist group al-Qaeda. For now, we would like to provide a brief outline of its cultural and contextual framework, to illustrate the cultural and contextual outline with a specific example. The material used for this purpose is a distillation of facts from documents from the movement itself and official publications preceding and following September 11.

Cultural Aspects of the Group's Identity

Al-Qaeda is an organization that identifies with the radical fundamentalist Islamic movement that considers Western, especially American, influence and culture as a threat to the integrity of Islam, and its sovereignty and sacred sites. In the words of its leader, "Our religion is under attack. America has started a crusade against the Islamic Nation." The United States, according to al-Qaeda, is guilty of sending troops into the home of the two holy sites of Islam (Saudi Arabia) and of corrupting its regime. The group believes that true believers in the teachings of Islam should strike at the enemy, which is represented by infidels, and that there is no room for accommodation or compromise.

The group's cultural identity finds its roots in the Arab world, especially Saudi Arabia and Egypt, where many of its leaders come from. Such identity is more ideological than ethnic, as its radical view of Islam crosses ethnic and geographical borders to include people from Chechnya, the Philippines, Indonesia, Sudan, Somalia, the Arab countries, Afghanistan, and even the United States. Adherents therefore speak different languages, belong to different states, and greatly differ in their cultural customs and backgrounds. But all share the same credo and philosophy. This considerably widens both the group's reach and the differences among its cells, making it one of the most complex and polymorphic terrorist movements in history.

Cultural Meaning of the Group's Behavior

Anti-Western sentiment in many areas of the world where Islam is the official religion is not a new phenomenon. In most Islamic countries, the Koran, Islam's main religious text, is interpreted as nonviolent. A diametrically opposed view is held by militant fundamentalists, who find in the same book a message justifying extreme forms of violence.

As an example of the passages that can be interpreted as possibly inciting to violence is this: "And when the sacred months are passed, kill those who join other gods with God wherever ye shall find them; and seize them, besiege them, and lay wait for them with every kind of ambush." The group's leader has repeatedly cited this passage.

It is mostly the threat by unbelievers that is the basis of radical Islamic movements. Perhaps the cultural meaning of the group is best captured by the following assertion by Bernard Lewis, a scholar of Islam: "What is truly evil and unacceptable is the domination of infidels over true believers. For true believers to lead misbelievers is natural, since this provides for the maintenance of the holy law and gives the misbelievers both the opportunity and the incentive to embrace the true faith. But for the misbelievers to rule over true believers is blasphemous and unnatural, since it leads to the corruption of religion and morality in society and to flouting or even abrogation of God's law" (Sullivan, 2001). Al-Qaeda's central view on terrorism is based on this core belief system, perhaps not a novelty in the landscape of Islamic fundamentalism but certainly one that found vast resonance in a large and diverse group of fundamentalists, as attested by the sizable number of people who signed on.

Cultural Aspects of the Group's Perceived Causes of Terrorism

The reason and internal logic of the group's terrorist act can be found in the declaration of war (*fatwa*) that was issued against the United States in 1996: "The latest and the greatest of the threats incurred by Muslims since the death of the Prophet is the occupation of the land of the two Holy Places (Mecca and Medina, considered sacred by Muslims), the foundation of the house of Islam, the place of the revelation, by the army of the American crusaders and their allies." In 1998 the groups went even further and issued another edict, this time jointly with Egypt's Jihad group. This *fatwa* declares there is "an explicit declaration by the Americans of war on Allah. We give all Muslims the judgment to kill and fight Americans and their allies to abide by Allah's orders by killing Americans and stealing their money anywhere, anytime and whenever possible." The group justifies its terrorist activities on the basis that they aim at instigating anti-Americanism, which will lead to the fall of governments it considers non-Islamic, with the consequent expulsion of Westerners and non-Muslims from those countries, the ultimate goal being a pan-Islamic caliphate throughout the world.

Cultural Aspects of Social Stressors

Adherents to the group come from all over the world and are motivated by very diverse social stressors. There are, however, two countries where the movement had its inception, Saudi Arabia and Egypt.

It is well known that the majority of the key members of the organization are Egyptian and that the merger between the group and the Egyptian Jihad represents a turning point in the organization both from an ideological and strategic view-point. Over the last twenty years, a growing sense of rage and powerlessness has been brewing among many Egyptians. This is due in part to high unemployment rates, a lack of professional opportunities, and a stalling economy. This hatred is felt not only in the overcrowded slums of Cairo, but also among the thousands of young people with brand-new university degrees who are unable to find a job suit-ed to their degree. These young professionals are often forced to work two or three jobs to be able to survive. In this country of 63 million people, more than 55 per-cent of the population is under the age of 25, and the resentment of this young and swelling population continues to grow. Powerful outsiders, especially the United States, are easier targets than the government. The mastermind of the attack of September 11 was one such disenfranchised young Egyptian, who went to study abroad to get a specialized degree, hoping to enhance his professional status at home. As with other members of al-Qaeda, his leap from being a quiet person with radical religious views to becoming a full-fledged terrorist happened in a Western country, where his views on who was at fault for the injustices in the Arab world were taken to an extreme.

Cultural Aspects of Social Support

Social support for the organization is widespread throughout the Muslim world. Anti-American resentment runs deep in many countries where Western values are seen as corrupt, anti-Muslim, and deliberately in favor of Israel and against the Palestinian cause. *Madrasahs* in Pakistan and schools in Saudi Arabia indoctrinate young students with radical views of Islam and hatred for the West. Manifestations of jubilation and incendiary anti-Western sermons were common in some coun-tries after September 11. Among these were countries such as Sudan and Afghani-stan that had given haven and support to the group members. Such support was not only moral but also material, with financing coming from religious organiza-tions, private donations, charitable organizations, and governmental support.

Cultural Aspects of the Group's Level of Functioning

As for level of functioning, al-Qaeda is run like a business, with a CEO, a coun-cil, and various committees that work on all aspects of its activities. Revenues are derived from legitimate businesses, such as construction companies and cattle breeding farms in Sudan; from organized crime involved in the traffic of heroin; from financial networks such as companies that wire money; and from petty frauds and crime such as credit card and insurance scams. To communicate, the organiza-tion takes advantage of the global technology, using e-mail, faxes, satellite cell phones, and Web sites. The foot soldiers are organized in cells that operate individ-ually in different countries and have no contact with other cells or the upper levels of the organization. Integration in the host culture is emphasized and encouraged.

A member can be an active member of society for years, with a family, a social life, and a regular job, before he is called to action. Assimilation within the cultural fabric is a departure from the clandestine nature of most terrorist groups.

Cultural Aspects of the Relationship Between the Individual Terrorists and the Group Leadership

The bombings of the American embassies in Nairobi in 1997 and in Tanzania in 1998 provide a glimpse into how the hierarchy of the organization works. The individual terrorists have never met the head of the organization, who only communicates his plans in person to a handful of close advisers. The only way the group leader communicates with his followers is through propaganda tapes that serve as recruitment tools and can be found on the Internet. The decisions of the small group of leaders are communicated to lower members, who in turn convey them to the leaders of the cells. The foot soldiers may not know about the operation until just before the execution of the plan. From their notes, there is even evidence that most of the plane hijackers on September 11 expected to spend a long time in prison rather than to die.

In this sense, bin Laden sees his role as an instigator rather than a person who oversees his troops (ABC News, 1999). The cells can rely on highly efficient support networks in various part of the world and are given ample discretion on how to organize and carry out their plans. Nevertheless, as the events of September 11 have shown, very little is left to chance because they operate according to the al-Qaeda manual's three operational stages: research, planning, and execution. The group's meticulous planning means that it may take months before an operation is carried out. Investigators identified three distinct groups of the nineteen terrorists who participated in the attack: Atta, the mastermind, and three other leaders who chose the dates and flew the planes; three individuals in charge of logistics such as providing documents or renting apartments; and twelve soldiers, whose only responsibility was restraining the flight crew while the leaders took control of the plane. The businesslike organization of this structure and of the relationship among its members reflects its leader's experience in his father's large construction company.

Historical Context

The movement has its historical point of reference in medieval Islam, a school of thought called *Salafiyya* (the venerable forefathers). Linking themselves to the Prophet Mohammed, the Salafis believed that Islam had lost its purity and had been contaminated by idolatry. While the movement was conciliatory with the West in the past, in the course of the twentieth century, after the subdivision of the Ottoman empire, it moved to radical positions, believing that the Islamic world was under the threat of extinction by barbaric forces coming from the West. The organization's philosophy was heavily influenced by the writings of an Egyptian writer, Sayd Qutb, who stated that the rulers of Muslim states had strayed from Muslim teachings and should be considered infidels. Later al-Qaeda used this argument against Saudi Arabia, which had allowed the crusaders to desecrate the Arab peninsula.

Under the umbrella of the *Salafiyya* school falls the Wahhabi movement, to which Osama bin Laden and his followers strictly adhere. The sect, founded by Muhammad bin Abd al-Wahab in the ninth century, sees modernization as a curse on Islam as it deviates from the teachings of the prophet Mohammed. The group believes in spreading its conservative message and in backing the people's will to fight for their cause. The Wahhabi dynasty was instrumental in the birth of the monarchy and the state of Saudi Arabia, but its followers, who are not in the ruling structure, are only supportive of their rulers if they follow the strict teachings of Islam, which are practiced to this day in that state.

Socioeconomic Context

Al-Qaeda has attracted and trained aspiring terrorists from very diverse socioeconomic backgrounds, from the poor and uneducated of northern Pakistan to middle- and upper-class Egyptian college graduates. Many are from areas of religious, ethnic, or political conflicts that have lasted for decades, where economic conditions have been dismal, and powerlessness is a way of life. Imbued with religious fervor and militant fanaticism, they are attracted by the promise of victory over injustice and eternal happiness after martyrdom.

Perhaps if there is a common theme among these lives turned into instruments of terror, it is how much they seem to be affected by social change. This social change is very much the focus of al-Qaeda, which refuses a socioeconomic order based on modernity and freedom, seen as not only depraved and evil but as a threat to the only possible world order, the one based on Islamic fundamentalism, whose rules were written centuries ago. The two socioeconomic systems are irreconcilable and there is no room for compromise. This world, with a set of social values based on Islamic brotherhood and with modernity—embodied by the United States—as its sworn enemy, promises to overthrow corrupt governments and replace nation states to form a nationless Islam, a terrifying prospect for secular governments.

Political Context

The Soviet invasion of Afghanistan in 1979 represented the defining political context for the young would-be leader of al-Qaeda, who fought valiantly against the Russians, at the same time financing and organizing militant Islamic fighters. During that war the United States backed these fighters, mostly indirectly through funds provided to the Pakistani Secret Service, which in turn funneled money to fundamentalists training fighters. After the Soviets left in 1989, al-Qaeda's leader returned to his homeland with the status of a folk hero, with radical Muslim fundamentalist views, emboldened by the victory over a superpower. Iraq's invasion of Kuwait in 1990 prompted the Saudis to turn to the United States, which sent troops to be stationed in Saudi Arabia. This event proved to be crucial to bin Laden's radicalization. In fact, he has often mentioned it as one of the main reasons for his fight. In 1991 he was exiled by the Saudi royal family, disowned by his own family, and stripped of his citizenship. He moved to Sudan, where an Islamic dictatorship was sympathetic to his cause. It was in Sudan that al-Qaeda flourished both as business venture, with bin Laden as CEO, and as a terrorist group spreading its tentacles to different areas of the world. During his stay in Africa, bin Laden's group financed the bombing of the World Trade Center in 1993, was involved in the killing of twelve U.S. peace-keeping soldiers in Somalia, sent fighters to Chechnya and Bosnia, and carried out a series of attacks on embassies in Africa and U.S. targets in the Middle East. Crucial during this period were his alliances with the Iranian-backed Hezbollah, Algeria's Armed Islamic Group, and Egypt's Jihad Group. In 1996, after the United States put pressure on the Sudanese government, bin Laden and his group moved back to Afghanistan, where, protected by the fundamentalist Taliban government, he continued his expansion, propaganda, and planning for destruction that culminated in September 11.

Media and Communication Context

Al-Qaeda is a group that, for all its hatred for modernity, uses modern tools to maximum advantage. Since its days in Sudan, the group has gradually refined its media department, taking advantage of the global network of communications. The group uses simple yet effective means of communication, such as sending messages through chat rooms, sharing encrypted information, and sending electronic mail whose language has been modified to avoid detection. The nineteen terrorists of September 11 were able to travel freely with terrific logistic support (money, transportation, and documents) that allowed them to rehearse their plot meticulously.

Moreover, the group enjoys copious coverage by the Western media as well as by Arab satellite stations that broadcast in real time worldwide. The group's masterful timeliness in the use of the media as a propaganda tool was demonstrated with the release of tapes of the group's executive committee inciting Islamic militants throughout the world and praising God for the carnage inflicted upon the United States. The timeliness and focus of the tapes speaks to a preparedness and organization that the group clearly wishes to flaunt, both to embarrass its enemy and to expose its vulnerability. To be sure, the clockwork precision of the chain of events of September 11 could not have been achieved without complete control of fast and hidden means of communication. In sum, this group has clearly demonstrated how efficiently destructive modern communication advances can be.

Overall Cultural and Contextual Framework

To summarize what we know about al-Qaeda's overall cultural and contextual framework, the group's cultural identity is rooted in radical fundamentalist Islam and its anti-Western stance. Its ethnic identity, though heavily Arabic (Saudi and Egyptian), is as diverse as the many geographical areas of the world from which its adherents come from and in which they operate. The group's actions are based on a violent reading of the Koran and of radical writers who derived their ideas from the conservative Wahhabi Islamic sect. The group's joint *fatwa* with Egyptian Jihad incites and justifies the killing of Americans and their allies because they desecrated with their occupation the sacred home of Islam and thus represent a threat to the entire nation of Islam. Since its followers come from diverse sociocultural situations, they are influenced by different social stressors, such as a fight for independence, poverty, and the lack of professional opportunities. Support for the group and its activities is widespread and runs deep in community, religious institutions, and, until recently, some states. The group is highly organized and is structured like a business. Its members belong to cells that are distributed worldwide and they are bona fide members of the society in which they operate. Most members do not have any contact with the group's leader but interact with other members to research, plan, and operate according to directives and the group's manual.

The group's historical point of reference is medieval Islam and the Salafiyya school. The two defining political moments for the group were the Soviet invasion of Afghanistan and subsequent defeat of the Russians, and the invasion of Kuwait by Iraq, which led to American troops being stationed in Saudi Arabia. The group has ties with most of the other radical Islamic movements throughout the world. The group's adherents, coming from all types of socioeconomic conditions, use state-of-the-art communication advances that allow them to operate without interference and to spread the propaganda through mass media with skill and timeliness.

IMPLICATIONS FOR POLICY MAKING

Policies addressing measures to counter terrorism need to take into consideration the terrorist organizations' cultural and contextual realities. It is naive to think that a policy that worked with one group will be successful with another group. And even within the same group, cultural and contextual differences will need to be addressed. For example, even though al-Qaeda operatives in the Philippines and Somalia belong to the same organization, different strategies will be needed to defeat them. Of the cultural and contextual aspects mentioned in this article, some are more accessible to intervention than others. Cultural identity is particularly difficult to challenge because most of these groups are extremely suspicious of governments. Nevertheless, policies conveying a message that one's culture and sense of identity can be preserved even in the face of swift social changes can discourage individuals from drifting into radicalism. Regarding the meaning and explanation of the terrorist activity, policies should incorporate information on tolerance of diversity and respect of human rights. Repressive governments that show little respect for human rights should be held accountable by international organizations that monitor the implementation of such policies, as human rights should not be sacrificed in the name of fighting terrorism. Moreover, social stressors have to be addressed if a policy is to work. This may mean expensive investment in social programs that may not be very popular. Nevertheless, there is ample evidence that even small changes in macroeconomics can have a huge macro-social impact (World Health Organization, 2001).

Policies aiming at undermining the support of groups should be based on individuating and addressing culturally specific reasons for discontent and discouraging institutions from fomenting rage and using violence to resolve conflicts. Understanding of cultural patterns of relating within terrorist groups may be helpful in devising counterterrorist tactics aimed at disrupting crucial links at various levels of the group's structure. Given the global reach of the terrorist threat, international cooperation in monitoring and fighting terrorism is essential for the success of transnational antiterrorist policies, which at the same time should be formulated with respect for national differences and local realities. Contextual considerations—whether political, historic, or socioeconomic—should be incorporated in such policies both at the national and international level.

CONCLUSION

The events of September 11 and other recent terrorist acts have demonstrated how obsolete conventional means of preventing and fighting terrorism have become. Newer, more creative methodological approaches to studying terrorism in all of its aspects are needed if more effective ways to counteract this phenomenon are to be devised. Understanding the terrorist group's way of thinking and how it views itself and the world from its own perspective within its own cultural/contextual milieu may be one such approach. To do this, we need to replace our Western lenses with others that may be better suited to focus on cultural realities that are so far away from ours.

We propose that the cultural and contextual framework outline can help to systematically address some of terrorism's multiple layers of complexity, by summarizing in a narrative way the most salient aspects of the terrorist groups' values, motivations, belief systems, modus operandi, and contextual background. The outline's ultimate goal is to complement a psychological formulation of individuals and groups that engage in terrorist activities, since material on cultural and contextual aspects may be easier to obtain than psychological ones. Integrating cultural and contextual aspects with psychological ones will be a challenging task for future research in this field. New approaches to preventing and fighting terrorism will greatly benefit from an integrated and comprehensive approach.

REFERENCES

ABC News (1999, January). Osama bin Laden interview with Rahimullah Yusufzai.
Ajami, F. (2001, October 7). Nowhere man. *Time*, pp. 19–20.

Bandura, A. (1973). *Aggression: A social learning analysis.* Englewood Cliffs, NJ: Prentice-Hall.

Bandura, A. (1986). *Social foundations of thought and action: A social cognitive theory.* Englewood Cliffs, NJ: Prentice-Hall.

Bracket, D. W. *Holy terror: Armageddon in Tokyo.* New York: Weatherhill, 1996.

Bragg, R. (2001, October 14). Shaping young Islamic hearts and hatreds. *New York Times*, p. A1.

Caracci, G. (2000). Using DSM-IV cultural formulation to enhance psychodynamic understanding. *Dynamische Psychiatrie [Dynamic Psychiatry], 182/183,* 245–256.

Caracci, G., & Mezzich, J. E. (2001). Culture and urban mental health. In J. E. Mezzich & O. Fabrega (Eds.), Cultural psychiatry: International perspectives. *Psychiatric Clinics of North America, 24,* 581–593.

Cordes, B. (1987). Terrorism in their own words. In P. Stewart, P. Wilkinson, & M. Aberdeen (Eds.), *Contemporary research on terrorism* (pp. 318–36). Aberdeen, Scotland: Aberdeen University Press.

Crenshaw, M. (1987, September). How terrorism ends. Paper presented at the meeting of the American Political Science Association, Chicago.

Crenshaw, M. (1990a). The logic of terrorism: Terrorist behavior as a product of a strategic choice. In W. Reich (Ed.), *Origins of terrorism* (pp. 7–24). Washington, DC: Woodrow Wilson Center Press.

Crenshaw, M. (1990b). Questions to be answered, research to be done, knowledge to be applied. In W. Reich (Ed.), *Origins of terrorism: Psychologies, ideologies, theologies, states of mind* (pp. 247–260). Washington, DC: Woodrow Wilson Center Press.

Crenshaw, M. (Ed.) (1995). *Terrorism in context.* University Park, PA: Pennsylvania State University Press.

Fournier, L. (1984). *FLQ: The anatomy of an underground movement.* Toronto: NC Press.

Gurr, T. D. (1990). Terrorism in democracies: Its social and political bases. In W. Reich (Ed.), *Origins of terrorism* (pp. 86–102). Cambridge, England: Cambridge University Press.

Hamouda, A. (1986). *The assassination of a president* (4th ed.). Cairo: Sinai.

Huntington S. P.(1998). *The clash of civilizations and the remaking of the world order.* New York: Simon and Schuster.

Jansen, J. J. G. (1986). *The neglected duty: The creed of Sadat's assassins and Islamic resurgence in the Middle East.* New York: Macmillan.

Kelman, H. C. (1973). Violence without moral restraints: Reflections on the dehumanization of victims and victimizers. *Journal of Social Issues, 29,* 23–61.

Laqueur, W. (1999). Terrorism and history. In *The new terrorism: Fanaticism and the arms of mass destruction* (pp. 8–48). New York: Oxford University Press.

Mezzich, J. E., et al. (1993). Cultural formulation guidelines. In J. E. Mezzich et al. (Eds.), *Revised cultural proposal for DSM-IV: Technical report.* NIMH Group on Culture and Diagnosis, Pittsburgh, PA.

Ministry of Interior, Federal Republic of Germany (1981). *Analyzen zum terrorismus* (pp. 82–84). Darmstadt: Deutscher Verlag.

Mydans, S. (2001, January 14). Singapore stunned as ordinary men are tied to terror. *New York Times*, p. A9.

Post, J. M. (1986). Hostilité, conformité, fraternité. *International Journal of Group Psychotherapy, 36,* 211–214.

Post, J. M. (1990). Terrorist psycho-logic: Terrorist behavior as a product of psychological forces. In W. Reich (Ed.), *Origins of terrorism* (pp. 25–40). Washington, DC: Woodrow Wilson Center Press.

Reich, W. (1990). Understanding terrorist behavior: The limits and opportunities of psychological inquiry. In W. Reich (Ed.), *Origins of terrorism* (pp. 261–278). Washington, DC: Woodrow Wilson Center Press.

Schmid, A. P. (1988). *Political terrorism: A new guide to actors, authors, data bases, theories, and literature* (rev. ed.). Amsterdam: North-Holland Publishing.

Stern, J. (1999). *The ultimate terrorist.* Cambridge, MA: Harvard University Press.

Sullivan, A. (2001, October 7). This is a religious war. *New York Times Magazine*, p. 52.

Weinberger, L., & Eubank, W. L. (1987). *The rise and fall of Italian terrorism.* Boulder, CO: Westview Press.

World Health Organization (2001). *Macroeconomics and health project.* Geneva, Switzerland: Author.

4

Honing a Tool Against Terrorism: Making United Nations Peace Operations More Rapid and Effective

Henry Breed[1]

Half a year after the World Trade Center fell, the secretary-general of the United Nations, Kofi Annan, reflected in an interview on "the world's failure over a decade to act on warning signs in Afghanistan, [as it was] battered by political, economic, and natural disasters." He went on to outline " . . . a clear, if complicated, trail from the absence of engagement with Afghanistan in the 1990's to the creation of a terrorist haven there to the attacks on the World Trade Center" (Crossette, 2002).

In making and linking these points, he gave voice and focus to what many had come to sense: that the attacks and the forces behind them had not arisen in a vacuum and that they could not be addressed in one. Yet agreeing on precisely what forces had shaped that moment, and in what manner and measure, would prove to be an elusive and explosive pursuit. And, since progress in addressing a problem is predicated on progress in understanding its causes and currents, deciding how best to respond would prove even tougher.

Many forces were put forward as factors in the terrorist attacks, the situation in Afghanistan, or both. Many organizations leapt into the breach to address them. Many new options were examined, and many existing activities and programs were reinvigorated or reinforced.[2] Of the latter, the United Nations alone had already created and galvanized its membership behind more than a dozen different counterterrorism conventions and instituted specific programs to forward the goals they contained. It had also already set up specific programs and offices to address political, humanitarian, social, and developmental challenges confronting Afghanistan, albeit on a scale constrained by the contributions received from United Nations member states and by competing crises elsewhere. Other multilateral organizations, governments, and nongovernmental organizations (NGOs) had undertaken similar initiatives of their own, frequently facing similar constraints.

Yet there was one option that, though often examined, was not employed in this context: a United Nations peace operation.

The coalition operation that went into Afghanistan had many of the characteristics and components that its United Nations equivalents had had, might have, or could have. Further, only shortly before the attacks occurred, the United Nations Panel on Peace Operations had been convened and had concluded a significant set of recommendations on ways in which these operations needed to be amended and adjusted so that they might better respond to the challenges ahead. Additionally, in the wake of the attacks, the man who had chaired that panel and guided that process, Lakhdar Brahimi, was appointed by the secretary-general as his special representative for Afghanistan. In that capacity, he turned to and implemented many of the conclusions and recommendations that the panel had put forward, in both the political process and the peace operation that evolved there. In short, there were many links, but there was no bond.

Yet, even though no specific United Nations peace operation was deployed in this context, there was clearly a great deal of cross-fertilization, mutual benefit, and growth. One of the main means by which this chapter will examine the links (both present and possible) between this context on one hand and United Nations peace operations on the other is precisely by identifying both the relevant recommendations, readjustments, and realignments that emerged from the panel's report and the ways that they are being applied (in Afghanistan and situations like it) or might be applied. The point of doing so is not to reflect on the road not taken, but— much more importantly—to identify the ways in which these recommendations and operations might best be put to use in addressing the evolving challenges before us, to assess the synergies they have to offer in and to a rapidly changing context, and occasionally even to anticipate the ways that the lessons learnt in applying the recommendations might be applied to the recommendations in turn.

But what precisely is (or could be) the link between the context in question here (in which terrorism has greatly changed both the challenges before us and our perception of them) and peace operations (the means employed by the United Nations to address those challenges on the ground)? What light can that link shed on our understanding of the psychological origins and aspects of that context in general and terrorism more specifically? How can it illuminate the ways in which we choose to address them? What specific measures will need to be taken? By whom? What are some of the most promising and productive means of pursuing the goals that emerge? And what are some of the weaknesses or worries associated with them? How, in the final analysis, can a clearer understanding of the psychological aspects of this dynamic better undergird our actions and directions?

By looking first at the overall context and then at the evolution of peace operations as a response to it, it is these questions that this chapter explores.

CONTEXT

What is the overall context from which the challenges now before us emerged?

A decade ago, Jacques Attali (1991), president of the European Bank for Reconstruction and Development, wrote *Millennium*, a book in which he sketched the profile of the challenges that he believed would confront us now, at the threshold of a new thousand years. In the wake of September 11, 2001, it has become hauntingly prescient. In *Millennium*, Attali explained that

> [l]ike all past civilizations, which sought to endure by establishing an order to ward off the threat of nature and other men, the coming new order will be based on its ability to manage violence. Unlike previous orders, however, which first ruled by religion, and then by military force, the new order will manage violence largely by economic power. Of course, religion and military might will continue to persist, especially in the peripheral developing countries. . . . [But] the central organizing principle of the future will be economic.
>
> . . . [C]onflict is more likely now that the Cold War has ended and the market has triumphed. For it is precisely because so much of the world now shares the same desire for a prosperous order based on choice that conflict will arise. . . . For inequality will cleave the new world order as surely as the Berlin Wall once divided east from west.
>
> [There will be . . .] economic refugees and migrants on an unprecedented scale. . . . If the North remains passive and indifferent to their plight, and especially if Eastern Europe is brought into the orbit of prosperity through the full force of Western generosity while the South is neglected, the peoples of the periphery will inevitably enter into revolt and, one day, war.
>
> But there is an even more ominous and less visible threat on the horizon. It has to do with the very warp and woof of the new world order and its liberal ideology of consumerism and pluralism. The essence of both democracy and the market is choice. Both offer the citizen-consumer the right to adopt or reject options, whether candidates or commodities, politics or products. . . . This capacity to change . . . is the principal feature of the culture of choice on which the consumerist consensus rests. It informs both our political system and our economic order. Both are rooted in pluralism, and what might be called (perhaps

awkwardly) the principle of reversibility. We have come to believe that
nothing is (or should be) forever. Everything can be exchanged or dis-
carded. Such a principle, however convenient in the short term, cannot anchor a civilization. Indeed, it undermines the chief imperative of
all previous civilizations: to endure.

. . . The social vertigo induced by the principle of reversibility, which
sanctifies the short term and makes a cult of immediacy, is already provoking reaction. The broad revival of religious fundamentalism . . . the
fanatic rejection of industrial life . . ., the nostalgia for hierarchical
social structures and tradition, raise the spectre that the democratic
values and market principles inherent in the culture of choice will be
constantly attacked, perhaps even overturned. (pp. 2–18)

Attali's explanations are searing, and their implications are frightening. Is the
culture of "reversibility" a monster that we have ourselves created, at least in part?
Is the "social vertigo" that Attali anticipates the equal and opposite—and perhaps
inevitable—reaction to it? Were those who felled the World Trade Center targeting the "culture of choice"?

Attali's analysis brilliantly anticipates the context in question here, but it does
not (and could not) anticipate the attack itself. Yet, if the world is to attempt successfully to address its new situation, some attempt to understand both that event
and its perpetrators' motives must be made. "The religious fundamentalism, . . .
fanatic rejection of industrial life, . . . and nostalgia for hierarchical social structures
and tradition" that Attali mentions cannot but bring to mind the World Trade
Center bombers, as does another prescient and perceptive reference.

In a speech he gave on terrorism in Jerusalem nearly thirty years ago, U.S. Senator Henry Jackson recalled the words that George Bernard Shaw had given Joan of
Arc (in his *Saint Joan*) when she was informed that she was to be burned at the
stake:

If I go through the fire, . . . I shall go through it to their hearts for ever
and ever. (Safire, 1992, p. 534)

One cannot help but wonder whether, from however perverse a perspective, the
terrorists who destroyed the World Trade Center saw themselves and their "fundamental" mission in the same light. If they did so, they did so with some reason. In
very different ways, they did reach every human heart, even if—in the great vast
majority of them—they inspired horror, fear, and outrage. In doing so, they reminded the world of a truth that the philosopher Miguel de Unamuno had uttered
nearly a century before: "Martyrs create faith; faith does not create martyrs" (De
Unamuno, 1913). The impact of their messianic mission, however, was none the
less for that.

From both a multilateral and psychological perspective, nonetheless, it is important to try to garner some sense of what motivated these individuals—and what

they hoped to achieve. What kind of faith were they propounding? What following were they hoping to generate?

To each of these questions, illuminating responses can be found in *The Law of Love and Violence*, a work that Leo Tolstoy wrote at the end of his long life, with the shadow of both World War I and the Russian Revolution bearing down on him, along with that of his own end. It is the political, philosophical, and psychological testament of someone whose sense of the currents of civilization was uniquely tuned. In it, expressing concern about the misuses of faith, such as those that resulted in the terrorist attacks, he avers that

> one can neither weigh nor measure the evil that false religion has caused and is still causing. Religion is the establishment of the relation that exists between man, God, and the universe, and the definition of man's mission that results from it. How miserable our lives would be if this relation and this definition were false. (p. 29)

In addition to indicating the falseness of this base, he also considers the structures and strictures constructed from it, and the actions that result. He explains that

> perceiving the constant increase of their misfortunes, [men] employ the only means of salvation that, according to their conception of life, they consider rational: the oppression of part by the rest.

> Certainly, it is possible [for such men] to push a man forcibly in the direction that he refuses to take. . . . But how shall one understand the reasoning by which violence is a means of inviting men to do everything we wish them to do?

> Constraint always consists in forcing others, by threats of suffering or death, to do what they refuse to do. That is why they act against their own wishes as long as they consider themselves weaker than their oppressors. From the moment that they feel themselves stronger, they will not only cease to obey, but, irritated by the struggle and by all that they have suffered, they will first gain their liberty, and then in their turn they will impose their will upon those who disagree with them. So it should be evident that the struggle between oppressors and oppressed, far from constituting a means of social organization, leads to disorder and . . . disagreement. (pp. 15–18)

The pattern Tolstoy describes and the particular kind of "groupthink" that it profiles seem almost tailored to fit both terrorists or terrorist groups (such as al-Qaeda) and those who come within their grasp. The vital difference, in the context in question, is that, with luck, the tools that we are honing against precisely that cycle of constraint—in which repressor replaces repressor and violence begets violence—might stand a better chance of breaking it. To improve their odds, however, understanding both the psychology of the situation and of those caught in it will be crucial. So will be understanding the means at our disposal to address that situation and assist those individuals and groups.

Alongside the line that stretches from Attali's understanding of causes and currents to Tolstoy's understanding of their results and ramifications, another line—describing and proscribing the ways in which the world responds and can respond—needs also to be drawn. In drawing it, the first and foremost question that needs to be asked is: How can the international community support efforts—by and in Afghanistan and countries like it—to emerge from the terror and violence that have subsumed them?

HOW CAN WE RESPOND?

When speaking of terrorism in Jerusalem thirty years ago, Senator Jackson asked "What can be done?" and answered with five suggestions:

- We must "acknowledge that international terrorism is a 'collective problem'"
- We "must work against . . . efforts to define away terrorism. The idea that one person's terrorist is another's 'freedom fighter' cannot be sanctioned"
- "We must turn the publicity instrument against the terrorists, and we must expose . . . state support of terrorist groups whenever we identify it. . . . When an act of terrorism occurs, [we] should unite in sponsoring resolutions in the United Nations condemning the act. Where we have evidence of support for the terrorists by some other state, this support should be censured in the strongest terms
- We "must work together to apply sanctions against countries which provide sanctuary to international terrorists"
- "Within each of our own countries, we must organize to combat terrorism in ways consistent with our democratic principles and with the strong support of our citizens." (Safire, 1992, pp. 537–539)

Thirty years ago, at a point in time when it could be rightly claimed that "terrorism is not a new phenomenon; what is new is the international nature of terrorism" (Safire, 1992), this list might have been seen as complete as well as concrete. In the midst of the Cold War and the multilateral limitations it entailed, restricting the United Nations' role to one of sanction and censure might have been perceived as reasonable. Today, neither of those is the case.

In the context in question here, in the shadow of the challenges it portends, as the secretary-general noted at the time,

> the United Nations is uniquely positioned to advance this effort. It provides the forum necessary for building a universal coalition and can ensure global legitimacy for the long-term response to terrorism. United Nations conventions already provide a legal framework for many of the steps that must be taken to eradicate terrorism—including the extradition and prosecution of offenders and the suppression of money laundering. (Annan, 2001)

The United Nations is also advancing this effort, in Afghanistan and in other conflict areas, by engaging actively in the political aspects of resolution, in humanitarian assistance, and in peacekeeping—as it has done throughout its existence.

During the Cold War, many of these efforts focused on addressing the impact of conflicts between countries. In the decade that followed it, peace operations within and without the United Nations broadened to embrace a broader spectrum of activity. Former Secretary-General Boutros Boutros Ghali's "Agenda for Peace" defined a continuum encompassing four areas of action—preventive diplomacy and deployment, peacemaking, peacekeeping, and post-conflict peacebuilding (United Nations, 2000c, para. 10). In places such as Cambodia, Guatemala, and El Salvador, all of these elements came into play at one moment or another; or even simultaneously. Peacekeeping in particular emerged from its Cold War functions of truce observation and burgeoned into a complex means of addressing multidimensional conflicts with numerous needs. Great optimism was felt, and great strides were taken. In the short space of five years, however, and again particularly in peacekeeping, many of these efforts had badly faltered. Somalia, Bosnia, Rwanda, and Burundi are but the best known and most painfully recalled of these.

Realizing that extensive reform was needed in both what the organization did and how it did it, the secretary-general convened a Panel on Peace Operations on March 7, 2000, to look into the problems existing and the solutions that could be found to them, to

> undertake a thorough review of United Nations peace and security activities, and to present a clear set of specific, concrete, and practical recommendations to assist the United Nations in conducting such activities better in the future. (United Nations, 1998, covering letter)

In its report (which subsequently became known as the Brahimi Report, after the chair of the panel), the Panel on Peace Operations did not focus on when or why to deploy an operation, though some both inside and outside the United Nations feel that it should have. It did not try to prescribe or proscribe specific conditions under which the organization must act or should. Realistically, it knew that decisions of this kind were and would be taken by member states, and on a case-by-case basis rather than under fiat.

What, then, were the parameters that the panel did define? And how did it deal with its subject within them?

First of all, the panel addressed the concern that, too often, in areas precisely like Afghanistan, "United Nations operations did not deploy into post-conflict situations but tried to create them" (United Nations, 1998, p. ix). In many of these situations, the prerequisites of peace—or of peace operations—were often not present. Though some of the operations thus created were able to surmount that impediment, a consensus developed that deployment in and under such conditions needed seriously to be reconsidered. Difficulties encountered reminded us that

> there are lessons that must be learned if we are to expect the peoples of the world to place their faith in the United Nations. There are occasions when Member States cannot achieve consensus on a particular response to active military conflicts, or do not have the will to pursue what many might consider to be an appropriate course of action. The first of the general lessons is that when peacekeeping operations are used as a substitute for such political consensus they are likely to fail. There is a role for peacekeeping—a proud role in a world still riven by conflict; but . . . if the necessary resources are not provided—and the necessary political, military, and moral judgements are not made—the job simply cannot be done. (United Nations, 2000e, para. 498[3])

Essentially, while peace operations could be used to address conflicts, they "should not be used as a substitute for addressing the root causes of conflict." (United Nations, 1998, para. 49) To use one of the few psychological terms to emerge from the multilateral lexicon, what they require most is "political will."

With that point established, the other principal consideration to which the panel turned was the vital need for more rapid and effective deployment. Experience had taught that rapid reaction and arrival alone were useless without the mandate, means, and direction required to make presence effective. Yet it had also shown that a clear direction and solid support would not stave off crisis if they arrived too late. Rwanda, perhaps more than any other operation, had borne agonizing witness to the inability of the international community in general and the United Nations in particular to respond promptly or effectively to utmost need—and to the effects of that inability.

Many authors have emphasized that the first stages of conflict, like the first stages of dénouement, can be both the most fragile and the most threatening. Looking back at the situation in Rwanda, Alan J. Kuperman advanced the astounding assertion that, of the up to 800,000 people who perished in that country's five-month-long 1994 genocide, as many as 250,000 were slaughtered in the first two weeks of it alone, at "the fastest genocide rate in history" (Kuperman, 2000, p. 98). At that very moment, the United Nations Assistance Mission in Rwanda (UNAMIR) was infamously reduced, first by unilateral contingent withdrawal, then by a Security Council resolution, from a strength of more than 2,000 to less than 270, and it would not be reinforced until the end of the year, well after the slaughter had ended. Even in retrospect, a less-rapid, less-effective deployment than this seems inconceivable. The low-water mark of United Nations peace operations had been reached. Above all, this was what needed to be avoided or averted in the future. But how?

Against this grim history, the panel had to balance the realities, weaknesses, and impediments of the organization. It also, however, needed to take a long, hard look at each actor in the political process, whether an individual or an organizational unit, and it had to recommend ways in which the actions and interactions of those actors could be put to greatest service.

From a theoretical standpoint, based on game theory, Robert Axelrod offers a number of insights into how that progress might best be achieved:

> Mutual cooperation can be stable if the future is sufficiently important relative to the present. . . . When the future casts a large shadow, . . . it pays to cooperate . . . and . . . cooperation based on reciprocity is stable. . . . There are two basic ways of [enlarging the shadow of the future]: by making interactions more durable, and by making them more frequent.

> Hierarchy and organization [can be] especially effective at concentrating [such] interactions. . . . By binding people together in a long-term, multilevel [situation], organizations increase the number and importance of future interactions, and thereby [can] promote the emergence of cooperation among groups too large to interact individually. This in turn leads to the evolution of organizations for the handling of larger and more complex issues. (Axelrod, 1981, pp. 126–131)

It seems at many points that this is the perspective that the panel adopted, wittingly or not, in hammering out its assessments and recommendations. Moving from one actor to the next, we will see how that perspective is reflected.

The panel knew, for example, that the presence or absence, strength or weakness of any action taken by the United Nations was and is entirely dependent upon the political will manifested by (or through) its member states. It knew not only how thinly that life-blood could trickle, but also how far through the labyrinth of structure and administration it had to course.

One of the ways in which member states had long been laboring to achieve an increasingly greater say in peace operations was through meetings of "troop contributors," both general and mission-specific.

Troop contributors meetings and briefings are convened to involve "prospective troop contributors [in] consultations at the earliest possible stage in order to provide them access to the information required to enable them to make an informed decision on participation" (United Nations, 1998, para. 53). A political committee within the United Nations made up of member states has repeatedly underlined "the importance of consultations with troop-contributing countries," but has also pushed farther, volleying for "strengthening and formalizing the consultation process" and holding meetings "*at the request of* troop-contributing countries, particularly when a new mandate is being considered." It has further suggested that countries that have committed personnel to a mission "should be invited to participate in meetings of the Security Council in which the Secretariat provides it with information on changes to the mission's mandate and concept of operations that have implications for the mission's use of force" (United Nations, 2000a, paras. 8–12, italics mine). Clearly, those countries that risk the lives of their young for peace deserve both the fullest knowledge of the situation available and the maximum protection that that knowledge can offer. If their interest and participation is to be sustained, it is essential. There is a balance to be considered, however. If the point were reached where the increasing involvement of troop contributors became a de facto broadening of the Security Council, the very rapidity and effectiveness that those troop contributors and others are seeking would be hampered, if not endangered. Yet a better balance must unquestionably be found; one that— whether through invitation to Security Council meetings on mandate formulation or some other means—gives possible troop contributors the comfort, confidence, reassurance, and input they require to be able to commit their contingents early and fully.

Two of the panel's recommendations do a great deal not only to maintain the fragile balance between these parties and others, but also to further effectiveness and rapidity. The first is that "the Security Council . . . assure itself that [peace agreements involving the creation of peacekeeping operations meet] threshold conditions, such as consistency with international human rights standards and practicability of specified tasks and timelines." Recalling the international negotiations on Afghanistan that took place in Germany and their impact, one understands better both the need to insist upon these threshold conditions and the benefits to be gained by so doing. The second and more ingenious recommendation is that

> the Security Council should leave *in draft form* resolutions authorizing missions with sizeable troop levels until such time as the Secretary-General has firm commitments of troops and other critical mission support elements . . . *from Member States.*" (United Nations, 2000c, para. 64, italics mine)

This single brilliant stroke, if ever implemented, would alone address a host of problems that the panel and others have had to face: force strength, mandate, and security primary among them. For those very reasons, its future will be something to watch with concern—concern, however, and hope.

The other really hopeful sign as regards the Security Council is the growing trend of its deploying fact-finding missions to peace operations on the ground. The panel itself lamented (United Nations, 2000c) the way that the Secretariat felt increasingly constrained to refrain from telling "the Security Council what it needs to know, not what it wants to hear." That frustration was compounded by the realization of how little firsthand insight or experience those handling the mission from New York were gleaning from the ground. Those experiences convinced the panel of the utility—even the necessity—of fact-finding missions. Given the expenses that operations now entail, as the panel itself noted, such missions are wise investments entailing relatively minute expenditures, which can nonetheless be carefully accounted, audited, and defended. They should prove a "force multiplier" in every sense, and it is very encouraging that the council in particular is seeing their value and making use of them.

Concerning these missions, the panel argued that

> [o]n a political level, many of the local parties with whom peacekeepers and peacemakers are dealing on a daily basis may neither respect nor fear verbal condemnation by the Security Council. It is therefore incumbent that Council members and the membership at large breathe life into the words that they produce, as did the Security Council delegation that flew to Jakarta and Dili in the wake of the East Timor crisis last year, an example of effective Council *action* at its best: *res, non verba*. (United Nations, 2000c, para. 276)

This lesson, learned in East Timor, might, under other circumstances, have been learned or applied in Afghanistan. More importantly, the fruit it has borne will encourage those involved in addressing future challenges and crises to apply it to them. A number of such recent missions have also shown (and the panel has noted) that, just as there is benefit to be reaped from early missions to an operation by Secretariat staff and the Security Council, there is also benefit in ensuring that

> the entire leadership of a mission [is] assembled at Headquarters as early as possible in order to enable their participation in key aspects of the mission planning process, for briefings on the situation in the mission area and to meet and work with their colleagues in mission leadership. . . . The Secretariat should routinely provide the mission leadership with strategic guidance and plans for anticipating and overcoming challenges to mandate implementation and, whenever possible, should formulate such guidance and plans together with the mission leadership. (United Nations, 2000c, para. 101)

Experience in Afghanistan and other recent crises has underlined that these steps are equally important in situations where, without the benefit of a United Nations peace operation, a special representative of the secretary-general (or the equivalent) has been assigned to address a crisis and guide a political or peace process.

The secretary-general, in his report on the implementation of the panel's recommendations (United Nations, 2000d, para. 64) made the analogous point that "those who will ultimately have to start up and run a mission on the ground should be involved in the planning of that mission."

One of the innovations recommended by the panel would help achieve precisely this. The panel advocates the participation of "advisor-observers" during peace negotiations to ensure that

> tasks to be undertaken by the United Nations are operationally achievable . . . and either contribute to addressing the sources of conflict or provide the space required for others to do so. Since competent advice to negotiators may depend on detailed knowledge of the situation on the ground, the Secretary-General should be pre-authorized to commit funds from the Peacekeeping Reserve Fund sufficient to conduct a preliminary site survey. (United Nations, 2000d, para. 58)

Clearly, the preliminary site surveys would form another and welcome strand in the net of deeper, earlier contacts with the field that includes the missions by the Secretariat and Security Council that the panel also supports. Aside from assisting in determining such crucial issues as proposed mission strength and deployment, however, these site surveys would undoubtedly be of use precisely in assessing what support and material a mission would require, and how best it might receive it. Interestingly, in the case of Afghanistan, the advisor-observer function was not only present, it far exceeded in both range and rank anything anticipated by the language of the panel. Further, in a natural-enough division of labor (particularly given the coalition composition of the mission on the ground), the site survey work was actually undertaken by or through the contributing countries. From both of these initiatives, a greater ability to react rapidly and effectively resulted.

There is a vital and promising link to be made between the various points, possibilities, and options just covered. "Burnout" is always a risk of long involvement with one issue. And fresh perspectives can often be extremely useful. But the points that the panel and the secretary-general make above on early and extended participation are extremely important and promising. Too rarely has enough foresight been exercised to envisage the presence of a United Nations (or any other) peace operation early in a peace process. More rarely still has the United Nations become involved in or been brought in for the purpose of designing that presence in conjunction with and support of that peace process. And rarest of all have been the incidences where rapports and reputations on the ground have already been well established, where institutional memory is already broad and solid.

Other good and valuable recommendations on senior staffing emerge from the panel's report and those who react to it. The enhancement of "on-call" lists for special representatives of the secretary-general (SRSGs) and other senior staff will encourage rapidity and effectiveness, particularly if the panel's recommendation to broaden them to include senior officials in specific areas such as electoral assistance and human rights is fully followed. One United Nations political committee, in considering the smooth filling of these posts, recommended (United Nations, 2000a, para. 17) that "all mission leaders must be interviewed by the senior leadership, as a general rule, at United Nations Headquarters." If the mission is still nascent and New York is still its nexus, this clearly makes sense. Yet, in balancing effectiveness and rapidity, it needs to be remembered that the process of filling field posts is already notoriously cumbersome and slow. If these steps—admittedly good and necessary—are to be taken, where will the slack for them be found or created? And at what stage of implementation does it make more sense for senior officials (apart from the SRSG and deputy SRSG themselves) to be interviewed in the mission area? In considering questions of civilian personnel, the panel recommends that hiring authority be delegated to the field. The line between these two recommendations—the point at which ongoing contact with (and therefore an interview in) New York becomes essential—needs to be more fully and carefully drawn. But will that need to be decided on a mission-by-mission basis? And perhaps by the SRSG himself, whether in New York or once deployed?

Whether this decision is taken by the SRSG or someone else, the question of filling posts in the field is also tied, in a very practical way, to building local capacity and cooperation, as people locally hired are frequently local. This reality has in turn a profound psychological impact on the local population and their outlook on the mission. Often, in their own minds, local recruitment is used as a litmus test to gauge the (perceived) extent to which the international community is actually (and literally) working with them and investing in them. Their conclusions frequently determine (or at least affect) the degree of their cooperation and support.

The strengthening of the role of the SRSG is actually an area in which one of the panel's most cogent and promising recommendations emerges. Both the panel and the secretary-general recommend (United Nations, 2000c, para. 47a) that

> a small percentage of a mission's first-year budget should be made available to the representative or special representative of the Secretary-General leading the mission to fund quick-impact projects with the advice of the country team's resident coordinator.

Though they are unacknowledged, the proposal draws on lessons learned from two operations: The successes achieved by SRSG Aldo Ajello in Mozambique, in part through the use of precisely this kind of fund, and the frustration and failure encountered by the United Nations in Rwanda for lack of it or anything similar. Ajello's funds, it needs to be noted, were provided not by or through the United Nations, but rather by his own government, which took great interest in the Mozambican peace process. It was for this reason that the United Nations was unable to respond to similar requests in and from Rwanda: There has been, to this day, no United Nations fund from which to draw for such projects and expenses.

Small acts of support or good faith by Ajello—often rapid responses to slight requests of a logistical or material nature—proved invaluable in sustaining the parties, their good faith, and their participation in the peace process. Like local recruitment, these were sound and solid psychological investments. The United Nations Assistance Mission in Rwanda, in contrast, was never able to emerge from under the cloud of misgivings of both the parties, partly due to its inability to offer precisely this kind of gesture of good will and support. During its tenure and beyond its departure, both Hutu and Tutsi lamented both the larger failure of the mission to achieve its mandate and its many smaller failures to provide the resources or support that would have aided the country in its reach toward recovery.

To imply that such initiatives were entirely absent is neither accurate nor fair. But as Shaharyar Khan, the SRSG in Rwanda, noted in a cable to New York shortly before the mission closed, they were taken "mainly through military and technical units, operating over and above their mandated tasks" (United Nations, 1996b, p. 1).

To prove this point, Khan then recounted a list of achievements that is both impressive and moving, including: rebuilding four bridges, repairing thirteen roads and building three new ones, assisting in the reconstruction of Kigali Airport and the restoration of national telephone and radio networks, treating up to 1,600 patients in the mission's clinics and immunizing 62,000, as well as training hospital staff and performing life-saving surgical operations on Rwandan citizens, transporting large quantities of food and up to a million refugees, and providing generators and engineering services (United Nations, 1996b, pp. 3–5). The end-of-mission report submitted by his force commander, only a few days later, closes with a similar synopsis. Both, however, acknowledge that the mission was still "looked upon with misgivings by both the ethnic parties" and conclude that "the peace as it exists can best be described as fragile" (United Nations, 1996a).

As one analyst explained,

> [t]he local population . . . is generally not able to comprehend the failure of their "trustees" to expend allocated funds promptly to deal with obvious and urgent needs and may grow resentful in the face of apparent indifference. . . . UN rules make it difficult for a mission to expend resources on anything other than the mission itself. This may not be problematic for most peace-support operations, but it would be helpful for an operation whose purpose is to facilitate the emergence of a new state, or at least to promote substantial autonomy, to permit the use of UN resources . . . by fledgling indigenous institutions. UN procurement rules should be revised to allow transitional administrators greater authority to buy goods and services directly. (Caplan, pp. 74–76)

These observations fully reinforce the need both for this kind of assistance and for a fund that would allow it to be provided more rapidly, effectively, fully, and freely. The end-of-mission report by the force commander, General Sivukumar, places such stock in just such an arrangement that he recommends that "a permanent advisor to the Agencies and NGOs [for coordinating this kind of quick-impact project] . . . would prove beneficial to the functioning" of the mission. Noting that part of the new focus of United Nations peace operations is "to create and strengthen political institutions and to broaden their base," the secretary-general's Millennium Report (United Nations, 2000b, paras. 221–222) argued that this kind of assistance is essential because "[p]eople will quickly become disillusioned with fledgling institutions, and even the peace process itself, if they can see no prospect for any material improvement in their condition." This is a risk that is still being run in Afghanistan and other conflict areas like it, where needs are identified, a small fraction of the aid needed to meet them is promised, and, even when promised, it tends to arrive too little and too late to meet many needs and expectations. The goals espoused—and the situations themselves—will continue to be placed in unnecessary peril as long as this continues. At a psychological level, the message transmitted by inaction is as strong as that transmitted by action; it is simply its equal and its opposite.

To help the SRSG address these challenges and situations, the role of the deputy SRSG (whether the local humanitarian coordinator or resident representative) was somewhat retailored as well. To signal the symbiosis required between the SRSG and the deputy, the Secretariat, and the United Nations' agencies and programs on the ground, the secretary-general emphasized in his reform proposal (United Nations, 1997, para. 119) that "in the field, the Special Representative . . . will have authority over all United Nations entities," but that the SRSG would receive senior-level support from the humanitarian coordinator or resident representative, recommending that that individual serve as deputy, as appropriate. Again, as Axelrod (1981) would note, the durability, frequency, and immediacy of interaction has been underscored. The net has again been strengthened and tightened. Greater, broader, and more sustained contact with the local population, leading to greater support and cooperation from them, is again the goal, the psychological and political purpose.

To achieve these aims, effective leadership is vital—across each and all of the areas discussed. Equally essential, however, is commensurate reform at the working level and on the ground. In recommending the creation of Integrated Mission Task Forces (IMTFs), the panel addresses the first of those needs.

Admitting that the task forces that had previously been convened to address specific situations or to guide the initial deployment of specific missions had functioned "more as sounding boards than executive bodies that . . . meet infrequently and . . . disperse once an operation had begun to deploy" and acknowledging that "missions have no single working-level focal point at headquarters that can address all of their concerns quickly," the panel argued that the IMTFs should constitute

> an entity that includes all of the backstopping people and expertise for the mission, drawn from an array of headquarters elements that mirrors the functions of the mission itself. The notion of integrated, *one-stop support* for United Nations peace-and-security field activities should extend across the whole range of peace operations, with the size, substantive composition, meeting venue, and leadership matching the needs of the operation. . . . The supporting cast would remain substantially the same during transitions [between phases and responsible departments]. . . . [The IMTF's] size and composition would match the nature and the phase of the field activity being supported. *Task Force members should be formally seconded* to IMTF for [the period needed] by their home division, department, agency, or programme.

> . . . An IMTF should be much more than a coordinating committee or task force of the type now set up at headquarters. It should be a temporary but coherent staff created for a specific purpose, able to be increased or decreased in size or composition in response to mission needs. Each Task Force member should be authorized to serve not only as a liaison between the Task Force and his or her home base, but as its *key working-level decision-maker* for the mission in question.
>
> IMTFs offer a flexible approach to dealing with time-critical, resource-intensive, but ultimately temporary requirements to support mission planning, start-up, and initial sustainment. The concept borrows heavily from the notion of "matrix management" used extensively by large organizations that need to be able to assign the necessary talent to specific projects without reorganizing themselves every time a project arises.
>
> IMTFs, with members seconded from throughout the United Nations system, as necessary, should be the standard vehicle for mission-specific planning and support. (United Nations, 2000c, paras. 200–217, italics mine)

Clearly, in an organization where most officers bear responsibility for more than one mission (and sometimes more than one area), this innovation would entail substantial revisions and reforms. The definition of roles and timings alone will prove very sensitive. And it will be important not to destabilize the current decision-making process while the IMTFs are being put into place and into motion. Yet, regardless of those requirements (among others), there is undoubtedly a great deal to be gained from having a hub that is indeed more unified, where all headquarters actors are in both immediate and frequent contact with each other, and where, perhaps most importantly, they are each and all empowered to be "key working-level decision-makers." Structurally, devolving that degree of authority to that extent would both simplify and expedite decision and action. The underlying assumption—or safeguard—would seem to be that the checks and balances now imposed sequentially by a vertical hierarchy could be adequately replaced by simultaneous lateral consultation within the context of the IMTF itself. To the extent that this proves true—and sufficient—the process, the organization, the mission, and the mission area will clearly gain a great deal from the change proposed.

Seconding the officers concerned, freeing and forcing them to focus solely on the mission in question and its needs, will also make line reactions and responses more rapid and effective, given that adequate ties and reporting to their "home bases" are assured. Further, involving those identified from the beginning, achieving the fullest and broadest representation possible, and ensuring smooth transitions between phases will maximize the retention of institutional memory and avoid the frustrating slippage so often encountered by the current system, most notably during handovers or reassignments.

These changes again recall Axelrod's perception on the psychological dynamic of such constructs, which "[b]y binding people together in a long-term, multilevel [situation], . . . increase the number and importance of future interactions, and thereby [can] promote the emergence of cooperation" (Axelrod, 1981, pp. 126–131). Early indications from the United Nations missions in East Timor and other areas where IMTFs have been employed confirm that they have indeed brought progress toward the goals sought—and that they hold even greater potential for future operations.

The strength and success of the IMTF mechanism will also, of course, depend upon the support provided through it to elements and activities on the ground, and on their strength in turn. In three of those elements (military personnel, civilian police, and civilian personnel), the panel recommended changes that could help bring about that greater strength and success.

While all the actors and aspects examined thus far play crucial roles in achieving rapid and effective deployment, three elements actually *are* deployed, rapidly and effectively or not: military personnel, civilian police, and civilian personnel. Of these, military personnel are usually among the very first to arrive in the theater, and they are also usually at the core of efforts to plan and implement an operation's deployment. Their efforts, therefore, go to the heart of achieving the goals that the panel identified.

The inadequate provision of military personnel has been the bane of peacekeeping in the last decade, at times with disastrous results, and it has often seemed that the broader the mandates and needs of an operation have become, the wider the gap has gotten. There is a certain logic in this, of course, but there is also a certain irony.

The language of the panel's recommendation reflects this. Both moving and telling, it also demonstrates a sensitivity to the psychological needs and vulnerabilities of a population emerging from conflict that is rarely given voice in official documents:

> . . . the Panel believes that, until the Secretary-General is able to obtain solid commitment from Member States for the forces that he or she does believe necessary to carry out an operation, it should not go forward at all. To deploy a partial force incapable of solidifying a fragile peace would first raise and then dash the hopes of a population engulfed in conflict or recovering from war, and damage the credibility of the United Nations as a whole. (United Nations, 2000c)

It is in this context and for these reasons that the panel believes that resolutions should be left in draft form, and it also points (United Nations, 2000c, para. 61) to ways in which it believes that such "commitment gaps" can be filled or diminished.

Among these, four are key. The formation of brigades (by member states or regional or other organizations) that can be quickly deployed has the advantage of units that are pre-formed and pre-trained. But interoperability has yet to be achieved among them, and they still require parliamentary approval at the national level (which is not always speedily received) to be deployed.

"On-call lists" would be made up of up to a hundred officers of various specialties and nationalities, pre-qualified, pre-trained, and deployable within seven days. "Interacting with the planners of the Integrated Mission Task Force" and assembled to coordinate the planning of the mission, the task of

> the "on-call team" would be to translate the broad strategic-level concepts of the mission . . . into concrete operational and tactical plans, and to undertake immediate coordination and liaison tasks in advance of the deployment of troop contingents, [. . . remaining] operational until replaced by deployed contingents. (United Nations, 2000c, para. 112)

In addition to these initiatives, the panel recommended the deployment of teams to assess the readiness of contingents before they deploy, and it also noted the need for "enabling forces, which include the provision of specialized units for movement control, communications, terminal or air-traffic control capability . . . [and] strategic lift assistance to troop contributors" (United Nations, 2000c, para. 84).

Parallel to these military measures, two important innovations were being propounded that relate specifically to the civilian police, as part of both

> a doctrinal shift . . . in how the Organization conceives of and utilizes civilian police in peace operations . . . [and] an adequately resourced team approach to upholding the rule of law and respect for human rights through judicial, penal, human rights and policing experts working together in a coordinated and collegial manner. (United Nations, 2000c, para. 40)

That coordinated and collegial collaboration would need to be accomplished at two levels: a new and independent rule-of-law unit that would report to the civilian police commissioner in the United Nations' Department of Peacekeeping Operations, and rule-of law teams that would participate in IMTFs and other aspects of early mission deployment. In setting out resource requirements to implement the panel's recommendations, to expand civilian police mandates and create rule-of-law teams, the secretary-general cautioned that

> [t]he ability of the United Nations civilian police to carry out their mandates is intrinsically linked to the ability of the local judicial and penal systems to carry out their responsibilities effectively. Yet, civilian police in peace operations are often deployed in areas where not only the local police, but also local judicial and penal institutions, have

been severely weakened or have ceased to exist. In such areas, these institutions must be rapidly strengthened if United Nations civilian police are to succeed. (United Nations, 2000f, para. 5.99)

To extend Axelrod's concepts, for frequent and durable interaction to occur, for cooperation to thrive and for progress to be made, there must be parallel and analogous actors on each side. But yet, even in the absence of this, as the panel rightly noted

United Nations civilian police monitors are not peacebuilders if they simply document or attempt to discourage . . . abusive or other unacceptable behaviour of local police officers—a traditional and somewhat narrow perspective of [their] capabilities. Today, missions may require civilian police to be tasked to *reform, train, and restructure local police forces according to international standards* for democratic policing and human rights, *as well as having the capacity to respond effectively to civil disorder and for self-defence.* (United Nations, 2000c, para. 39, italics mine)

Again, as was the case with military personnel, the situation demands the strengthening of both mandate and means to achieve it. Again, in response to those demands, a forward bulwark is set that comprises elements both new and reinforced. In Afghanistan and the areas of conflict that follow it, success will continue to be measured by the extent to which that bulwark is reinforced, empowered, and defended, the extent to which these new structures have flesh put on their bones and are brought to life, the extent to which new links are made and strengthened.

As important to that success as the elements discussed thus far will be, another option—perhaps another challenge—has arisen alongside them that is both making different demands and offering new prospects: transitional administration.

If a line were drawn from traditional peacekeeping through the "wider peacekeeping" efforts undertaken in places like Cambodia and Mozambique, and withheld in Rwanda, then onward through the rule-of-law measures examined above, the next logical point on that line would be transitional administration.

In characterizing transitional administration operations, the panel notes (United Nations, 2000c, para. 77) that they

face challenges and responsibilities that are unique among United Nations field operations. [They] must set and enforce the law, establish customs services and regulations, set and collect business and personal taxes, attract foreign investment, adjudicate property disputes and liabilities for war damage, reconstruct and operate all public utilities, create a banking system, run schools and pay teachers, . . . rebuild civil society and promote respect for human rights, in places where grievance is widespread and grudges run deep.

This is clearly the kind of work that the United Nations has taken on successfully in East Timor, and strongly similar to the body of work currently under way in Afghanistan. Yet there are misgivings about whether "the United Nations should be in this business at all" and whether such undertakings should be "considered an element of peace operations or managed by some other structure." The panel recognizes each of them (United Nations, 2000c, para. 78). At a very practical and immediate level, however, and partly in consideration of the kinds of crises now before us, the assumed response to each of these queries is positive.

Looking at the list of duties just detailed, one realizes immediately how vital to their success it is to have rapid access to and support from a broad range of civilian specialists. Given the breadth of demands represented, it is equally clear that collaboration with agencies, programs, and bodies outside the United Nations will also need to be strengthened. At the same time, the realization strikes that, incomplete as United Nations efforts have been to line up personnel for military and civilian police duties, they have been weaker yet in the civilian sector. One reason for this is that United Nations involvement in these activities has previously been primarily advisory; only recently has the organization actually been required to implement them. That, however, does not mitigate the need for rapid and effective response in these areas.

To ensure the greater presence, broader support, and quicker response that current and coming crises will require, the panel recommends that three options of interest in this context be examined and possibly implemented. Two of them—assigning "sectoral responsibility" to national contingents from individual member states and/or creating an international Civilian Standby Arrangements System (CSAS)—can be seen either as alternates or as complements. A third—the cementing of closer ties with a broader range of actors—would clearly be essential in any case.

Between the first two options offered, at least from my view, the promotion and solidification of the CSAS as proposed holds far more promise than the bloc assignment of entire national contingents to specific sectors of responsibility. Because specialized teams in given missions would need very specific expertise, both individually and collectively, the option of being able to draw prepared and pre-approved *individuals* from an Internet-based roster and hire them in the field better ensures adequate coverage, both of disciplines and of mission needs. It allows a more tailored fit between the mission and the mission area. The roster proposed differs more in degree than kind from the more informal rosters now maintained, though it suggests greater range and rapidity. Nonetheless, the CSAS, if implemented as designed, would provide the mission and the organization greater fluidity, flexibility, and strength than the assemblage of national sectoral groups, large or small. It would result in a single woven fabric, not a patchwork quilt.

Additionally, better than national sectoral responsibility, CSAS would complement the effort to reach out to and involve nongovernmental organizations in a way that would assist the United Nations not only in the provision of personnel but also in the creation of broader understanding and political support, further strengthening the base of cooperation, as Axelrod suggested. This would be achieved in part by giving

> [t]he relevant members of the United Nations family . . . delegated authority and responsibility, for occupational groups within their respective expertise, to initiate partnerships and memoranda of understanding with intergovernmental and non-governmental organizations, for the provision of personnel to supplement mission start-up teams . . . (United Nations, 2000c, para. 144)

This possibility, however, brings Rwanda once again to mind. Hobbled by a lack of the kind of discretionary fund that had been used in Mozambique (and that the panel now recommends be used generally), the mission nonetheless made constant efforts both to reach out to the agencies and nongovernmental organizations (NGOs) and to coordinate with them. The first of these were moderately successful; the latter met with more resistance. Why?

While it is important for agencies and NGOs to be acknowledged as players and provided a place at the table, it is equally important, from their view, that they be able to retain objective distance from the United Nations and its mission and remain free of association with them. The identity and the credibility of these organizations often rest both on the specificity of their mandate (human rights, famine relief) as it fits into the larger mosaic of international community action and on the fact that they are precisely *nongovernmental.* They are answerable solely to their donors and directors, not to the General Assembly or the Security Council. Thus, from their perspective, communication with the United Nations and its mission is clearly and mutually beneficial. Collaboration is possible and sometimes fruitful. But *coordination* of NGO efforts by the United Nations or under its auspices is an idea that, usually, has met with a lukewarm reception at best. As past crises have underlined and as present crises have reconfirmed, this option is thus not without limitations.

Yet, it is entirely possible, and imminently necessary, to make firmer and greater strides in creating broader understanding and political support. It was in this context that the panel recalled (United Nations, 2000c, para. 269) that

> [t]he Secretary-General has consistently emphasized the need for the United Nations to reach out to civil society and to strengthen relations with non-governmental organizations, academic institutions, and the media.

NGOs have already proven both vital and effective in this effort. As organizations not made up of member states, the criticisms that they could sometimes level at specific countries or situations often complemented positions or tacks taken by the United Nations.

Yet, however effective such NGO pronouncements might be in helping the United Nations highlight problems in a given area and in attempting to address them, it is ultimately the media that conveys, fails to convey, or decides not to convey these stories. The spark that ignites interest, creates debate, and generates movement toward action is theirs alone.

Despite this, public information activities and outreach are grossly undersupport-
ed—financially as well as politically, at the level of the United Nations, regional
organizations (some of the U.S. coalitions being possible exceptions), member states,
and mission areas. Though it is true that financing for public information remains
a serious concern and an abiding frustration, the real problems facing the sector are
deeper, more endemic. They touch on mode and method as well as means.

The panel, realizing this, identified a number of aspects and areas of public
information that could benefit from reform, including: expanding and reinforcing
communication within missions; identifying competent spokespeople; developing a
peace operations extranet (POE) and co-managed Web sites to help spread the mission's message; strengthening public information approaches and activities in
expanding sectors (such as human rights and civilian police), and developing local
capacity.

Quite clearly and correctly, the panel argued (United Nations, 2000c, para.
147) that "[f]ield missions need competent spokespeople who are integrated into
the senior management team and project its daily face to the world" to help achieve
this. This recommendation (which is followed by a request that the Secretariat
"increase its efforts to develop and retain a pool of such personnel"), however, rais-
es another concern.

It is equally important (United Nations, 2000a, para. 31) that "consideration
must be given to the promotion of local capacity" in public information. Creating
such capacity is acknowledged to build an important bridge into the community,
strengthen communication across it, and look toward the point at which information functions, like those of civilian police, will be assumed from within the theater.

Yet strengthening such capacity both in the public information sector and far
beyond it will depend not only on the creation of cooperation within the community, or within the mission itself. It will depend on a wider, broader, more vibrant, and
proactive outreach by the organization and the international community at large,
something that (particularly at critical moments) has often been sorely wanting.

Turning from the local back to the international, from a specific afflicted state
to the sum of all member states, from capacity on the ground back to capacity
across the globe, brings us full circle. It completes our consideration of the panel's
recommendations and the role and relation of each party in and to them. It squares
the entire net we have been examining here—the warp threads of rapidity, the
woofs of effectiveness, and the contribution that each party makes (or can make) to
tightening and strengthening the fabric.

CONCLUSION

Stepping back from that net for a moment, we can quickly see the greater strength
and broader range that it will have, in Afghanistan, East Timor, or the areas that
follow them, if the panel's recommendations are accepted and implemented. We
can easily identify the strands that can strengthen the net, such as early visits to

new mission areas by Security Council members; early United Nations presence in negotiations (possibly through "advisor-observers"); preliminary site surveys; early access by the secretary-general to $50 million to initiate deployment; early identification of possible troop contributors; early choice of mission leaders and rapid assembly of them at headquarters; preliminary missions to the area by the headquarters staff (both military and civilian) who will be handling an eventual operation; early and rapid constitution of an Integrated Mission Task Force (IMTF), and of pre-approved military contingents and civilian staff (possibly as CSAS members), expedited and facilitated by enabling forces.

While these measures concentrate on early and rapid deployment, other strands of the net concentrate on increasing a mission's breadth and effectiveness, through strengthening its mandate and definition of self-defense; deploying rule-of-law teams; broadening civilian police activity; emphasizing human rights and building sustainable local capacity in this area; building local public information capacity, without forgetting to reach out within the mission itself; engaging the agencies and programs by involving either the humanitarian coordinator or the resident representative as the Deputy SRSG; collaborating more closely with NGOs; and reaching out more effectively both to the media and to the local population.

Each of these strands—both the warps that extend as early into an operation's life as possible and the woofs that stretch as broadly as feasible across disciplines and mission areas—will be essential if the improvements sought are to be reached and grasped.

What are some of the most promising and productive means identified by the panel to pursue these goals? And what are some of the weaknesses or worries associated with them? In what ways and for what reasons will they need to be watched?

Quick impact projects, considered for a decade, hold great promise. Yet they require the SRSG who chooses and oversees them to be fully informed and in command of the situation from the very moment of his or her arrival. At the far end of the year foreseen for them, additionally, some consequent (whether it be local procurement, longer-term agency programs, or some other means) must then be ready to take over if their impact is to be realized fully. Because of the autonomy and delegation of authority they assume, their progress will need to be watched to see not only what support this initiative receives, but also what constraints and restraints are placed upon it.

IMTFs might indeed provide the more concise and consolidated headquarters support that missions require. Empowering line managers and desk officers could well result in more rapid reactions. But will this less vertical chain of command ensure the expertise required? And will the IMTFs actually receive, through full secondment of their members, the lifeblood, energy, and commitment that they will need to thrive? This initiative, encompassing the sensitive secondment issue in a Secretariat already overstretched, will be the bellwether of support within the house for the reforms set, and it should be watched carefully for that reason and indication.

Member states' commitment to reform will be tested more than anything else by whether they (in and through the Security Council) support and confirm the panel's recommendation that council resolutions authorizing missions remain in draft pending receipt of the support required to implement them. One of the oldest and deepest frustrations of the organization has been receiving mandates without means. Passing authorizing resolutions without providing the means they require has enabled member states to have their cake and eat it too—to avoid contributing to a mission and then lament the "failure" of the United Nations to acquit itself of the responsibilities they gave it. This is and has been a comfortable loophole to have. Will member states bear to see it closed, knowing that its closure will mean shouldering either responsibilities or costs? Their response on this issue will indicate their commitment to the reform for which they themselves have been calling.

The development, deployment, acceptance, and support of rule-of-law teams will prove a sure and sensitive indicator of the support (or lack of it) from the areas and countries where missions are deployed. Granted, peace operations are now created somewhat from a *menu à choix*, but as the continuum of international action moves through ethnic-conflict operations onward toward transitional administration, this element, the full and effective implementation of it, and the creation of the necessary local capacity to sustain it will all prove important indicators of the necessary longer-term view and commitment within the mission area itself.

Meeting the unique needs of public information, in rule-of-law and other emerging sectors, will test interest and commitment both within the organization and across a wider range. Regional organizations, member states, national broadcasting corporations, NGOs, and others, both within the mission area and beyond it, have shouldered some of the responsibilities in this area in the past. Will they be willing to take on the broader commitment now needed?

Finally, in Afghanistan and many other places like it, strengthening the range and reach of local capacity will test the willingness of the entire international community to redress, and not merely address, the crises that confront it. It will test commitment to the continuum that begins with the symptomatic response of a peacekeeping operation and moves through the curative work of reconstruction and sustainable, systemic development. Quick-impact projects, local procurement, auctioning and donating equipment no longer needed, and building local capacity from the ground up through the ministries, in one area and country after another, will show the international community's willingness or unwillingness not only to reform, but to reaffirm as well.

In convening and mandating the panel on United Nations Peace Operations, the secretary-general (United Nations, 2000a, covering letter) charged it to

> undertake a thorough review of United Nations peace and security activities, and to present a clear set of specific, concrete, and practical recommendations to assist the United Nations in conducting such activities better in the future.

It has acquitted itself of those responsibilities. The very real and pregnant question now is: will those to whom it has turned now acquit themselves of theirs?

Years ago, the Independent Task Force of the Council on Foreign Relations commented (Soros, 1996) that

> some of the . . . challenges of recent years . . . have led to quick claims that the difficulty lay not in the problem but in the institution trying to deal with the problem.

As both experience and analysis have proven, that accusation—while not entirely baseless—is inaccurate, incomplete, and unfair. Other organizations have encountered similar obstacles and impediments. Coalitions, member states, and other entities have been confronted with similar challenges. Further, the United Nations is not a monolith, but rather a body of various members and organs, each with its own form and function, each with its own agendas and activities. The panel has made cogent, productive, and positive recommendations regarding each of them.

Reflecting on those recommendations, considering the causes and currents that Attali described, remembering the results and ramifications that Tolstoy noted, and looking both at Afghanistan and beyond it, the question that began this chapter returns anew: What can we do?

Remembering the linkage made by the secretary-general between "the world's failure over a decade to act on warning signs in Afghanistan" and the "clear, if complicated, trail from the absence of engagement with Afghanistan in the 1990's to the creation of a terrorist haven there to the attacks on the World Trade Center" (Crossette, 2002), we now need to ask: Where does that trail lead from here?

In some ways, we are still too close to the point of the attack to see where that trail will or might take us. Objective distance will come only with time. Writing on diplomacy years ago, Henry Kissinger admitted that

> [w]henever the entities constituting the international system change their character, a period of turmoil inevitably follows. (Kissinger, 1994)

In the interim, however, there are still important points to consider. Bertrand Russell once made an illuminating comment on the nature of "religious power" that links back to Tolstoy's point on false religion, noting that

> religious power is much less affected by defeat in war than secular power. . . . St. Augustine, in the *City of God*, which was inspired by the sack of Rome, explained that temporal power was not what was promised to the true believer, and was therefore not to be expected as the result of orthodoxy. (Russell, 1992)

This ominous outlook recalls Osama bin Laden's comment when he was informed that he was wanted "dead or alive"—that if he were removed, that action would serve only to bring forward ten thousand more like him. Clearly, if left unaddressed, the kind of "social vertigo" that this comment reflects could spiral out of all scale. Terrorism could become an eternal threat and a perpetual problem. Can't that be avoided?

Attali offers one option:

> "To avert this possibility, the market and democracy will have to be bound. . . . not by conservative values that preserve the past, but by conserving values that preserve the future. . . . In order to survive the triumph of our secular ideals, we need a new definition of the sacred. (Attali, p. 12)

The secretary-general (Annan, 2001) makes an analogous point:

> Terrorism threatens every society. As the world takes action against it, we have all been reminded of the need to address the conditions that permit the growth of such hatred and depravity. We must confront violence, bigotry, and hatred even more resolutely.

These two thoughts, between them, provide at least an initial indication of the direction we will need to take—and of the ways in which we will need to undergird the operations of the interim. They also underline the distance that we yet must travel to reach a deeper understanding of the events through which we are living, the responses we are making to them, and—perhaps more importantly—the psychology behind them.

REFERENCES

Annan, K. (2001, September 21). Fighting terrorism on a global front. *New York Times*, p. A35.

Attali, J. (1991). *Millennium: Winners and losers in the coming world order* (pp. 2–18). New York: Random House.

Axelrod, R. (1981). *The evolution of cooperation.* New York: Basic Books.

Caplan, R. (2002) *A new trusteeship? The international administration of war-torn territories.* London: Oxford University Press (for the International Institute of Strategic Studies).

Crossette, B. (2002, March 7). Annan says terrorism's roots are broader than poverty. *New York Times*, p. A13.

De Unamuno, M. (1954). *The tragic sense of life.* New York: Dover. (originally published 1913)

Kissinger, H. (1994). *Diplomacy.* New York: Simon & Schuster.

Kuperman, A. J. (2000). Rwanda in retrospect. *Foreign Affairs, 79,* 94–119.

Russell, B. (1992). *Power.* New York: Routledge.

Safire, W. (1992). *Lend me your ears.* New York: W. W. Norton.

Soros, G. (1996). *American national interest and the United Nations: Statement and report of an independent task force* (p. 13). New York: Council on Foreign Relations.

Tolstoy, L. (1948). *The law of love and violence.* New York: Rudolph Field.

United Nations (1996a). End-of-mission report by Assistance Mission to Rwanda. April 19, 1996.

United Nations (1996b). UNAMIR Cable 1996/1771, "UNAMIR's Assistance to Rwanda." April 18, 1996.

United Nations (1997). Report of the secretary-general entitled "Renewing the United Nations: A programme for reform. A/51/950.

United Nations (1998). Report of the Special Committee on Peacekeeping Operations. A/53/127.

United Nations (2000a). Comprehensive review of the whole question of peacekeeping operations in all their aspects. Report of the Special Committee on Peacekeeping Operations. (Extraordinary session to examine the recommendations of the Panel on United Nations Peace Operations.) A/C.4/55/6.

United Nations (2000b). Report of the Millennium Assembly of the United Nations ("We the peoples: The role of the United Nations in the twenty-first century. The Millennium Report"). A/54/2000.

United Nations (2000c). Report of the Panel on United Nations Peace Operations. A/55/305-S/2000/809.

United Nations (2000d). Report of the secretary-general on the implementation of the report of the Panel on United Nations Peace Operations. A/55/502.

United Nations (2000e). Report of the secretary-general pursuant to General Assembly resolution 53/55, entitled "The fall of Srebrenica." A/54/549.

United Nations (2000f). Resource requirements for the implementation of the report of the Panel on United Nations Peace Operations. Report of the secretary-general. A/55/507/Add. 1.

SUPPLEMENTARY BIBLIOGRAPHY

United Nations Documents

2001

A/55/977. Implementation of the recommendations of the Special Committee on Peacekeeping Operations and the Panel on United Nations peace Operations. Report of the Secretary-General.

A/55/713 and Add. 1. Programme budget for the biennium 2000–2001. Report of the Fifth Committee.

A/RES/55/247. Procurement reform.

A/RES/55/215. Towards global partnerships.

A/RES/55/175. Safety and security of humanitarian personnel and protection of United Nations personnel.

A/RES/55/155. Establishment of the international criminal court.

A/RES/55/135. Comprehensive review of the whole question of peacekeeping operations in all their aspects.

A/RES/55/109. Enhancement of international cooperation in the field of human rights.

A/RES/55/107. Promotion of a democratic and equitable international order.

A/RES/55/101. Respect for the purposes and principles contained in the Charter of the United Nations to achieve international cooperation in promoting and encouraging respect for human rights and for fundamental freedoms and in solving international problems of a humanitarian character.

A/RES/55/99. Strengthening the rule of law.

A/RES/55/73. New international humanitarian order.

A/RES/55/64. Strengthening of the United Nations Crime Prevention and Criminal Justice Programme, in particular its technical cooperation capacity.

S/RES/1353 (2001). Strengthening cooperation with troop-contributing countries.

United Nations Department of Public Information. Background note on United Nations peacekeeping operations, June 15, 2001.

United Nations Department of Public Information. Background note on United Nations political and peace-building missions, June 1, 2001.

United Nations Department of Public Information. Political Bulletin #3. March 19, 2001.

2000

A/54/839. Report of the Special Committee on Peacekeeping Operations (2000).

A/55/676. Implementation of the report of the Panel on United Nations Peace Operations. Report of the Advisory Committee on Administrative and Budgetary Questions.

A/54/670. Report of the secretary-general on the implementation of the recommendations of the Special Committee on Peacekeeping Operations.

A/54/549. Report of the secretary-general pursuant to General Assembly resolution 53/55, entitled "The fall of Srebrenica."

A/RES/54/282. Draft United Nations millennium Declaration.

A/RES/54/82. Questions relating to information.

A/RES/55/28. Developments in the field of information and telecommunications in the context of international security.

S/2000/194. Progress report of the secretary-general on standby arrangements for peacekeeping.

S/2000/101. Report of the secretary-general on the role of United Nations peacekeeping in disarmament, demobilization and reintegration.

S/PV.4109. Verbatim Report of the 4109th Meeting of the Security Council (March 9, 2000). ("Maintaining peace and security: Humanitarian aspects of issues before the Security Council.")

S/RES/1327 (2000). Implementation of the report of the Panel on United Nations Peace Operations.

S/RES/1296 (2000). Protection of civilians in armed conflict.

Office of the United Nations High Commissioner for Refugees. Catalogue of emergency response tools. Document prepared by the Emergency Preparedness and Response Section. Geneva, 2000.

Office of the United Nations High Commissioner for Human Rights. Annual appeal 2000: Overview of activities and financial requirements. Geneva, 2000.

1999

A/54/549. The situation in Bosnia and Herzegovina.

A/54/87. Report of the Special Committee on Peacekeeping Operations (1999).

A/54/1. Annual report on the work of the organization ("Preventing war and disaster: A growing global challenge").

A/RES/53/142. Strengthening the rule of law.

A/RES/53/59. Questions relating to information.

S/1999/1257. Report of the independent inquiry into the actions of the United Nations during the 1994 genocide in Rwanda.

S/1999/957. Report of the secretary-general on the protection of civilians in armed conflict.

S/1998/883. Report of the secretary-general on protection for humanitarian assistance to refugees and others in conflict situations.

S/1999/361. Progress report of the secretary-general on standby arrangements for peacekeeping.

S/RES/1269 (1999). Responsibilities of the Security Council in the maintenance of international peace and security.

S/RES/1265 (1999). Protection of civilians in armed conflict.

ST/SGB/1999/13. Observance by United Nations forces of international humanitarian law.

1998

A/53/127. Report of the Special Committee on Peacekeeping Operations (1998).

A/53/1. Annual report on the work of the organization. ("Partnerships for global community").

A/AC.121/42. Report of the secretary-general on the implementation of the recommendations of the Special Committee on Peacekeeping Operations.

E/AC.51/1998/4 and Corr.1. Report of the Office of Internal Oversight Services entitled "Triennial review of the implementation of the recommendations made by the Committee for Programme and Coordination at its thirty-fifth session on the evaluation of peacekeeping operations: Start-up phase."

1997

A/51/950. Report of the secretary-general entitled "Renewing the United Nations: A programme for reform."

A/RES/52/167. Safety and security of humanitarian personnel.

A/RES/52/125. Strengthening the rule of law.

A/RES/52/118. Effective implementation of international instruments on human rights, including reporting obligations under international instruments on human rights.

A/RES/52/12. Renewing the United Nations: A programme for reform.

Goulding, Marrack. "Practical measures to enhance the United Nations effectiveness in the field of peace and security." Report submitted to the Secretary-General of the United Nations. New York: June 30, 1997.

1996

A/RES/50/243. Financing of the United Nations Preventive Deployment Force.

A/RES/51/207. Establishment of an international criminal court.

A/RES/51/137. Convention on the safety of United Nations and associated personnel.

A/RES/51/96. Strengthening the rule of law.

A/RES/51/63. Strengthening the United Nations Crime Prevention and Criminal Justice Programme, particularly in its technical cooperation capacity.

A/RES/51/55. The maintenance of international security—prevention of violent disintegration of states.

United Nations. *The blue helmets: A review of United Nations peacekeeping.* New York: United Nations (3rd ed.).

1995

A/50/60-S/1995/1. Supplement to an agenda for peace: Position paper of the secretary-general on the occasion of the fiftieth anniversary of the United Nations.

A/RES/50/179. Strengthening the rule of law.

E/AC.51/1995/2 and Corr.1. Report of the Office of Internal Oversight Services entitled "In-depth evaluation of peacekeeping operations: Start-up phase."

United Nations, Department of Peacekeeping Operations, Lessons Learned Unit. UNOSOM I and II: Summary of Lessons Learned.

1994

A/RES/49/194. Strengthening the rule of law.

A/RES/49/189. Regional arrangements for the promotion and protection of human rights.

A/RES/49/158. Strengthening the United Nations crime prevention and criminal justice programme, particularly in its technical cooperation capacity.

A/RES/49/143. Financial situation of the United Nations.

A/RES/49/59. Convention on the safety of United Nations and associated personnel.

A/RES/49/57. Declaration of the enhancement of cooperation between the United Nations and regional arrangements or agencies in the maintenance of international peace and security.

A/RES/49/53. Establishment of an international criminal court.

S/RES/960 (1994). Endorsement of the results of free and fair elections in Mozambique.

United Nations, Department of Peacekeeping Operations, Lessons Learned Unit. ONUMOZ: Lessons Learned in Planning.

1993

A/47/277. Report of the secretary-general pursuant to the statement adopted by the summit meeting of the Security Council on 31 January 1992, entitled "An Agenda for Peace: Preventive diplomacy, peacemaking and peace-keeping."

A/RES/48/132. Strengthening the rule of law.

A/RES/48/84. Maintenance of international peace and security.

A/RES/48/44. Questions relating to information.

A/RES/48/43. Strengthening United Nations command and control capabilities.

A/RES/48/42. Comprehensive review of the whole question of peacekeeping operations in all of their aspects.

S/RES/868 (1993). United Nations peacekeeping operations.

Books and Periodicals

Annan, K. (1994). Peace-keeping in situations of civil war. *New York University Journal of International Law and Politics, 26,* 623–631.

Annan, K. (1994, March 10). Peacekeeping's prospects. An address to the Archivio Disarmo, Rome.

Armon, J., Hendrickson, D., and Vines, A. (1998). The Mozambican peace process in perspective. *Accord: An International Review of Peace Initiatives, 3.*

Berdal, M., & Malone, D. M. (Eds.) (2000). *Greed and grievance: Economic agendas in civil wars.* Boulder, CO: Lynne Rienner Publishers.

Berman, E. (1996). *Managing arms in peace processes: Mozambique.* Geneva: United Nations Institute for Disarmament Research.

Butler, R. (1999). Bewitched, bothered, and bewildered. *Foreign Affairs, 78,* 9–12.

Byman, D. L. (2001). Uncertain partners: NGOs and the military. *Survival, 43,* 97–114.

Canada, Government of (1995). *Towards a rapid reaction capability for the United Nations.* Ottawa: Department of Foreign Affairs and International Trade and Department of National Defence.

Childers, E., & Urquhart, B. (1992). *Towards a more effective United Nations: Two studies.* Uppsala, Sweden: Dag Hammarskjöld Foundation.

Des Forges, A. L., & Kuperman, A. J. (2000). Shame. *Foreign Affairs, 79,* 141–144.

DeSoto, A., & del Castillo, G. (1995). Implementation of comprehensive peace agreements: Staying the course in El Salvador. *Global Governance, 1,* 2.

Doll, W. J., & Metz, S. (1993). *The army and multinational peace operations: Problems and Solutions.* Carlisle, PA: Strategic Studies Institute, U.S. Army War College.

Eriksson, J. (1996). *The international response to conflict and genocide: Lessons from the Rwanda experience: Synthesis report.* Odense, Denmark: Steering Committee of the Joint Evaluation of Emergency Assistance to Rwanda.

Falk, R. (1995). The Haiti intervention: A dangerous world order precedent for the United Nations. *Harvard International Law Journal, 36,* 341–419.

Forman, S., Patrick, S., & Salomons, D. (2000, February). *Recovering from conflict: Strategy for an international response.* New York University, Center on International Cooperation.

Frye, A. (2000) *Humanitarian intervention: Crafting a workable doctrine.* New York: Council on Foreign Relations Books.

Gardner, R. N. (2000). The one percent solution. *Foreign Affairs, 79,* 2–11.

Glennon, M. J. (1999). The new interventionism. *Foreign Affairs, 78,* 2–7.

Gordon, P. H. (2000). Their own army. *Foreign Affairs, 79,* 12–17.

Griffin, M., & Jones, B. (2000, Summer). Building peace through transitional authority: New directions, major challenges. *International Peacekeeping, 7,* No. 3.

Guéhenno, J.-M. The impact of globalisation on strategy. *Survival, 40,* 5–20.

Gurr, Ted R. (2000). Ethnic warfare on the wane. *Foreign Affairs, 79,* 52–64.

Henkin, A. H. (Ed.) (1995). *Honouring human rights and keeping the peace: Lessons from El Salvador, Cambodia and Haiti.* Washington, DC: Aspen Institute.

Holm, T. T., & Eide, E. B. (Eds.) (1999, Special Winter Issue). Peacebuilding and Police Reform. *International Peacekeeping, 6.*

Jamison, L. S. (2001). *The U.S. role in United Nations peace operations.* Washington, DC: Council for a Lovable World Education Fund.

Jett, D. C. (2000). *Why peacekeeping fails.* New York: St. Martin's Press.

Kuhne, W., Weimer, B., & Fandrych, S. (1995). *International workshop on the successful conclusion of the United Nations operation in Mozambique.* New York: Friedrich Ebert Foundation.

Lehmann, I. A. (1995). Public perceptions of UN peacekeeping. *The Fletcher Forum of World Affairs, 19,* 109–120.

Lewis, W. H. (Ed.) 1993. *Peacekeeping: The way ahead?* Washington, DC: National Defense University.

Lind, M. (1999). Civil war by other means. *Foreign Affairs, 78,* 123–144.

Lipschutz, R., & Crawford, B. (1995). Ethnic conflict isn't. Policy Brief. San Diego, CA: Institute on Global Conflict and Cooperation.

Luers, W. H. (2000). Choosing engagement. *Foreign Affairs, 79,* 9–14.

Moore, J. (Ed.) (1998). *Hard choices.* Geneva: Lanham, Maryland, Rowman and Littlefield for the International Committee of the Red Cross.

Moore, J. (Ed.) (1996). *The U.N. and complex emergencies.* UNRISD.

Pugh, M. (1997). *The UN, peace and force.* Portland, ME: Frank Cass.

Rifkind, M. (1993, April). Peacekeeping or peacemaking? Implications and prospects. *RUSI Journal,* 1–5.

Rothstein, L. I. (1993). Protecting the new world order: Is it time to create a United Nations army? *New York Law School Journal of International and Comparative Law, 14,* 107–142.

Sanger, D. E. (2001, February 24). Bush tells Blair he doesn't oppose European force. *New York Times,* pp. 1, 4.

Thornberry, C. (1995). *The development of international peacekeeping.* London: LSE Books.

Thomas, J. P. (2000). *The military challenges of Transatlantic coalitions.* (Adelphi Paper 333) New York: Oxford University Press.

Tucker, R. W. (1999). Alone or with others. *Foreign Affairs, 78,* 15–21.

United Kingdom, Government of. Inspector General of Doctrine and Training (1995). *Wider peacekeeping.* London: HMSO.

Volcker, P., & Ogata, S. (1993). *Financing an effective United Nations: A report of the independent advisory group on U.N. financing.* New York: Ford Foundation.

Wallensteen, P., & Sollenberg, M. (1998). Armed conflict and regional conflict complexes, 1989–1997. *Journal of Peace Research, 35.*

Weiner, R. O., & Aolain, F. N. (1996). Peacekeeping in search of a legal framework. *Columbia Human Rights Law Review, 27,* 293–354.

NOTES

1.   Mr. Breed is writing in his personal capacity and the views he has expressed here are his own.

2.   Collectively, all of these are well beyond the reach and remit of any single chapter. Individually, many of them could be very fruitfully examined in this context, and a number already have.

3.   The passage is taken from the Report of the Secretary-General on the fall of Srebrenica.

Part II:
Roles and Impacts of Religions

5

On the Psychosis (Religion) of Terrorists

Jerry S. Piven

> Our terrorism against America is blessed terrorism.
>
> —Osama bin Laden (on video)

> The acme of this religion is jihad.
>
> —Osama bin Laden (Bergen, 2001, p. 41)

> Lo! Allah loveth not aggressors.
>
> —The Koran, 2:190 (Pickthall, 1999)

> Allah is forgiving, merciful.
>
> —The Koran, 2:192 (Pickthall, 1999)

RELIGION AND FANTASY

Numerous religious leaders and friends of Islam have pleaded with us not to hate Muslims, for their religion is not a violent one and does not sanction murder. The mistake is to assume Islam is about aggression, they say.

> If you study the life of Prophet Mohammad, peace and blessings be upon him, you will see the most gentle man. He would never allow innocent people to die, never. Never. (Muslim cleric Imam Siraj Wahhaj, in Bergen, 2001, p. 92)

Consider that the Muslim cultures that were attacked during the Crusades were among the most spiritual and cultured of peoples. One cannot say with intelligence that Islam is inherently violent. Eighty percent of Afghan Muslims belong to the Sunni Hanafi sect, considered the most liberal and tolerant Sunni school of thought (Rashid, 2000, p. 83).

Nevertheless, the same Christians who went on the Crusades also had faith in a religion that is ostensibly pacifistic and commands us to turn the other cheek. Religion (any ideology) serves whoever utilizes it to justify their interests—and their fantasies. In other words, terrorists are not violent because their religion commands them to be so.[1] In fact, one *can* find justification for violence in the Koran: "kill the idolaters wherever you find them . . ." (2:191). One can also read many Jewish stories about the vengeful hand of God in the Hebrew *Tanach*. One can even find validation of slavery in the Bible (see Ephesians 6).

But that is not the point. Again, adherents will interpret these texts in any way that sanctifies and validates the actions they wish to take. The Koran, Surah 2:191, commands followers to slay only aggressors who persecute Muslims, and specifically abjures initiating hostilities (2:190). Rather than claiming that religion instructs people to be violent, religions must be understood as fantasy systems, many (but not nearly all) of which validate the desired beliefs and actions with divine sanction, truth, and authority. If God tells you to murder people, then there can be no opposition, no disagreement, and no blame. If there is ever a question of opposing worldviews, sanctification by God is the highest authority and renders every act in "his" name irrefutably righteous.

Psychological dependence on a projected fantasy of a deity is an immensely gratifying position. One feels protected, nurtured, loved by the parental surrogate, and one attains approval in carrying out his commands, and feels absolved and adored for pleasing the God with sacrifices and acts of gratitude. The devotee feels the satiation of absolving feelings of badness, self-loathing, inferiority, and insignificance by pleasing the divinity, and feels immense gratification in destroying others and eliminating competing ideologies. One can destroy rivals, eliminate threats to the veracity of one's own system, mollify one's God, destroy death itself through violent domination of others, and channel obsession and rage. Furthermore, one can find a sense of nurturance in the religious group itself, a nearly maternal gratification in losing one's separateness in that group and participating in a communal merger (Chasseguet-Smirgel, 1975). And again, one is absolved of guilt—or evades the possibility of blame—when the group is performing a violent act under the auspices of a God (Arlow, 1964; Freud, 1921). Religions of compassion and love have also sanctified such acts historically, from ancient acts of slavery to the Inquisition.

Spirituality is not necessarily the issue either. The wisdom or enlightenment of religious texts has little to do with how people adjust those messages to accord with their wishes. Religion is *not* a spiritual system, if by the term *spiritual* one means an inward meditative relation to humanity, nature, divinity, cosmos, and so forth. *Spiritual* also has other meanings, such as that which is explicitly opposed to the physical, which escapes the body, sexuality, and mortality; consequently condemning or despising sexuality, the body, and nature, and fleeing into fantasies of disembodied purification. *Spiritual* often connotes a need to punish the despised body. Be wary of the term, as it is sometimes a euphemism placing a positive spin on what may often be a pathological defense against sexuality, bodily weakness and need, the fear of decay, and being terrified and overwhelmed by physical desires.

Religion is first and foremost a fantasy system invented to merge with omnipotent forces that protect communities and individuals from death, predation, the terror of the unknown, and the viciousness of nature. This system enables people to feel secure, ensconced within a predictable system of meanings and realities that provide rules to follow, prohibitions enabling them to avoid disastrous evil or calamity, and rituals that magically alter the world to displace anxiety and hostility, unite the community, and control nature (Becker, 1973; Freud, 1927, 1930; Gay, 1979; La Barre, 1970, 1991; Roheim, 1932).

A significant component of many religions, as we have intimated, is evading death through both palliative illusions and violent acts of murder and sacrifice. Defining religion this way necessarily excludes philosophical meditations or wisdom (such as Zen) that need not define entities in the universe to whom people can pray, implore, or sacrifice—that is, anything that literalizes metaphors by projecting them onto the universe as distinct sentient beings. It also excludes experiences that, again, are not literal—for instance, a Christian theology that understands the Eucharist not as a magical act of consuming a real son of God, but a metaphorical and psychological transformation of the self through the act. It must exclude mythologies (like stories of Indra in Hinduism) that expose literalism, or narratives that fictionalize but do not provide beings or entities to worship or believe in (such as the story of Shakyamuni Gautama's enlightenment). By contrast, some versions of Buddhism expose our attachments to fictions, while Buddhism elsewhere condemns women for introducing death and desire into the world, and yet other Buddhisms command devotees to call Amida's name to get into Paradise. The Buddhisms that expose attachment to illusions are not religions (are *negative theologies,* so to speak), while the latter are religions in the most conventional and psychologically regressive sense—meaning they rely on literal belief that narrows and distorts reality in dependence upon that system at the expense of both reality and adherents' own individuation (Gay, 1979; Ostow, 1958).

I am making these distinctions because *not* all of what we call religion must be implicated, but one central characteristic of religion that I am separating from other philosophies, wisdoms, or spiritualities (in the positive sense) is its quality of being a system of literalized beliefs designed to sanctify fantasies of merger with omnipotence, escape from death, and, often, to enact immensely violent acts. As Jung said, religion can be a defense against the experience of God—Jung meaning here *not* a blissful feeling of merger or power with a literal God (conventionally taken as religious experience), but as an inward connection to one's psyche. So again a religion may or may not teach violence, but what is responsible for the violence is the vengeful fantasy itself, which either utilizes, twists, or invents a divine sanction (religious precedent) to justify what is psychologically *motivating* the fantasy.

THE GENESES OF MURDER, MISOGYNY, AND VENGEANCE

So why are these fantasies so full of rage? How can people commit such horrendous acts? These are questions I have heard repeatedly from friends, acquaintances, and victims alike. Political answers cannot explain why someone feels rage deep enough to murder civilians across an ocean. Political explanations can shed light on why cultures feel oppressed, and can explain the hardships and oppression that engender feelings of hatred and injustice. But vengefulness that translates into murder, and the absence of empathy that accompanies such violence, are *not* derived from political injustice alone. Violent aberration of empathy is the quintessentially pathological feature of the terrorist mentality. Such a dearth of empathy derives from much earlier experience and requires not just oppression, impoverishment, disaster, or suffering. The failure of empathy resides in having been repeatedly and consistently neglected and brutalized as a child (Athens, 1992; Gilligan, 1996; Goldberg, 1996; Kernberg, 1992; Kohut, 1971, 1972).

Oppressed people can love their children—they may indeed inculcate a heightened sense of empathy and brotherhood with the oppressed, as is taught in the Passover *Haggadah*. As Sue Grand (2000) writes, "To live in anticipation of extinction is to experience moments of extraordinary humanity . . ." (p. 89). This is not a conspicuous feature of terrorist emotion. Terrorists empathize with their own victimization and protest against cruelty toward their own people, but they simultaneously brutalize their own people and demonstrate a tangible absence of empathic regard for the rights of others to live. As will be explained shortly, this may resemble empathy but it is a pathological complex and is in fact antithetical to genuine empathy. Make no mistake—empathic people do not viciously abuse women and children or commit atrocities on their own people. They do not decide that others have no right to live. Terrorists feel nothing (but rage, fear, and disgust) for the women they punish and murder, they feel nothing for the children they neglect and abuse, they feel nothing at all for their victims, which is ostensively (ontologically and psychologically) sociopathic.[2] Such seething hostility among terrorists precludes genuine empathy, and this is precisely the problem.

Absence of empathy can only derive from having been neglected and emotionally injured. The child's sense of empathy for others—recognizing them as other separate human beings with needs as legitimate as his or her own, being able to identify with them and experience their pain—fails to develop both in deprivation of empathic parenting, where those around the child fail to attend to his or her needs, and in injurious parenting where supposed caregivers brutalize a child through physical and emotional violence (Kohut, 1971).

In the former case, the child cannot internalize the trust and nurturance, psychological impressions of a nurturing mother, a benign giving breast, or a source of security and love that will always protect the child (Erikson, 1950; Freud, 1905; Winnicott, 1965). The consequences are not only the absence of love, but rage as well. The child is deprived of all the emotional influences that enable it to enjoy others, trust them, love them, and feel a sense of nurturance toward them, and instead feels mistrustful and has a vacuum of loving and trusting feelings, alongside immense hostility toward absent caregivers who have deprived the child. The absence of the mental image of the nurturing breast is the evil withholding neglectful breast, which translates into rage against mothers, women, nurturers, and real and symbolic sources and images of love and generosity. The experiences of neglect and separation inculcate a catastrophic anxiety over being annihilated or killed (Loewald, 1975; Mahler, 1979; Rheingold, 1967). Separation becomes not a source of adventure, but of abandonment, terror of death, and exposure to an unresponsive environment that will let the child cry and die. Malignant rage and misogyny tend to be the consequences of neglectful mothering.

Misogyny seems to be historically ubiquitous, but to varying *degrees*. One decisive means of identifying the psychopathology of an individual or culture is to examine the way it conceives women. Are women respected and admired, or are they despised and rebuked? To what degree can an individual or culture experience women as intellectual and sexual equals (perhaps superiors) with comfort, or to what degree do people need to abuse women, devalue them, abjure their sexuality and bodies as evil, and define their strengths as insidious or demonic? To what degree are women feared and despised? And finally, to what degree are women experienced as human beings, and how much is fantasy inventing and distorting them? Whether they become medusae or angels, either fantasy reflects the inability to experience women as they are. Devaluation and idealization are both defenses against the experience of the whole person, and splitting women into wholly medusal or angelic aspects is an extremely primitive means of protecting the self against annihilation and death. When men make monsters out of women and see them as ogresses, succubae, or inferior and contaminated things to be punished, we can be sure that the distorting individual is experiencing massive psychological derangements. These fantasies and distortions are symptoms of severe psychopathology.

Many cultures in the Middle East and the Arab world approach the most deranged abusiveness on the continuum of misogynistic pathology. As El Saadawi (1980) writes, little girls are inculcated with feelings of being inferior, unwanted, and incomplete from virtually the moment of birth. They are not welcome in the world. Depression, sadness, and violent abuse of the mother may follow the birth of a girl. "From the moment she starts to crawl or stand on her two feet, she is taught that her sexual organs are something to fear . . ." (p. 12).

> The education that a female child receives in Arab society is a series of continuous warnings about things that are supposed to be harmful, forbidden, shameful or outlawed by religion. The child therefore is trained to suppress her own desires, to empty herself of authentic, original wants and wishes linked to her own self, and to fill the vacuum that results with the desires of others. Education of female children is therefore transformed into a slow process of annihilation, a gradual throttling of her personality and mind, leaving intact only the outside shell, the body, a lifeless mould of muscle and bone and blood that moves like a wound up rubber doll. (p. 13)

She is a "girl who has lost her personality, her capacity to think independently and to use her own mind . . ." (p. 13). Girls are frequently sexually molested by their own families, blamed, shamed, punished, even poisoned or executed for the violations inflicted upon them (pp. 14–19). El Saadawi laments: "It is a well known fact that in our society young girls are often exposed to various degrees of rape" (p. 19).

Genital mutilations such as clitoridectomy and sewing shut the vaginal labia pervade the Arab world:

> The practice of circumcising girls is still a common procedure in a number of Arab countries such as Egypt, the Sudan, Yemen, and some of the Gulf states. The importance given to virginity and an intact hymen in these societies is the reason why female circumcision still remains a very widespread practice. . . . (p. 33)[3]

These operations are performed with rusty instruments or jagged pieces of glass. The clitoris is considered dirty, disgusting, or poisonous. Clitoridectomy is considered a cleansing or purifying procedure (p. 34). As the president of Pakistan's Commission on Women concluded, "the average woman is born into near slavery, leads a life of drudgery, and dies invariably in oblivion."[4] The Taliban are vicious and punitive toward women, inhibiting and oppressing them severely, controlling their dress and movement, their intellectual, sexual, and emotional freedom, even murdering them for minute transgressions of sartorial prohibitions, such as accidentally exposing an ankle (Rashid, 2000). The Taliban have seething contempt for women, which develops from massive emotional injury and neglect early in life. Osama bin Laden resonates with this hatred—one of his primary targets was former Pakistani Prime Minister Benazir Bhutto, the first woman to represent a modern Muslim nation (Bergen, 2001, p. 60).[5]

Those who despise women are terrified of women and need to wreak vengeance on them as displacements (transferences) of rage they feel toward their mothers. Misogyny thus connotes the rage over neglect and rejection, hence the misogynist also despises women for not giving him love, and finally himself for *needing* love. Women are simultaneously medusal castrators and seductive sirens who are loathsome for continually arousing men but depriving them of love. The misogynist then rages against himself for needing what he despises, and sees his own need for love and his dependence on such abominable creatures as disgusting weaknesses (Gruen, 1987). Intimacy with women becomes nearly impossible, as the misogynist craves intercourse but hates the object of his dependence, his own weakness for needing her for gratification, and the vagina that threatens castration and helplessness via the loss of ego boundaries that occurs with orgasm. Sexual and emotional merger are akin to death, as they render one vulnerable, exposed, and coalesced with the dangerous and castrating feminine. The misogynist must ejaculate quickly to avoid physical and emotional disaster within the castrating vortex of female sexuality, and his penis becomes a penetrating weapon that must be cleansed after intercourse with something so disgusting and lethal. In punishing women, the misogynist punishes his own pitiable and hence loathsome desire and vulnerability, the object that symbolizes self-disgust, rejection, and inadequacy.

Control, punishment, and loathing are proportional to fear, resentment, humiliation, and archaic feelings of neglect. No one who has internalized a nourishing breast seeks to violate and demean women, or to punish their intellect or sexuality, and those who besmirch women are suffering severe derangement and toxic internalizations. By contrast, those who have internalized loving relationships with their mothers do not fear or despise women, and do not have a psychotic need to violate and disparage women.

What this means, however, is that the women are so abused that they also develop severe pathologies, and they are virtually incapable of empathy, just like the men. As El Saadawi writes:

> Most mothers suffer hunger, deprivation and a state of exhaustion which renders them unfit to nourish their babies or even look after them. Without food their breasts dry up, without the basic needs of life their affection withers. Deprived of everything they lose their capacity to give. Withered to the core by years of labour in the fields and in the home, their youth ebbs away in a matter of years, leaving a broken body and a drying soul—a useless forgotten being whose lot it is to be cast aside. . . . (p. xiv)

One must also consider the effects of being brutalized in terms of their own identification with the system that deranges them. El Saadawi remembers her mother's blithe smile and oblivious contented conversation while her daughter was lying in a pool of her own clitoridectomal blood (p. 8). While many women clearly recognize their suffering (how could they not!), others participate in the violence and attain a measure of approval and esteem for following the ethical imposition. One must also take into account the expression of unconscious aggression in these acts, the disavowed hostility that mothers inflict upon their own daughters (Lopez-Corvo, 1997; Rheingold, 1964). As El Saadawi concludes regarding brutalized and genitally mutilated women, "most of them, if not all, became the victims later on of sexual or mental distortions as a result . . ." (p. 9). To put it another way, it is virtually impossible for such victims not to be vastly traumatized and emotionally mutilated from such violence, an ordeal inculcating intense shame and rage, the dread of bleeding to death in a ceaselessly gushing pool, the shock of absolute betrayal, the corruption of one's body, of being invaded, suffocated, and raped, the excision of life (Accad, in Ransohoff, 2001, p. 160). The woman who emerges from such brutality (and its analogues) escaping without emotional scars and her own hostile conflicts is as rare as the boy immersed in that misogynistic hostile society who emerges without becoming a violent aggressor.[6] As El Saadawi laments, mothers are themselves so exhausted and victimized that they cannot sustain an emotionally nurturing relationship with the child, who is both neglected and subject to her own emotional chaos.

Hence male misogynists are engendered by their mothers as well as fathers. El Saadawi reflects that men "are also victims of a society that segregates the sexes, and that considers sex a sin and a shame . . ." (p. 13). In this sense, the men who distort women into demons have been injured in such a way as to *inherently* imagine women as evil (Kohut, 1977). They distort women, but they cannot help doing so because of the way they were malnourished psychologically, and the degree of misogyny becomes the indicator of the psychopathology of the child and his or her culture.[7]

Who is to blame here? While I am writing of abusive parenting, neglect, and toxic influences, it must be understood that people are largely the products of the culture that nourishes or neglects them. Hence the abusive vicious mother who destroys her child is inflicting the abuse and derangement she received from those who oppressed her. Blaming the mother means blaming the men who abused her, which then means blaming the mothers who bore them, ad infinitum. Isolating one parent or generation only works with exceptions, and recognizing the social complex of violence precludes blaming one parent or gender. The point here is that the culture becomes a ceaseless cycle of vicious parenting and transgenerational abuse.

I have thus far emphasized neglectful parenting and the paucity of nurturing internalizations. The additional case of physical and emotional abuse only complicates the pathological scenario. Alongside the absence of positive nurturance, the missing internalization of positive structures, and the failure to develop a stable emotional-cognitive personality are the hostile feelings and images that are forced into the child by the hostility of those around the child (Kernberg, 1992). A mother or father looking angrily at the child, using physical violence, yelling at the child, or screaming at a boy for crying or for not being a man—these behaviors can be infinitely damaging. The child internalizes rage and hostility and is traumatized and terrified in ways he or she cannot process or comprehend. Athens (1992) describes this as the "belligerency stage of violentization."

Not only is the child angry, terrified, and mutilated by neglect and injury, by the absence of positive structures, and by the overabundance of hostile ones. The child actually comes to identify with the violence and hostility of the surrounding environment. The only source of strength for a child is caregivers, and should these be vicious, the child will come to depend on this cruelty to master his or her own environment. The child will look to that violence as the only source of strength, the only means of survival, the only way to transform passive, helpless victimization to active, non-helpless domination. And the child will seek to dominate others in order to deny this helplessness and victimization, to feel the aggressive power in dominating insecurity and death, and to participate in the very society that has elevated that violence to an ethic of masculinity, toughness, and righteous indignation over those who have oppressed the child.

The male child comes to be initiated into a society of violent hateful people whose only source of self-esteem is participating in the violent aggression of the group. In behaving like his father or brother, the child has made the only connection to those who would not love him, and meanwhile has found the only way to gain any approval whatsoever. Finally, he has displaced his hostility from the vicious, abusive father toward an external enemy because he cannot express rage at the father whom he now needs as emotional support (communally and ideologically), and because the father can still brutalize him. Hence he will express rage toward an evil enemy that substitutes for father and oppressive authority. Though he feels victimized (and may in reality be terribly victimized by his own society as well as by an enemy who decimates his culture), the enemy is scapegoated (Durkheim, 1965; Freud, 1921; Moscovici, 1988; Volkan, 1988). Enemies are dehumanized, even chosen as oppressors who must be obliterated to exterminate *evil*. As Ernest Becker (1975) has stated, the most violence perpetrated in history has been to *eradicate* evil. Evil then must be understood as a symbolic displacement rather than a rational process.

In effect, the terrorist inflicts on others both what has been inflicted on him and what he wishes to inflict on his father (and mother). He need not repeat the exact abuses that were heaped upon him, but he seeks to punish, violate, and retaliate for his own feelings of having been violated, abused, punished, and victimized. The rage is proportional to the manifold sources and intensity of the abuse, violence, neglect, humiliation, and malignant internal structures that possess him. This state is possession—in the demonic and psychological sense. The terrorist is possessed by the internalized imagery—the hostile faces, crushing fists, the weapons that dominated him. They act as ghosts and revenants moving through him, and he speaks with their voices though he imagines they are his own.

Internalized images and structures (psychoanalysts may call such people "objects" or "part-objects") have a life of their own and are no mere speculation. There are often many people inside us. Schizophrenics believe they are possessed by others, or by God. Those with the debatable diagnosis of multiple personality disorder (or dissociative identity disorder) are possessed by internalized others, alternate personality structures that emerge in response to those voices and situations. Those possessed by demons, those who speak in tongues, or those who channel spirits are literalizing a symbolic representative of internalized malignant object relations. The malignance varies, as does the influence of the voice depending on the psychological stability and maturity of emotional structures. For those abused and brutalized mercilessly from an early age, those who survive without being overtly disintegrated and dysfunctional have increasing potential to become murderous (Gilligan, 1996; Goldberg, 1996).

Again, their vengefulness is a reflection of having been brutalized and identifying with that aggression as the only means of strength and survival. They meanwhile lack human empathy and in fact have immense hostility toward the abusive parent, the neglectful parent, and finally the weak, helpless self they wish to murder in utter shame and degradation. They do not just lack concern for human life, they have a malignant hatred for the living, for the happy, and for all that thrives and enjoys. Disgust for helplessness impels expulsion of rage into repositories that must suffer and be destroyed in punishment and vengeance.

DEIFICATION, MADNESS, AND SURVIVAL

The identification with the childhood image (internalized character) of father and authority is elevated and deified to an eternally vengeful and sanctimonious justification. Deification means not just validation and worship of that which becomes eternally important, it also means the extent to which the authority of father has dominated the child, and the extent to which the image of father must be elevated to avoid being killed by the terrorist's unconscious rage (which would kill an ordinary human being).

Deification is thus partly a response to the need for authority to be sanctified, as well as the need to insure that the father will not be killed by one's own rage; thus he must be invulnerable. Acting out his will also ensures that one's own rage does not instigate God's reprisal. Inflict your rage on enemies instead of on the father and not only will you please him, but he won't kill you for hating him. Of course, the hatred is again unconscious and displaced onto the enemy. To understand terrorism this way is to recognize how pathological, and hence how pitiable, are people who must have been so brutalized that they are so vengeful and unempathic as to compulsively hate and murder displacements of who were, deep down, their parents and cousins. Indeed, they murder to displace their own self-contempt for having submitted to brutal authority (Gruen, 1987).

This does not mean that terrorists have no love for anyone—quite the opposite. They love their friends, family, country, and God deeply and passionately. But this love is purchased by evacuating severe hatred toward those same figures and inflicting it on their enemies. Otherwise the hatred would be overwhelming and intolerable. There would be complete psychological breakdown if their true feelings were experienced consciously. Thus empathy for others is (and must be) entirely excluded.[8] One is saying, "The fact that I have been brutalized is infuriating and I want to murder you. But if I do so I will be alone and unloved. I can love you only if I hide my overwhelming hatred for you and project it on someone else. Then I can love you as a brother and victim, the same kind of victim as I. Loving you then becomes a way to protest my own victimization by protecting you. I will then hate others instead of you, and proportionally to the way I hate you for having brutalized me." This is emblematic of the psychotic paranoid process, and it resonates as group fantasy (Meissner, 1978, 1988).[9]

I have termed it psychotic because such a dearth of empathy and such malignant rage, alongside such distorted and paranoid displacements constitute a massive deformation in personality development and reality testing (Gruen, 1987). Psychotic is not to be equated with a drooling, raving, incapacitated patient in a mental ward. If Hannah Arendt (1963) and Robert Jay Lifton (1986) have shown us anything in their studies of murderers such as Eichmann and the Nazi doctors, it is that deluded, malicious, sadistic, genocidal executioners can be distant and dissociated from the horrific elements of their cruelty, can describe their violence, human liquidation, and torture with dispassion, aplomb, joyful satiety, and serenity (or even remorse that they could not fulfill their dreams of complete genocidal cleansing). One can be a calm psychotic, as one can smile and be a villain (Hoffman, 1998; Shakespeare, 1603). One need not confuse a quiet dissociated smile amid the intense joy of death with emotional health. Psychosis can be ambulatory and functional given a social system organized around similar resonant fantasies (Gruen, 1987; Hitschmann, 1949).

Many social structures and religious illusions may be defenses against psychotic regression, fragmentation, chaos, and anomie (Kaufman, 1939; Jaques, 1955; La Barre, 1991; Spiro, 1978). Paranoid and vengeful worldviews of such intensity are expressions of psychotic injury as well as psychotic reality distortion and serve as attempts at *reconstruction and survival* against nearly overwhelming experiences of brutalization, helplessness, and despair (Arlow & Brenner, 1964; Eigen, 1986; Lifton, 1986). Recent studies in "terror management" correlate violence and worldview defense with the fear of death (Solomon, Greenberg, & Pyszczynski, 2002). Identifying with rage and violence is the means of psychological survival (Gruen, 1987).

However, it is highly debatable whether a whole society could be considered psychotic. Fromm (1955) spoke of the "socially patterned defect," and I have been illustrating how excessive neglect and brutality could injure the child psychologically, creating malignant psychological structures, starving the child of benign structures, and inhibiting the establishment of a developmentally stable or mature personality. Cultures that routinely brutalize one another, murder their citizens, and victimize and execute women and children (such as can be seen with the Taliban) may be understood as suffering from gross culturally patterned psychological injuries. Nevertheless, *not* all citizens perform these actions and *not* all are terrorists.

The situation becomes more complicated when we are discussing the vengeful group or culture. If we are speaking of terrorists as a select or extreme few, then it is easy to isolate them as the psychotic anomaly of the culture. But in many cultures brutality is the norm and we must then ask to what degree terrorists are representative of a culture or of aberrant deviations. Those who fly airplanes into skyscrapers are a minority, but those who are paranoid, murderous, and revel in destroying the enemy are *not* anomalous, *not* the exceptions. Mass violence, murder, and celebration over mangling victims are so common as to be *banal*, as Arendt (1963) wrote.

Whether we are discussing the Nazis, the Turks who committed genocide over Armenians, Japanese who raped and murdered in Manchuria and Nanking, the atrocities in Kosovo, or vengeful Muslims screaming for *jihad*, we are here speaking of groups who are too often representative of a culture and *not* of the rare individuals or anomalous fanatics. They may be extremists, but they are also so banal, so historically fermentative, that it would be a mistake to consider them mere fringes. Psychotic murder is not unanimous, but it is by no means peripheral. To see it as such is denial—of the sheer frequency with which cultures have succumbed to mass violence. As Becker (1973) has said, it is the so-called normal people who have laid waste to the planet—so-called because they *appear* normal to their culture, but normalcy may be incredibly brutal, misogynistic, even delusional. Under ordinary conditions, most people are not psychotic, but far more than we want to admit are both brutalized into psychosis early in life, or are raped into psychotic regression and delusion as a psychological means of survival and even fulfillment.

The degree to which violence can be a matter of psychological survival or emotional fulfillment is a critical nuance. The Egyptian militant Sheikh Rahman, "who had been blinded by diabetes when he was a baby, wept as he heard the crashing of artillery shells in the distance, bemoaning the fact that he could not see for himself his dream of jihad in action" (Bergen, 2001, pp. 53–54). Though terrorist actions are enacted as though they were redressing injustices, the words of terrorists themselves often reveal an intense pleasure in the act of killing. There is an orgasmic relief expressed in descriptions of their violence. From his interviews with terrorists, psychiatrist Gustav Morf writes:

> The sexual importance is sometimes striking. For some, when a bomb goes off, it is like an orgasm. . . . One fellow told me he felt "liberated" every time he heard a bomb explode. Some others told me they would place a bomb, then sit out on a balcony and listen. When the "boom" came, it was a great relief. (in McKnight, 1974, p. 149)[10]

This illuminates another disturbing component of the psychology of terrorism and mass violence—that it is not merely a matter of following orders, losing control, or being possessed by rage. The vengeful fantasy is enacted in a sexual release, a euphoric conquest of one's enemies, over ideologies that threaten the truth of one's own sacred beliefs, over helplessness, humiliation, and death. Sadism absorbs the fear of death (Becker, 1975, p. 113). Stomping the guts of others can be an ecstatic triumph over mortality itself, and such ecstasy can be so orgasmically fulfilling that it becomes seductive and addictive. People may thrive on violence as a means of overcoming feelings of rage, humiliation, helplessness, impotence, and the dread of death. As Hitler said, "the joy of killing brings men together" (Bormann, 1953).

This is another eerie confirmation of Lifton's (1986) assessment of the Nazi doctors. Ordinary people can be seduced into violence as a fulfilling sensual triumph over death, and indeed this may be a survival strategy for those brutalized by their society or by the lamentable violence around them.[11] All too readily ordinary people may become addicted to genocidal aggression and participate in its banal righteousness, dissociating culpability, even enjoying bloody mastery. As Becker writes, "Men spill blood because it makes their hearts glad and fills out their organisms with a sense of vital power . . ." (1975, p. 102). No one ordered the Japanese to slaughter babies or rape women in Nanking. No one required Turks to kill pregnant women and chop up their unborn babies (Kalayjian, Shahinian, Gergerian, & Saraydarian, 1996). If terrorists are the anomalous few (and even they differ significantly in character from one another), we should not make them into monsters by believing we are a distinct and more civilized species. "Normal" people have also been seduced into genocidal behavior, and the fortunate among us have not been so emotionally tortured from infancy to thrive on vengeance under ordinary conditions.

Given the findings of Becker (1973, 1975), Lifton (1986, 1988, 1990), and Lifton and Mitchell (1999), psychotic violence, genocidal behavior, and "normalcy" may be closer than we would like to imagine (Gruen, 1987). The fact is that violence and neglect in infancy dispose individuals toward psychopathic violence, while nurturing tends to enable a loving and empathic personality. But history continues to demonstrate how seductive ecstatic violence can be for the "ordinary" person as well. As Tiger (1996) muses, "inhumanity may be panhuman" (p. 96). Becker (1975) concurs:

> . . . not only weak, or mechanical, or pathological, or "primitive and elemental" types aggress, but also fat, jolly ones—people who have had abundant childhood care and love! The man who dropped the atomic bomb is the warm, gentle boy who grew up next door . . . man aggresses not only out of frustration and fear but out of joy, plenti- tude, love of life. *Men kill lavishly out of the sublime joy of heroic tri- umph over evil.* (p. 141)

Given the complexities of these phenomena, several elusive questions emerge: Under what conditions can "ordinary" and "civilized" people succumb to wanton aggression? Under what conditions do individuals resist such seductive violence? How vicious is one's society, how much abuse and trauma are necessary for indi- viduals to *require* violence in order to displace rage, endure the terror of death, and survive psychologically? In other words, how does a society encourage and sustain such vicious behavior?

I have mentioned religion as an expression of cultural fantasy and discussed the influence of the group. Since in these cases we are dealing with an inherently social influence, the question must be asked to what degree the emotional pattern can be understood as derived from childhood injury or the social structure, since the social structure necessarily impacts upon the sanity of the group. Group situations inher- ently foster regression to more archaic psychological states where individuation, judgment, rational thinking, and ethical feelings are far more chaotic and inchoate (Becker, 1973; Bion, 1955; Freud, 1921). The group is always inclined toward regression into fantasy and it is truly the exception who is rational in the group situ- ation, especially when the social structure is designed to merge the group aggressive- ly or religiously (Ostow, 1958). This is not just a consequence of the group, but is a motive of group formation in the first place. Group fantasy may be regressive but that is often the desired result, as the communal merger intensifies and the fantasy is reified. Hence, the group reflects the pathological state of its constituents but also enables individuals to validate the fantasy through communal reinforcement.

So are they psychotic or regressed willfully to a near-psychotic state? What would the psychic state of the terrorist be without communal reinforcement? My guess is that the individual would feel less charged, validated, courageous, sancti- fied, and zealous, and would feel exposed as an individual to feelings of despair and helplessness that the group magically dissipates (Ostow, 1972). The individual would feel far less protected, far more vulnerable, and would feel an absence of the nourishment of hostile fantasies that the group provides. The individual might fragment in terror or become the fanatical advocate of his threatened worldview, since the worldview is a protective fantasy. Manic compensation tends to avert psychotic disintegration when such an individual is sequestered from the group—in other words, it provides emotional reinforcement of what has now been threatened by his isolation. The group encourages more primitive and euphorically aggressive emotions, but safety in the group and social validation of the fantasy actually protects the individual against feeling exposed and vulnerable. Hence, the group behavior and zealousness may be seen as maniacal and frenzied, but the individual is saved from fragmentation through the communal merger and support.

Would the injury suffered as a child be sufficient without group reinforcement of the fantasy system? I would suggest that without communal support, despite its regressive influence, the individual might be even less stable, and probably would not even be sufficiently emotionally equipped to transform helplessness, rage, and malignant influence into his own aggression, since there would be no source of violent support with which he could identify and from which draw strength. Survival is based on this identification, which for him means the difference between incapacitating psychotic fragmented breakdown, and directed psychotic vengefulness. This is why, as mentioned previously, the social system is a defense against psychosis even while it simultaneously represents psychotic derangement and injury. In a sense, paranoia, even as a psychosis, is an achievement over schizophrenic incapacitation. Paradoxically, the religion *represents* the psychopathology, but is also a defense *against* debilitating insanity, annihilation, and death (Greene, 1969; Jaques, 1955; Kaufman, 1939; Leverenz, 1975).

MASOCHISM AND ESCHATOLOGICAL FANTASIES OF REBIRTH

I have argued that the religious language of terrorists allows them to sanctify their violent fantasies and acts. By describing terrorists as psychotically paranoid, we must not forget a central component of the fantasy system—the masochistic deployment of self-injurious behaviors. Paranoids often orchestrate the conditions by which they are victimized. They invite and induce others to victimize them so they will have proof that others are in fact to blame. This enables the paranoid to reinforce the fantasy that he is victimized while others are evil (Juergensmeyer, 2000; Meissner, 1978; Moses-Hrushovski, 1994).

After the World Trade Center attacks, we received a recorded message from Osama bin Laden explaining how reprisal would be met with further vengeance. But this message was recorded before America began bombing Afghanistan. In other words, bin Laden arranged an attack knowing that the United States would retaliate, so that our retaliation would be proof that we were evil and would also be justification for his vengeance. He planned an attack that he knew would bring destruction to his people, and rather than perceiving the logical order, used our reprisal as proof that we should be destroyed—as though American retaliation was inappropriate but his reprisal was justified even though he initiated the whole thing. Were this merely a strategy to start a war, we might say he was using the same technique as Lincoln or Roosevelt (as some have argued). But he behaves as though he were the eternal victim, which justifies mass extermination of the West.

The masochistic element is not to be underestimated. Masochism can mean many things, but here the motive is to sanctify the self through victimization. And blaming the other as evil not only displaces blame *from* the self. It also allows one to punish and murder *oneself* so that one can be loved by the parent—or God, in this case. During the Afghan war with Russia, "the Arabs would pitch white tents out in the open in the hopes of attracting Soviet fire, hoping for martyrdom." One reporter witnessed a man crying because he *survived* an air assault. A Muslim killed in *jihad* is *shaheed*, a martyr assured entry into Paradise (Bergen, 2001, p. 12). Paradise is the fantasy of immortality through union with omnipotent object (parent). One is willing to die for immortality and eternal reunion.

As he lay dying from wounds inflicted by an explosion, Mansoor al-Barakati pleaded for death, crying, "I am fed up with this worldly life. I really love Allah." Bergen writes that a witness recounted how "a beautiful scent the likes of which I have never experienced in my life" emanated from the corpse (2001, p. 59). The fantasy of death is so seductive that a corpse becomes an olfactory hallucination of bliss.[12] The medieval Muslim scholar Taqi al-Din ibn Tamiya, often quoted by bin Laden, wrote "Death of the martyr for unification of all the people in the cause of God and His word is the happiest, best, easiest and most virtuous of deaths" (Bergen, 2001, p. 41). The Koran reads: "And repute not those slain on God's path to be dead. Nay, alive with their Lord, are they richly sustained; Rejoicing in what God of his bounty hath vouchsafed them, filled with joy for those who follow after them. . . . Filled with joy at the favours of God, and at his bounty . . ." (3:163-5).[13]

This fantasy of death and rebirth is situated within an apocalyptic mythology. On the theological plane, the terrorist wishes to die and be reborn in Paradise, but he also desires apocalyptic destruction and the instantiation of paradise on earth. As Ricoeur writes (1967) in *The Symbolism of Evil,* "By negation, order reaffirms itself" (p. 42).

> . . . any coherent theology of the holy war is founded on the first mythological "type" of Evil. According to that theology, the Enemy is a Wicked One, war is his punishment, and there are wicked ones because first there is evil and then order. In the final analysis, evil is not an accident that upsets a previous order; it belongs constitutionally to the foundation of order. (p. 198)

Innumerable examples demonstrate the apocalyptic rebirth fantasies of terrorists. Every apocalyptic vengeance involves *ekpyrosis*, mythic cataclysmic destruction and rebirth through fire.[14] As N. O. Brown (1991) states, *jihad* is an eschatological reality: "In the Islamic sense of time we are always in the last days" (p. 84).

This imagery is not confined to Islamic apocalyptics. Jewish and Christian fanatics also speak in terms of redemption and rebirth. Rabbi Meir Kahane wrote of the "final redemption" that would be achieved by destroying Arabs, and the infamous "Temple Mount" operation was designed "to facilitate the resurrection of a Jewish Third Temple and enable the Messiah's return." The terrorists sought annihilation of Israel's Arab enemies, establishing a new theocratic "Kingdom of Israel" (Hoffman, 1998, pp. 102–103). The Cave of the Patriarchs massacre in 1994 was also an attempt to generate cataclysm and the return of the messiah. In this case, Dr. Baruch Goldstein opened fire on Muslim worshippers in the Ibrahim (Abraham) Mosque with an M-16, killing 29 and wounding 150 before the shocked congregants bludgeoned him to death. Goldstein envisioned his massacre in the mythic tradition of Mordecai, a fifth-century B.C.E. Jew who liberated his people from their arch-enslaver Haman (p. 104).

American Christian white supremacists also seek racial and religious purifying redemption through murder and massacre. Diverse groups of paranoid militias believe in a coming apocalypse, require "blood to cleanse" them, and speak of their "holy war" (pp. 105–111). One militia group organizer spoke from his pulpit, "Soon we will be asked to kill, but we will kill with love in our hearts because God is with us" (p. 111). A brochure entitled *This Is Aryan Nations* asserts:

> WE BELIEVE that there is a day of reckoning. The usurper will be thrown out by the terrible might of Yahweh's people as they return to their roots and their special destiny. (in Hoffman, 1998, p. 113)

Such rhetoric revolves around phrases such as "racial and religious Armageddon" (p. 114) and "the ultimate holocaust" (p. 116).[15]

Despite divergent religions and cultures, a central defining psychological characteristic of the terrorist agenda is the fantasy of apocalyptic destruction and rebirth. If one asks why apocalyptic fantasies are so critical to terrorism, one must deconstruct fantasies of murder, universal destruction, and the renaissance emerging from the ashes of the cataclysm. As I have been arguing, such fantasies derive from excruciating rage and humiliation that translate into visions of destroying the world, the desire for death and reunion with loved ones, inscribed into a theological and heroic doctrine (Ostow, 1986, 1988). Suicide almost invariably contains the fantasy of rebirth and reunion with love objects by whom one has felt abandoned or neglected (Maltsberger & Buie, 1980; Socarides, 1988), while the theological dimension transforms an infantile, helpless, and humiliating wish into a heroic cosmologically righteous act of stolid morality and puissance.[16]

Osama bin Laden has stated that he wishes to be destroyed so that he can meet Allah. His fantasy of merger with his father—displaced onto the image of a divine benefactor—requires him to be punished and killed because he has such trenchant feelings of badness and self-loathing; only by being punished can he be forgiven and loved by his father (Bunker, 1951). The Freudian death drive is the wish to merge with the parent through dying, as living itself is a hostile and deeply regrettable separation from parental merger. ". . . the 'martyr' acquires the right to enter heaven and liberate himself from all the pain and suffering of this world" (in Hoffman, 1998, p. 99). Punishing himself and externalizing evil purifies and absolves himself, all for the purpose of evacuating his own self-loathing so that he may final-ly attain the love of his father—who in real life was as unempathic, unloving, un-nurturing, and demeaning as are the fathers who inculcate a terrorist culture of patriarchal abuse and rage. Let us not be fooled into believing that the inheritance of cash can be equated with loving parenting.

Further, rage against the West must be understood as a displacement of wrath against his father. It is not that there are no other reasons for hostility toward America, but that his reactivity, hatred, and disgust have amplified the United States to mythic and demonic proportions, and the dynamics of transference and fantasy must be recognized in this process of cosmic vilification.[17] Evil is *symbolic* when amplified to cosmic proportions that cast the other in the role of arch infidel (Ricoeur, 1967). The theologically fanatical language and paranoid delusionality of the fantasy bespeak the intrapsychic conflict projected upon the external world (Glass, 1985; Volkan, 1988). In the process of fantasizing death and blissful reunion with father in Paradise, all rage and toxins contaminating the ideal image of the omni-benign father must be purified and siphoned. Hate for the abusive father must be repressed and displaced, and hence the United States becomes the Devil. The Christian Devil—any Manichean enemy of horrific proportions—is the same fantasy deriving from the need to split off rage against the father and God, who must be benign and pure and who must also not be incited to vengeance against his son for illicit feelings (Fauteux, 1981).

Thus again, bin Laden needed to invent an enemy in order to love and be loved by his father. It is no mere Freudian sophistry to see the destruction of the Twin Towers as a conspicuous castration of the father, displaced from his own to the invented enemy. Injuring the duplicate phalloi was simultaneously the destruction of competing immortality projects, the eradication of eternal monuments that defied death, and the castration of a national "erection" reminding him of his self-loathing, insignificance, and impotence (Arlow, 1964).[18] Immense phallic towers rising into the sky broadcast narcissistic self-glorification to the world, and this is an excruciating insult to those pathologically envious of and malicious toward the arrogance of wealth and confidence, an invitation for resentful malicious retaliation (Berke, 1988).[19]

This last point about destroying his self-loathing complicates the analysis of the terrorist personality and cannot be underestimated when reaching for an under-standing of masochism and paranoia. The psychotic paranoid experiences a com-plex revolving around narcissistic humiliation, rage, neediness, and the intense need to destroy the father, the mother (as both vicious and rejecting erotic femi-nine), the vulnerable self, and the sexual self. The punitive paranoid fantasizes his divinely endowed righteousness. If he needs to punish, eradicate, or castrate that which is oppressive, heretical, or infidelitous, he must be painfully aware of his sense of finitude in the face of such grandiosity. Divine sanction amplifies his own meager existence to the point of irrevocable omnipotence and morality, and hence utilizing the fantasy of a God is not just projecting one's father upon the universe. It is a narcissistic inflation of megalomaniacal proportions. One responds to the brutal humiliation, victimization, and helplessness of childhood by oneself becoming the vengeful invulnerable God (Arlow, 1951; Atwood, 1978; Meissner, 1990, 1991).[20]

However, as the victim of neglect, abuse, and humiliation, the terrorist then derides that which is weak and helpless and strives to eliminate his own despicable self-image. He must fantasize his godhood as an antidote to such contemptible weakness and self-disgust, and he becomes the dispenser of divine vengeance against himself acted out on both himself and others. This means that those oppressive persecutory others who are punished become surrogates for the father who victimized the young frail boy (as mentioned), but also his weak and vulnerable self that is despised precisely because it is weak and humiliated. One becomes a vengeful God to punish the loathsome weak and contemptible self (Bakan, 1971). The terrorist identifies with the aggression of his victimizers, and draws strength from their violence even though it brutalized him.

Thus his vengeance is manifold. He punishes his contemptible self and anything perceived as weak and passive, and he equates the weak and helpless with the feminine—he therefore despises anything perceived as effeminate, including children and women, and anyone yearning for love—who must be punished to kill off his own echoing remembrances of weakness. He thus targets a decadent culture like the United States for being soft, sensual, sexual, indulgent, feminine, and maternal, even as its grand phalloi represent the oppressive father who must be castrated and the symbolic immortality that excludes him and threatens the veracity of his own grandiose fantasies. The Devil is father and mother, brutal patriarch, cannibalistic non-nurturing mother, erotic and threatening feminine, sexual self, and effeminate, desiring self as well. Meanwhile, as intimated, he orchestrates the destruction of his own people because he has a compulsive need to punish that same despised self.

The self that was castrated and shamed must be destroyed alongside the self that needs love and is therefore weak and needy. These inferior selves must be destroyed in hostile self-loathing, thus he destroys his own culture and simultaneously projects sinful qualities upon those contemptible sensualists who act out their decadent licentious prurience (Gruen, 1987). Reminders of his own unfulfilled wishes, which were punished and beaten out of him, are infuriating symbols of his own brutalization, rejection, and neediness. The terrorist kills in vengeance against those who originally rejected and victimized him, against his own loathsome helpless self, and against his own despicable need for love.

CONCLUSIONS

The question for us is whether we can pity a person capable of such violence. I wrote this article not to reify the fantasy that Muslims are evil—far from it. It was not the Islamic prophet Mohammed but the pious Christian saint Thomas Aquinas (1956) who wrote, "*Ut beatitudo sanctorum eis magis complaceat, et de ea uberiores gratias Deo agant, datur eis ut poenam impiorum perfecte intueantur*"—"In order that the bliss of the saints may be more delightful for them and that they may render more copious thanks to God for it, it is given to them to see perfectly the punishment of the damned" (Question 94, Article 1). This is delight through the agony of others. Our own theological tradition enjoys the suffering of our enemies far too often, and I would warn us to be aware of this particularly insidious psychopathology.

Nor have I argued that Afghanis are evil, but that a certain contingent of their society has been brutalized to such an extent that they are possessed by murderous rage and the absence of empathic structures. In effect, I hope that compassion will prevail for those who have been so deprived of love. Political strategies aside (since I cannot suggest what we *should* do), my interest is in enabling readers to see terrorists as battered children forced into madness, not as monsters. What suffering must a person have endured to kill in cold blood, to hate so much. This analysis applies to varying degrees to many abused and psychologically damaged people all over the world who have become deranged enough to commit immense violence and, if my message is clear, we should wonder how much of our own psychological makeup is also suffused with rage and unempathic disregard for life, justified through our own fantasies and rationalizations.

It may also be that we invited this violence in a psychological sense. While I am in no way blaming the United States, we must consider to what degree American policy was also designed to incite bin Laden to envy and rage so that we might have an enemy, so that we might also have an evil demonic threat that would galvanize the American people and enable us to displace our rage and anxiety. I am not saying this must always have been a conscious decision. However, we must always ask to what degree we invite enemies to fulfill our fantasies as well. I do not mean that the support of Israel incited bin Laden—this is true in some sense but it is futile to argue that support of Israel justifies the murder of thousands of American civilians. The question is how much we also needed an enemy to scapegoat, to fulfill our fantasies, and how much we invited his reprisal to maintain the fantasy of our goodness and moral sovereignty.

We too have our fictions and our murderous propensities, disguised by myths and a propaganda of self-righteousness. We have had our slaves, witch trials, and insidious exploitation of Native America, and though we are always striving to improve, we have not outgrown our brutality. Democracy is a compassionate and humane political system, but our current president wishes to have closed military trials composed of a jury of soldiers—who must by definition be inherently biased because they are members of an army dedicated to eliminating the enemy—endowed with the power to execute suspected terrorists without appeal. This is unconstitutional, fascistic, and *sick*. The U.S. governmental system was designed to be humane and to prevent abuse of power, but fanaticism and malice thrive.

As for the people, America largely ignores the consequences of the atomic aftermath in Japan (Lifton & Mitchell, 1995). We rarely discuss the millions of Germans who starved to death following World War II. We most often strive to avoid knowing about the hundreds of thousands of Iraqi children who died of starvation and disease following our military aggression a few years ago. We cannot profess humanely that everyone killed deserved to die. If sometimes people die as the tragic consequences of unavoidable military actions, denial of the inherent atrocity does not eliminate its reality, though it helps us sustain the fiction of moral purity. How much death is tragic consequence and how much is the results of our veiled, rationalized aggression is something we must consider in its complexity. This is not to be done as an indictment of democracy or a means of punishing American history— but as a means of coming to terms with our own individual as well as social irrationality, illusions, and violence, especially if these phenomena are sometimes seductive and pleasurable, enabling us to feel we are righteous, avatars of democratic freedom, smiting and hunting down evil, while we surreptitiously conquer death by inflicting it on others.

The American paranoia following September 11 demonstrates just how easily people can slip into paranoid violence, as citizens targeted Muslims and Arab-looking people in reprisal. I counseled a woman of Latin descent who had escaped from one of the Twin Towers moments before it collapsed. She suffered from severe post-traumatic stress symptoms and would cry uncontrollably in fear and sadness for the victims. The day after she escaped, a man unleashed his dog against her in revenge against terrorism because she resembled a Middle Eastern person.

We have not lived lives of brutality and ubiquitous warfare, but we certainly regressed to a hostile, vengeful, delirious state almost immediately after the attacks. Political speeches and images in the media only fueled the paranoia and hostility, by the righteous rhetoric and imagery of justified revenge and obliteration of the enemy. Many people were compassionate, resisting the seduction of violence. Many worked frenetically to help others. And still the imagery of vengeance spread round the country, and this united many of us in a cozy and sentimental patriotic hatred.[21]

> There is only one way to begin to deal with people like this, and that is you have to kill some of them even if they are not immediately directly involved in this thing.
>
> Former Secretary of State Lawrence Eagleburger
> (CNN, September 11, 2001)

> The response to this unimaginable 21st-century Pearl Harbor should be as simple as it is swift—kill the bastards. A gunshot between the eyes, blow them to smithereens, poison them if you have to. As for cities or countries that host these worms, bomb them into basketball courts.
>
> Steve Dunleavy (*New York Post*, September 12, 2001)

> America roused to a righteous anger has always been a force for good. States that have been supporting if not Osama bin Laden, people like him need to feel pain. If we flatten part of Damascus or Tehran or whatever it takes, that is part of the solution.
>
> Rich Lowry, *National Review* editor, to Howard Kurtz
> (*Washington Post*, September 13, 2001)

TIME TO TAKE NAMES AND NUKE AFGHANISTAN.
Caption to cartoon by Gary Brookins
(*Richmond Times-Dispatch*, September 13, 2001)

At a bare minimum, tactical nuclear capabilities should be used against the bin Laden camps in the desert of Afghanistan. To do less would be rightly seen by the poisoned minds that orchestrated these attacks as cowardice on the part of the United States and the current administration.
Former Defense Intelligence Agency officer Thomas Woodrow, "Time to Use the Nuclear Option" (*Washington Times*, September 14, 2001)

Bill O'Reilly: "If the Taliban government of Afghanistan does not cooperate, then we will damage that government with air power, probably. All right? We will blast them, because . . ."
Sam Husseini, Institute for Public Accuracy:
"Who will you kill in the process?"

O'Reilly: "Doesn't make any difference."
("The O'Reilly Factor," Fox News Channel, September 13, 2001)

This is no time to be precious about locating the exact individuals directly involved in this particular terrorist attack. . . . We should invade their countries, kill their leaders and convert them to Christianity. We weren't punctilious about locating and punishing only Hitler and his top officers. We carpet-bombed German cities; we killed civilians. That's war. And this is war.
Syndicated columnist Ann Coulter
(*New York Daily News*, September 12, 2001)

I will conclude with a quote from Shakespeare, as remorseful commentary.

> . . . mothers shall but smile when they behold
> Their infants quarter'd with the hands of war;
> All pity choked with custom of fell deeds:
> And Caesar's spirit, ranging for revenge,
> With Até by his side come hot from hell,
> Shall in these confines, with a monarch's voice,
> Cry "Havoc," and let slip the dogs of war;
> That this foul deed shall smell above the earth
> With carrion men, groaning for burial.

Julius Caesar, III, i

James Hillman (1979, 1983) writes of hero myths as revealing not necessarily courage, but fear and rage: "aggression, violence, power, sadism—aren't shadow at all; that's the whole Western ego!" (*Inter Views*, p. 11).[22] We have a cultural mythology that thrives on gratifying vengeance, though we refuse to recognize it as such: "When you're in the middle of domination, you don't feel yourself in a *fantasy* of domination" (p. 11).[23] We have tangible enemies in the outer world, but we invent enemies as well, as fantasies ejected from our own imaginations as a means of destroying our terror.

Our own paranoia has tragic consequences, just as the psychotic and paranoid fantasies of terrorists demand murder in lieu of knowing their own helplessness and weakness, the complex marauding feelings of infantile rage, and the need for love. One meaning of *jihad* is "holy war," but the deeper meaning is one of struggle, of the psychological battle against oneself and one's demons. Holy war confuses internal enemies with external evil and lays waste to the world as a consequence. If we are not to rival their paranoia and exceed their violence, we need to know ourselves as well. We can read every analysis of terrorists, every declaration, conviction, and political strategy as (at least in part) a confession of our own fantasies, our irrational response to trauma, terror, and death. Ideally, we will arrive at some conclusions that deepen us rather than reinforcing our paranoid fantasies. I hope readers have learned something about terrorism, the paranoid process, and the immense suffering at the heart of violence—and learned it with self-knowledge and compassion.

REFERENCES

Aquinas, T. (1956). *Summa theologiae, III, supplementum.* Italy: Marietti. (Originally published 1273)

Arendt, H. (1963). *Eichmann in Jerusalem: A report on the banality of evil.* New York: Penguin.

Arlow, J. A. (1951). The consecration of the prophet. *Psychoanalytic Quarterly, 20,* 374–397.

Arlow, J. A. (1964). The Madonna's conception through the ear. *Psychoanalytic Study of Society, 3,* 13–25.

Arlow, J. A., & Brenner, C. (1964). *Psychoanalytic concepts and the structural theory.* New York: International Universities Press.

Ash, T. G. (2001, November 29). Are there good terrorists? *New York Review of Books, 48,* 30–35.

Athens, L. (1992). *The creation of dangerous violent criminals.* Urbana: University of Illinois Press.

Atwood, G. E. (1978). On the origins and dynamics of messianic salvation fantasies. *International Review of Psychoanalysis, 33,* 85–96.

Bakan, D. (1971). *Slaughter of the innocents.* San Francisco: Jossey-Bass.

Becker, E. (1973). *The denial of death.* New York: Free Press.

Becker, E. (1975). *Escape from evil.* New York: Free Press.

Beers, W. (1992). *Women and sacrifice.* Detroit: Wayne.

Bergen, P. L. (2001). *Holy War, Inc.: Inside the world of Osama bin Laden.* New York: Free Press.

Berke, J. H. (1988). *The tyranny of malice: Exploring the dark side of character and culture.* New York: Summit.

Bion, W. (1955). Group dynamics: a re-view. In M. Klein, P. Heimann, & R. E. Money-Kyrle (Eds.), *New directions in psycho-analysis* (pp. 440–477). London: Maresfield, 1977.

Bormann, M. (1953). *Hitler's table talk (1941–1944)* . London: Weidenfeld & Nicholson.

Brown, N. O. (1991). *Apocalypse and/or metamorphosis.* Berkeley: University of California Press.

Bunker, H. A. (1951). Psychoanalysis and the study of religion. In G. Roheim (Ed.), *Psychoanalysis and the social sciences* (Vol. III, pp. 7–34). New York: International Universities Press.

Carus, P. (1900). *The devil.* La Salle, IL: Open Court.

Chasseguet-Smirgel, J. (1975). *The ego ideal.* New York: Norton.

deMause, L. (2000). War as righteous rape and purification. *Journal of Psychohistory, 27,* 356–445.

Dundes, A. (1976). A psychoanalytic study of the bullroarer. *Man, 11,* 220–238.

Dundes, A. (1986). The flood: A male myth of creation. *Journal of Psychoanalytic Anthropology, 9,* 359–372.

Durkheim, E. (1912). *The elementary forms of the religious life.* New York: Free Press, 1965.

Eigen, M. (1986). *The psychotic core.* Northvale, NJ: Jason Aronson.

Eliade, M. (1963). *Myth and reality.* New York: Harper.

El Saadawi, N. (1980). *The hidden face of Eve: Women in the Arab world.* London: Zed Books.

Erikson, E. H. (1950). *Childhood and society.* New York: W. W. Norton, 1993.

Fauteux, A. (1981). "Good/bad" splitting in the religious experience. *American Journal of Psychoanalysis, 41,* 261–267.

Freud, S. (1953). *The standard edition of the complete works of Sigmund Freud.* London: Hogarth.

Freud, S. (1905). *Three essays on a theory of sexuality.* SE VII, 125–244. London: Hogarth.

Freud, S. (1921). *Group psychology and the analysis of the ego.* SE XVIII, 67–144. London: Hogarth.

Freud, S. (1927). *The future of an illusion.* SE XXI, 5–56. London: Hogarth.

Freud, S. (1930). *Civilization and its discontents.* SE XXI, 59–145. London: Hogarth.

Fromm, E. (1955). *The sane society.* New York: Rinehart & Company.

Gay, V. (1979). Against wholeness: The ego's complicity in religion. *Journal of the American Academy of Religion, 47,* 107–120.

Gilligan, J. (1996). *Violence.* New York: Vintage.

Glass, J. M. (1985). *Delusion: Internal dimensions of political life.* Chicago: University of Chicago Press.

Goldberg, C. (1996). *Speaking with the devil: Exploring senseless acts of evil.* New York: Penguin.

Grand, S. (2000). *The reproduction of evil: A clinical and cultural perspective.* Hillsdale, NJ: Analytic Press.

Greene, J. C. (1969). A "madman" searches for a less divided self. *Contemporary Psychoanalysis, 6,* 58–75.

Gruen, A. (1987). *The insanity of normality. Realism as sickness: Toward understanding human destructiveness.* New York: Grove Weidenfeld.

Hillman, J. (1979). *The dream and the underworld.* New York: Harper.

Hillman, J. (1983). *Inter views.* New York: Harper Colophon.

Hitschmann, E. (1949). Swedenborg's paranoia. *American Imago, 6,* 45–50.

Hoffman, B. (1998). *Inside terrorism.* New York: Columbia University Press.

Horney, K. (1930). The distrust between the sexes. In *Feminine psychology* (pp. 107–118). New York: Norton.

Horney, K. (1967). *Feminine psychology.* New York: Norton.

Horney, K. (1973). The dread of woman. In *Feminine psychology* (pp. 133–146). New York: Norton. (Originally published 1932)

Jaques, E. (1955). Social systems as a defense against persecutory and depressive anxiety. In M. Klein, P. Heimann, & R. E. Money-Kyrle (Eds.), *New directions in psycho-analysis* (pp. 478–498). London: Maresfield.

Juergensmeyer, M. (2000). *Terror in the mind of god: The global rise of religious violence.* Berkeley: University of California Press.

Kalayjian, A., Shahinian, D., Gergerian, E., & Saraydarian, L. (1996). Coping with the Ottoman Turkish genocide: An exploration of the experience of Armenian survivors. *Journal of Traumatic Stress, 9,* 87–89.

Kaufman, M. R. (1939). Religious delusions in schizophrenia. *International Journal of Psychoanalysis, 20,* 363–376.

Kernberg, O. F. (1992). *Aggression in personality disorders and perversions.* New Haven, CT: Yale University Press.

Kohut, H. (1971). *The analysis of the self.* New York: International Universities Press.

Kohut, H. (1972). Thoughts on narcissism and narcissistic rage. *Psychoanalytic Study of the Child, 27,* 360–400.

Kohut, H. (1977). *The restoration of the self.* Madison, WI: International Universities Press.

La Barre, W. (1970). *The ghost dance: The origins of religion.* New York: Doubleday.

La Barre, W. (1991). *Shadow of childhood: Neoteny and the biology of religion.* Norman, OK: University of Oklahoma Press.

Laqueur, W. (1977). *Terrorism.* London: Weidenfeld & Nicholson.

Laqueur, W. (1987a). *The age of terrorism.* Boston: Little, Brown, & Co.

Laqueur, W. (1987b). Reflections on terrorism. In W. Laqueur and Y. Alexander (Eds.), *The terrorism reader: The essential sourcebook on political violence both past and present* (updated and expanded ed., pp. 378–392). New York: Meridian.

Leverenz, D. (1975). Shared fantasy in Puritan sermons. *American Imago, 32,* 264–287.

Lifton, R. J. (1964). On death and death symbolism: The Hiroshima disaster. In E. Wyschogrod, (Ed.), *The phenomenon of death: Faces of mortality* (pp. 69–109). New York: Harper & Row.

Lifton, R. J. (1979). *The broken connection.* Washington, DC: American Psychiatric Press.

Lifton, R. J. (1986). *The Nazi doctors: A study in the psychology of evil.* New York: Basic.

Lifton, R. J. (1988). Life unworthy of life: Nazi racial views. In R. L. Braham (Ed.), *The psychological perspectives of the Holocaust and of its aftermath* (pp. 1–11). Boulder, CO: Social Science Monographs.

Lifton, R. J., & Markusen, E. (1990). *The genocidal mentality: Nazi holocaust and nuclear threat.* New York: Basic.

Lifton, R. J., & Mitchell, G. (1995). *Hiroshima in America: Fifty years of denial.* New York: Putnam.

Lifton, R. J., & Mitchell, G. (1999). *Destroying the world to save it: Aum Shinrikyo, apocalyptic violence, and the new global terrorism.* New York: Henry Holt.

Lightfoot-Klein, H. (1989). *Prisoners of ritual.* New York: Haworth.

Loewald, H. (1975). *Papers on psychoanalysis.* New Haven, CT: Yale University Press.

Lopez-Corvo, R. (1997). *God is a woman.* Northvale, NJ: Jason Aronson.

Mahler, M. (1979). On human symbiosis and the vicissitudes of individuation. In *Separation-individuation* (pp. 78–98). Northvale, NJ: Jason Aronson. (Originally published 1968)

Maltsberger, J. T., & Buie, D. H. Jr. (1980). The devices of suicide: Revenge, riddance, and rebirth. In J. T. Maltsberger & M. J. Goldblatt (Eds.), *Essential papers on suicide* (pp. 397–416). New York: NYU Press.

McKnight, G. (1974). *The mind of the terrorist.* London: Joseph.

Meissner, W. W. (1978). *The paranoid process.* Northvale, NJ: Jason Aronson.

Meissner, W. W. (1988). The cult phenomenon and the paranoid process. *Psychoanalytic Study of Society, 12,* 69–95.

Meissner, W. W. (1990). Jewish messianism and the cultic process. *Psychoanalytic Study of Society, 15,* 347–370.

Meissner, W. W. (1991). The phenomenology of religious psychopathology. *Bulletin of the Menninger Clinic, 55,* 281–298.

Moscovici, S. (1988). *The invention of society.* Cambridge, MA: Polity Press.

Moses-Hrushovski, R. (1994). *Deployment.* Northvale, NJ: Jason Aronson.

Nietzsche, F. (1889). *Der Antichrist.* Berlin: Walter de Gruyter.

Ostow, M. (1958). The nature of religious controls. *American Psychologist, 13,* 571–574.

Ostow, M. (1972). Religion and morality: A psychoanalytic view. In S. Post (Ed.), *Moral values and the superego concept in psychoanalysis.* New York: International Universities Press.

Ostow, M. (1986). Archetypes of apocalypse in dreams and fantasies, and in religious scripture. *American Imago, 43,* 307–334.

Ostow, M. (1988). Apocalyptic thinking in mental illness and social disorder. *Psychoanalysis and Contemporary Thought, 11,* 285–297.

Pickthall, M. M., trans. (1999). *The glorious Qur'an.* Elmhurst, NY: Tahrike Tarsile Qur'an, Inc.

Ransohoff, R. (2001). *Fear and envy: Why men need to dominate and control women.* New York: Painted Leaf Press.

Rashid, A. (2000). *Taliban: Militant Islam, oil, and fundamentalism in central Asia.* New Haven: Yale.

Rheingold, J. C. (1964). *The fear of being a woman.* New York: Grune & Stratton.

Rheingold, J. C. (1967). *The mother, anxiety, and death.* Boston: Little, Brown and Company.

Ricoeur, P. (1967). *The symbolism of evil.* Boston: Beacon.

Roheim, G. (1932). Animism and religion. *Psychoanalytic Quarterly, 6,* 59–112.

Schmid, A. (1984). *Political terrorism: A research guide.* New Brunswick, NJ: Transaction.

Schmid, A., Jongman, A., et al. (1988). *Political terrorism: A new guide to actors, authors, concepts, data bases, theories, and literature.* New Brunswick, NJ: Transaction.

Shapiro, D. (1965). *Neurotic styles.* New York: Basic Books.

Socarides, C. (1988). *The preoedipal origin and psychoanalytic therapy of sexual perversions.* New York: International Universities Press.

Solomon, S., Greenberg, J., & Pyszczynski, T. (2002). Fear of death and social behavior: The anatomy of human destructiveness. In J. Piven, P. Ziolo, & H. Lawton (Eds.), *Terror and apocalypse: Psychological undercurrents of history* (Vol. II, pp. 286–328). New York: Bloomusalem/iUniverse.

Spiro, M. E. (1978). Religious systems as culturally constituted defense mechanisms. In B. Kilborne and L. L. Langness (Eds.), *Culture and human nature.* Chicago: University of Chicago Press.

Tiger, L. (1996). Robert Jay Lifton and biology: The doctor is in—knock twice. In C. B. Strozier & M. Flynn (Eds.), *Trauma and self* (pp. 95–99). Lanham, MD: Rowman & Littlefield.

Volkan, V. (1988). *The need to have enemies and allies.* Northvale, NJ: Jason Aronson.

Winnicott, D. W. (1965). *The maturational process and the facilitating environment.* Madison, CT: International Universities Press, 1994.

SUPPLEMENTARY BIBLIOGRAPHY

Piven, J. (1999). Object splitting and separation-individuation phenomena in the derogation of women. *Tapestry: The Journal of Historical Motivations and the Social Fabric, 2 (1/2)*, 38–42.

Piven, J. (in press). Death, repression, narcissism, misogyny. *Psychoanalytic Review.*

Piven, J., & Lawton, H. (Eds.) (2001). *Psychological undercurrents of history.* New York: Authors Choice Press.

Piven, J., Ziolo, P., & Lawton, H. (Eds.) (in press). *Terror and apocalypse: Psychological undercurrents of history* (Vol. II). New York: Writers Showcase/Bloomusalem.

NOTES

1. I define terrorism provisionally as violence acted intentionally upon citizens rather than the military, which concurs with the U.S. State Department definition according to Title 22 of the United States Code, section 2656f(d) (Hoffman, 1998, p. 38). However, the term becomes as complex as the context of the "terrorism" in question. Attacks on military targets, while war is not officially declared, may be considered terrorism by those assaulted, while "terrorists" often see their own acts as justifiable and defensive responses to unjust occupation or military mobilization. Were guerrilla attacks by American revolutionaries a form of terrorism? Were the attacks on Hiroshima and Nagasaki terrorist attacks because civilians were targeted? There are undoubtedly complex answers here, but I am alluding to some sinister implications of what terrorism might be, if we challenge our perspective on our own tactics and perceive the perspectives of those we have taken action against. In other words, defining our enemies as terrorists sometimes reduces "them" to murderous assailants without valid grievances, while whitewashing our own potential culpability. This does not mean that terrorism is purely subjective, however, and it does behoove us to make distinctions between modes of violence (see Hoffman, 1998, in debate with Schmid, 1984, and Schmid et al., 1988; and Laqueur, 1977, 1987a). See also Ash (2001) as a perspicuous clarification.

2.   A case in point is bin Laden's rage against America for letting 500,000 Iraqi children die of disease and starvation following the American assault. He does not protest the murder of the Kurds, or their children, much less the vicious treatment of children in his own culture. This is not empathy, but paranoid fantasy demonstrating genuine disregard for life, and rage only when violence is inflicted on oneself or one's narcissistic self-objects.

3.   Clitoridectomy is not ostensibly practiced in Saudi Arabia (Ransohoff, 2001), though conflicting reports do implicate Saudi Arabia, Pakistan, and elsewhere in the Middle East. Regardless, misogyny and the violent derogation of women are the norm.

4.   For more information, see Nawal El Saadawi (1980), *The Hidden Face of Eve: Women in the Arab World,* especially chapter 6. See also William Beers (1992), *Women and Sacrifice,* and Hanny Lightfoot-Klein (1989), *Prisoners of Ritual.*

5.   When Bhutto returned to Pakistan in 1988, she was greeted by cheers from crowds numbering in the hundreds of thousands (Bergen, 2001, p. 61). Pervasive misogyny does not mean universal misogyny.

6.   This argument is once again not dependent on the fact of clitoridectomy, as so many extremely destructive abuses of women proliferate in the Arab world.

7.   Another indicator of their psychosexual pathology is their paranoid hostility toward homosexuals. As Bergen (2001) writes, "Taliban religious scholars labored over the vital question of how to deal with homosexuals," whether to throw them off roofs, bury them and drop walls over them, etc. (p. 9). This is confirmed by Rashid (2000), who also notes how prevalent homosexuality (and the rape of young boys) is despite being prohibited and despised (p. 115). From extensive experience with homosexuals and a highly masochistic population, my colleague Judd Grill believes that for men in such cultures, sodomy is inflicted in repetition of the violence performed on their mothers by the misogynistic fathers. Hence sodomy enacts the fantasy of simultaneously inflicting injury, contaminating the object, contaminating the self, and restoring the damage. It represents identification with the father, abuse of the mother, and reparative merger with the mother as well.

8.   As Kohut noted, in violence there may be sufficient empathy to know what causes pain, and thus inflict it on others. But this is more knowing one's own suffering and evacuating it punitively, rather than really understanding the feelings of others.

9.   Describing this process as both paranoid and psychotic may sound redundant, but I would argue that paranoia can be a cognitive style of "normal," neurotic, borderline, and psychotic degrees (see Meissner, 1978, and Shapiro, 1965). One conspicuous example of such paranoia is the belief that three Jews run U.S. foreign policy (Bergen, 2001, p. 5). Another is bin Laden's fantasy that the use of nuclear, chemical, and biological weapons constitutes *defending* his brethren (p. 85). He believes that U.S. military presence in the Middle East is a coalition of Jews and (Christian) "Crusaders" (p. 94), and that the deployment of women soldiers in Desert Storm was an ultimate insult (p. 99).

10.   I thank Lloyd deMause for bringing this to my attention and giving me permission to reference his citation.

11.   My argument here differs from Lifton's, for while he argues that numbing and "doubling" (a form of dissociation) are required for assailants to endure the horror of death and guilt of their actions, I have been suggesting that many assailants lack empathic structures and cannot feel the humanity of their enemies. Thus they dissociate culpability (acknowledging the wrongness of their actions), and the horror of death, but need not dissociate feelings of remorse for victims, as they have been brutalized into living the righteousness of murdering enemies. Supporting evidence may be found in deMause (2000), who cites the dual-brain research of Frederic Schiffer to explain the dissociation of social alters, alternate personalities located in separate hemispheres of the brain, ostensibly demonstrating

how violence can be enacted by ordinary people. One conscious side is unaware of the genocidal other half and genuinely does not know the viciousness the other half is enacting (pp. 366–371).

12.   This is also a denial of death as an ignoble, horrific, disgusting end—the corpse is not a mangled mass of putrescent flesh but a perfumed *shaheed* about to enter the enveloping womb of heaven. The fantasy transforms the horror and absorbs the humiliating blow to one's narcissism experienced in victimization. Recall the scene in Dostoevsky's *The Brothers Karamazov* where father Zosima's corpse is expected to emit a heavenly odor but instead putresces nastily. Reality is denied through blissful fantasies. As Nietzsche (1889) wrote, ". . . der Glaube unter Umständen selig macht . . ." ("under certain circumstances, faith makes [one] blissful"; *Der Antichrist*, p. 230).

13.   Another version translates the passage thus: "Think not of those who are slain in the way of Allah, as dead. Nay, they are living. With their Lord they have provision: Jubilant (as they) because of that which Allah hath bestowed upon them of His bounty, rejoicing for the sake of those who have not joined them but are left behind . . ." (3:169–70 in this version).

14.   Ekpyrosis is an early Stoic image of universal conflagration, attributed to Heraklitus, utilized also in Orphean terminology. There are any number of similar eschatological images, e.g., cataclysmic floods, the Vedic Mahapralaya (great dissolution), the Norse Ragnarok, etc., pervading religion, philosophy, and cult from the Vedas to Chiliastic imagery, Nazism, Aum Shinrikyo, and modern millennialism. I am incorporating the image as a recurring fantasy of death and rebirth through explosion or destruction, one that has even entered modern physics as "ekpyrotic theory" (which does not preclude its literal facticity—it merely signifies the vitality of the symbol in the imagination). See Eliade (1963), pp. 54–74.

15.   Despite the fact that most militia groups have not committed acts of violence, several of them have effectively demonstrated militancy and the kind of paranoid fantasy that forces us to take them as serious threats (Hoffman, 1998).

16.   I would add that re-merger is also experienced as the threat of annihilation and disintegration. Hence this re-merger is imagined in catastrophic terms, and rebellion against merging with the object whom one needs yet hates requires violent destruction. Finally, one must not overlook the fantasy of masculine gestation suffusing apocalyptic rebirths, and the concomitant envy of the woman's ability to give life. One despises but envies the woman's ability to give birth, and with the apocalypse one gives birth to paradise and oneself is purified (see Dundes, 1976, 1986; Horney, 1936; Ransahoff, 2001).

17.   Benjamin Beit-Hallahmi disagrees strongly with this reading, asking whether George Washington was displacing his rage against King George, or the Native Americans at Little Big Horn against General Custer (private communications). I agree that it would be reductive to claim that the hatred of oppression inherently derived from parricidal wishes. I would make some distinctions, however: bin Laden may perceive himself as defending his territory against oppression like those in the cited examples, but in this case our military presence is not imperialistically controlling the entire lands or government, and nor were the Native Americans or Washington paranoid sociopaths joyfully murdering thousands of civilians thousands of miles away. The Native Americans were literally fighting for their lives against invaders who would eliminate their culture and way of life. While the military presence in Afghanistan may be immoral, humiliating, and oppressive, it can also be argued that the American presence has something to do with preventing indigenous violence (not only oil interests). By contrast, the Afghan state is itself violent and oppressive, exemplifies no tangible interest in freedom except its own demand to subjugate its citizens in peace. America is not the source of Afghan misery or poverty (America supplied Afghan resistance against

the Soviets). It is not forcing Afghanistan to live by American laws or customs, is not policing citizens and punishing them when they wear makeup or attend their parents' graves, is
not demanding tithes, nor imposing leadership, nor gradually invading and commandeering
territory while expulsing the indigenous population. Again by contrast, if Washington had
supported the religious, undemocratic, punitive regulation of his people, declared his own
holy war against the British Empire, and dedicated himself to planning the murders of infidel civilians across the sea, this would approach similarity with bin Laden.

18.   Phallic and castrating language abound in al-Qaeda rhetoric. As but one example,
calls for attacks on U.S. troops in Somalia demanded loyal Muslims to "cut off the head of
the snake" (Bergen, 2001, p. 82).

19.   It should not be thought that just because bin Laden is wealthy that he does not
envy or resent the wealth of others. His envy resides not in greed but in the hatred of arrogant egotism, and in the need to avoid appearing wealthy and arrogant himself, which
would make him a conceited child upstart in the eyes of his father, family, and community.
Luxury and self-centeredness would connote individuation from the father and oedipal competition—in other words, the shameful boy telling father he is an independent, self-suffi-
cient adult—which threatens him with castration by father. Meanwhile, traveling among the
people enables him to father them without eliciting their oedipal rage, thus acting out his
fantasies of resolving the issues of a terrifying and hostile childhood. He can be a father and
love the way he was not loved, while fathering without eliciting the hatred of his sons. They
are surrogates for himself, and hence he avoids dethroning his own father if they love him,
while he avoids castration by father by being a nice daddy. Ironically, he symbolically cas-
trates himself to avoid castration from without. His humility bespeaks the massive need to
evade their envy and hatred (cf. Berke, 1988). His envy and hatred are therefore displaced
from his father, from himself, and from his own people, onto external enemies. A significant
component of the rage and envy relates not just to the father but to the other children who
absorbed the time and attention of father away from the needy insignificant child. An
anonymous son among fifty children resents the absence of love, attention, and recognition
every child needs, and hence violent anger against the father destroys competitors for love
and significance, especially those who are happy and do not feel his humiliating alienation
and envy. One is further enraged when the father is absent or dies—then one cannot express
one's rage, one feels guilty for wishing to do so, and guiltily responsible for feeling that one's
rage might have killed the father, as well as angry that the father is not powerful enough not
to have died, thus abandoning the hapless child and leaving no source of emotional support.
Paradoxically, a child can be angry at a father for being too weak, for dying. It is no psychoanalytic reductionism to call attention to the importance of a father's phallic strength for the
emotional security of his son. Children need to believe in their fathers and in their masculine strength (as much as they fear it). The destruction of the phalloi is revenge against the
phallic security father failed to provide.

20.   It is significant that bin Laden and company are excited by dreams of airplanes
(*New York Times*, December 16, 2001, Section 4, p. 5). Though airplanes are used as penetrating and destructive phalloi, and commandeering such massive instruments provides feelings of thrilling aggressive domination, the aerial dreams of bin Laden and his followers
symbolize transcendence and liberation. In addition to phallic-narcissistic grandiosity and
inflation, the historic context of airplanes as vehicles for rebellion, freedom, and destruction
amplifies the theological and mythological significance of their demolition of the Twin
Towers. Airplanes become the ideal symbol, or mythic signifier, of grandiose liberation and
cosmic, cataclysmic, apocalyptic destruction.

21.   The following quotes were posted to the Internet by Neil deMause, whose atten-

tiveness and perspicacity are to be commended.

22. See Hillman (1979), *The Dream and the Underworld.*

23. I am referring to the immense popularity of violent films such as *Rambo* and *The Terminator*, not to mention daily murder on television. Our cultural entertainment is extremely brutal, and overcoming the fear of death by killing enemies is a gratifying fantasy. There are even plans for a new Rambo film, in which the righteous hero wreaks vengeance on the Taliban. Not all media content is violent, of course. The remarkable conclusion of the 2001 *Harry Potter* film is overcoming enemies (persecutory anxiety) through love, not violence. This is no *political* solution (reality is sadly more complex), but it is a *psychological* improvement.

I would like to thank Howard Stein, Chuck Strozier, Paul Ziolo, Sheldon Solomon, Neil Elgee, George Victor, David L. Miller, Benjamin Beit-Hallahmi, Ruth Stein, Henry Lawton, Moshe Hazani, Arno Gruen, and Herman Piven for graciously reading this article and giving me patient feedback. My opinions do not necessarily reflect their own.

6

Psychological Legitimization of Violence by Religious Archetypes

J. Harold Ellens

INTRODUCTION

The Hebrew Bible conveyed to its adherents an ethical principle that was cryptic, direct, and pragmatic. It is simply stated in the Levitical and Deuteronomic codes and it readily became a rule for life in society and a metaphor for justice in a relatively barbaric world. "An eye for and eye and a tooth for a tooth" (Exodus 21: 23–25), the Bible legislates. We call it the *Lex Talionis*, or the law of the jungle.

Much has been written and preached to ameliorate those barbaric tones and their consequences since the ancient regulations were imposed purportedly by God or on God's authority. Jesus' own words seem the most powerful contradiction of the *Lex Talionis*. He declared, "You have heard that it was said, 'An eye for an eye and a tooth for a tooth.' I say to you, 'If anyone strikes you on the right cheek, turn to him the other also. . . . Love your enemies and do good to those who persecute you so that you may be children of your father who is in heaven'" (Matthew 5:38, 39, 44, and 45).

Few people in the Western world today would speak in favor of running society or their personal lives by the ancient barbaric law of the jungle. No one reading this book would favor a system consciously based on this precept. But the problem with metaphors, as Freud and Jung taught us so well, is that they are hatched in the unconscious, accrue their rich and fruitful meaning there, and carry out their function mainly at hidden levels of the psyche, not readily accessible to conscious analysis or discipline. Thus, the ancient cultures of the Eastern Mediterranean adopted that barbaric code; and while Arab societies today claim a Koranic grace as their code and the Israelis insist that their society is a democracy, that old barbaric metaphor shapes and justifies both the policies of *jihad* on the one side and the exaggerated mayhem of what is now being called proactive or preemptive defense on the other; all this in this twenty-first century, in this supposedly civilized Western world.

Freud and Jung were correct in arguing that metaphors, reflecting or tuned up to the power of psychological archetypes, function with effects and durability far beyond our wildest imaginations. By means of wholesome metaphors we create aesthetic and humane civilization, almost as though it were the normal product of daily life. By means of pathogenic metaphors, on the other hand, we continue to recreate destruction, even disaster, in each new generation, as though it were inherited in our genes.

Some awful things are inherited genetically, of course. However, much of what continues to defeat the groundswell of civilized decency and aesthetic transcendence, optimistically expected in each new era, is not only genetically inherited pathologies. What we inherit culturally in our dominant metaphors persistently defeats the gains in goodness for which we hope. We need not look across the ocean or to international politics to discern this unfortunate truth.

EXPOSITION

Of course, we human beings do not need exotic explanations of physical or cultural inheritance to account for our violence. We all seem perfectly capable of devising it quite on our own, without metaphoric prodding or genetic pathogenesis. The Israelis have no monopoly on violence; we need only to look within our own psyches or souls.

A Personal Illustration

A few days ago I was driving into my driveway when I suddenly decided to stop for my mail. The mailbox is just to the right of the driveway. I slammed on the brakes, threw my vehicle into reverse, and backed up, nearly putting two cyclists into the hospital in the process. They were innocent folks out for an afternoon's recreation on the fine municipal bike path, in what, I am sure, seemed to them a perfectly safe and peaceful suburb. When I again slammed on my brakes, the fellow right next to my window let out a violent tirade, informing me that I had been viciously irresponsible and incautious.

I am sure his tone was raised to a hysterical level because of the anxiety he felt about nearly being run down. My tone was also a bit hysterical because of my terror about the physical damage I had nearly done to two innocent human beings. I opened my window and yelled back at him, giving as good as I got, and bringing my diatribe to a fine rhetorical climax by telling him that this was my driveway, that he used the bike path at the pleasure of the community, meaning mainly me, and that he should shut up and pay more attention to what was going on around him.

The whole episode was scandalous for two purportedly decent old men; and scandalously violent. He seems to have recovered sooner than I did, for the next day there was an envelope taped to my mailbox that read as follows.

> To the motorist I encountered the other day. Pedestrian walkways, and bike paths are intended to keep non-motorized traffic out of busy roads—A great idea! These are located in right of ways and require no privilege. In fact, in Michigan, "Driving is a privilege, not a right." You have a great home and property which I have admired many times as I've passed by. However, it is located in a busy section of the city. This calls for extra caution. Cyclists, and pedestrians, need to be treated as the real traffic they are. When backing up, your range of vision is not as good as when moving and looking forward. Add a cell phone and concern for a mailbox and the risk goes up. PLEASE drive carefully! A couple of seconds are all that are needed to injure someone for life! Or, to avoid an injury. Sorry that I startled you that day!

I wrote him a letter in response and said the following.

> Friend, you are right and I was wrong for running off at the mouth. What ticked me off was what I perceived as your condescending scolding, but in retrospect I can understand your inclination to do so, given the circumstances, though obviously all of us were less cautious than we should have been. In any case, I apologize. I feel terror at what injury I nearly caused, as you note in your missive. The incident confirms what I have long suspected to be a ruling principle in life, namely, that when I feel justified to rise in righteous indignation, the indignation seems to operate automatically, but the righteousness never seems to quite kick in. In any case, thank you for going to the trouble of leaving the note on my mailbox. Perhaps we shall meet sometime for better reasons in a safer environment with opportunity for pleasant fellowship!

I placed this in an envelope with my name and return address. Because he did not sign his letter or indicate his identity, I taped the envelope to my mailbox with this sentence on it: "To the Consummate Cyclist and Gentleman Whom I Nearly Hospitalized." Unfortunately, the next day I found the envelope unopened, ground into the sand, with a discernible heel print on the face of it. Obviously, I had miscalculated in my cockiness and elitism. He is not a reader of nineteenth-century novels and he apparently thought that "consummate," in this context, was a curse word. I retrieved the letter from the ground, readdressed it, and put it back on the mailbox with a prayer that he would come to get it. I would like to see him and sit down over a good martini and redeem my iniquities—and his. Eventually my letter to him disappeared from my mailbox, but I have received no further word. The silence continues to be annoyingly noisy for me.

My point in relating this hilarious but painful narrative of gross dumbness is that humans—I at least, and most of us I fear—need little provocation for violence of one sort or another. There are things about us that seem to build it in. Even Jesus, despite his nice talk about loving one's enemies, was unacceptably violent in castigating Peter for getting the messianic terminology and vision wrong in what we call The Great Confession (Mark 8:27–33). Jesus was likewise unacceptably violent when he castigated his mother at the wedding at Cana (John 2:3–4), when he cleansed the temple of the money changers (Matthew 21:12–13 and Mark 11:15–17), and when he consigned the Jewish authorities of his day to a place somewhere below Sodom and Gomorrah in his equivalent of Dante's Inferno (Matthew 11:20–24, 12:38–42; Mark 8:11–12; Luke 11:16, 29–32).

A Sinister Problem

However, what I am concerned with here is something that seems to me to go far beyond that simple, though sinister, human inclination to daily personal violence. I am worried about what seems to me to be the societal and institutional violence that has plagued the Western world from its beginnings twenty-five hundred years ago. It is particularly troublesome to consider the role it has played since the rise of Christianity in the first century, the rise of Rabbinic Judaism in the third or fourth century, and the rise of Islam in the seventh century. Let me outline the logic of this concern simply and then tease out its details and implications.

While it is true that the early ethical code articulated in the Hebrew Bible is the *Lex Talionis,* it is more importantly true that the later prophets inveighed against this ethic. In fact, long before the close of that canon, its old barbaric code had been contested by and contrasted with what I will call the code of divine and human grace. Micah 7:18–20, for example, declares, "Who is a God like our God? He pardons iniquity, passes over transgression, will not keep his anger forever, delights in steadfast love. He is faithful to us when we are unfaithful to him. He tramples our iniquities under his feet and casts all our sins into the depths of the sea. Moreover, he has guaranteed this to us through our ancestors from the days of old" (author's translation). The Hebrew Bible is full of enjoinders for humans to do likewise.

It requires little argument to demonstrate that it is this Hebrew ethic of grace that Jesus, and thus the New Testament and the early Christian Movement, highlighted as the ideal code for the new and distinctive Christian life in the world, both for individuals and institutions. This had been the later Hebrew prophets' way and was to be the Christian Way. However, this ethic did not seem to hold up well in the earliest centuries of the church's life, as reflected in the factionalism and heresy trials of early church history. Moreover, this ethic seems to have *completely* failed as soon as the church was empowered by Constantine as the Queen of the

Empire in 313 C.E. Indeed, the conduct of individual Christians, Jews, and Muslims seems generally, throughout the last two thousand years, to have been considerably more grace-filled than that of most of the nations and other institutions of the Western world, which purportedly, in the view of many, were influenced by the rise and presence of Christianity and Rabbinic Judaism.

Let us take the example of the democratic republic of the United States of America. This nation, which has been influenced in discernible ways by the traditions of Judaism and Christianity, as well as Greek thought, thanks largely to the British philosopher John Locke, has readily and regularly resorted to gross violence to solve all of its major social and political problems, as well as its relational impasses, throughout its history. The Revolutionary War, if compared with the Canadian experience of disengagement from the British Empire, was an unnecessary seizure of violence, despite George Washington's Fabian tactics. The Civil War, which killed more than five hundred thousand American men and disabled, physically and psychologically, many more, did not discernibly accomplish anything that the abolitionists were not well on the way to accomplishing by 1860.

Even the secession of seven states would have done little of the damage that the war did, and by 1900 it would have been clear that the division of the union was so disadvantageous to both sides that a reunion would likely have been achieved. A more wholesome resolution of the issues that produced the Civil War would almost certainly have been achieved by 1900 than was achieved by the horrors of the war and Reconstruction. Moreover, as the slightest awareness of history readily suggests, every major war results—in the victorious society—in a sizeable increase in domestic social violence for a couple of postwar generations. It is no accident that after having waged the particular butchery of the Civil War, our society went on to channel those pathological energies into the Indian Wars. The United States did not negotiate for land; instead it employed theft, encroachment, abuse of treaties, and a policy of extermination of the Americans who happened to inhabit this continent before us.

We have always and we still do resort to gross violence as a nation to solve all of our major problems, despite the fact that this nation was established with what we claimed to be a new kind of spirituality and ethic: equality, liberty, justice, and the commonweal. Grace is the one word for that litany of what was supposed to characterize us. What we have proven by our history is the simple fact that we have behaved exactly on the violent model of all the European nations, going all the way back to the violent "Christianization" of the Roman Empire.

The Inherent Dissonance

What is the inherent dissonance in our system that prevents its clearly articulated idealism from ever grounding, perpetuating, or elaborating itself in a reigning role for grace, love, justice, and decency? What prevents us from seeking negotiated solutions to major problems in our Western civilization, and choosing statesmanship over manipulative politics? The urgency of this question is not decreased by the appropriateness of the United States' response to the destruction of the World

Trade Center towers on September 11, 2001. Why is it that, almost every time we perceive ourselves to be in a temporary crisis, we can readily, easily, and automatically *justify* a quick and radical resort to the grossest forms of violence? Why do we opt for violence as the exception to the rule of grace, violence that is always at hand in any emergency—violence that has not been the exception that proves the rule, as the old adage says, but has always functioned *as* the rule?

I want the emphasis in that sentence to fall on the word *justify*. Every decent human being will insist that the ethic of divine and human grace is the only worthy thing for human affairs, but we immediately suspend that rule or ethic as soon as we are faced with a really difficult relationship or negotiation, in our institutions or nation-states, and often in our personal affairs. We immediately *justify* the exception—*violence!*

I believe that this is not just a proclivity for the pragmatic. Most resorts to violence do not constitute the most pragmatic course of action available in any given situation. Barbara Tuchman has brilliantly documented this fact from a survey of Western history, in her fine book *The March of Folly* (Tuchman, 1984). Moreover, we tend in life and politics to allow things to get to a state in which we cannot think of any solution except violence. We do this precisely because we assume at some subconscious level that if things get bad enough it is justifiable to resort to violence. Thus, no great care need be taken in advance to prevent that eventuality from arising. Something is going on in our unconscious—as persons, communities, and nations—that leads us so easily to that *justification*. What is going on down there?

Is it possible that we have, fixed in our individual or collective unconscious, a metaphor that contradicts our conscious commitment to the decency of statesmanship—to the advantages of negotiated conflict resolution and to the redemptive ethic of that grace? Have we forgotten that the Hebrew and Christian prophets fashioned that ethic for us, so that it might stand against the pressures of the barbaric in ourselves and in our communal cultures? I believe that is *exactly* where the problem lies. My logic is simple. Let my explication of it, therefore, be brief.

Violent Religious Metaphors

Out of the Hebrew form of the *Lex Talionis* came a notion of atonement that corrupted the covenantal theology of grace in the Hebrew Bible. This notion of atonement was a shift away from the equation of a gracious God shepherding and caring for his people and committing himself to a perpetual covenant of grace with them. In that early model, the sacrificial system was the presentation to God of the first fruits of flock and field, in grateful response to his covenant of unconditional forgiveness and grace. In that equation God is congenial and good for our health. The relationship between God and humankind is one of pleasant companionship along the pilgrimage of life, albeit in many ways a tragic adventure.

The move away from this grace-equation to the notion of sacrificial atonement was engineered by the Zadokite priests after the decree of Cyrus the Great in 539 C.E., releasing the Israelites from Babylonian exile (Boccaccini, 2002). Their system was a shift toward the interpretation of the sacrificial system as a payment for sin. This was the result of post-exilic Judaism's trying to come to terms with the question of how God could possibly be present in history, given the tragedy of the exile to Babylon. The conclusion, that it could only make sense on the assumption that Israel had desperately sinned and God had sent the foreign nations as his servants to punish God's own rebellious people, led to the supposition that Israel's safety lay in its ability to mollify God with sacrifices that paid for the iniquity of God's people, individually and communally. This was a strategy for balancing the scales of divine justice, or at least resolving God's wrath and his intrapsychic dissonance.

In this model, God is a threat and his wrathful judgment can only be turned aside by sacrificial compensation, a very ancient pagan notion that was exactly the opposite of the Hebrew tradition of the covenant of grace. Pauline theology picked up this metaphor and identified it with the crucifixion of Christ as a propitiation for our sins. This atonement theology, elaborated by the early Christian theologians and epitomized in the juridical atonement theory of Anselm, represented God as sufficiently disturbed by the sinfulness of humanity that he had only two options: destroy us or substitute a sacrifice to pay for our sins. He did the latter; he killed Christ.

This concept has been elaborated in sentimental and well-frosted theological terms, and interpreted so as to make the cross, as substitutionary atonement, appear to be a remarkable act of grace. However, at the unconscious level it is, in fact, a metaphor of the worst kind of violence, infanticide or child sacrifice. The unconscious dynamics of this metaphor have to do with the image or model of God as being so enraged that his only choice is to kill somebody, us or Christ. In the narrative of the expulsion from the Garden of Eden, God cursed his own people (Genesis 3). With the flood of Noah he virtually exterminated them. With the Assyrian and Babylonian exiles he abused them. In the New Testament he crucified a substitute to settle the score (Miles, 1995, 2002), and that is represented in the texts as better behavior on God's part than the earlier Old Testament abusiveness.

That is, the crucifixion of Jesus of Nazareth is an image and a metaphor right at the center of the Master Story of the Western world for the last two thousand years, which radically contradicts the grace ethic it purports to express, and cuts the ethic's taproot by means of the dominant model of solving ultimate problems by resorting to the worst kind of violence. With that kind of metaphor at our center—and associated with the essential behavior of God—how could we possibly hold, in the deep structure of our own unconscious, any notion of ultimate solutions to ultimate questions or crises other than violence? How can we not opt for human solutions that are equivalent to God's kind of violence?

The God in Our Master Story

My father was without exception and by a wide margin the very best man I ever knew. He was the epitome of grace, patience, and self-control. I would like myself a lot better if I were more like him. He would not have spoken sharply to the cyclist, but would have acknowledged the humanness of the situation; and the affair would have ended in friendship and decency. I easily project upon God the image and metaphor that my father has become in my conscious and unconscious mind; and so to me God is the epitome of grace, patience, and decency. There is much in the Bible to illumine and certify this. I could never know or believe in any other kind of God. Any other kind is a monster, given the needs of the likes of us, caught as we are in our human predicament, which is not designed or selected by us. I need the God of Micah 7:18–20. But that is not the God of the Western world at the institutional level. Then who is the God at that level?

Is it possible that—beyond the mayhem that lousy chemistry wreaks upon us through psychologically sick human beings, and beyond the mayhem of our pettiness and fear that life's inadvertencies, such as running over cyclists, bring to the fore—there is at the core of our collective selves a divine monster, who, when he feels a little crazy about something like our human frailty, goes out looking for somebody to murder? Are we stuck with a monster god in our inaccessible psyches, who plays out his devilish game under the flag of our expediencies? Somebody ought to find out.

The American tragedy of September 11, 2001, is not just economic or political. It is not just the insupportable psycho-spiritual anguish about the death of thousands of people at the hands of terrorists, together with the immense grief and loss of the survivors and the families of the dead. All that is sufficiently overwhelming by itself. The real depth of the tragedy lies in the fact that a community of human beings, pseudo-Islamic fundamentalists, perpetrated this immense disaster upon another community of innocent humans, and did it under the banner of a religious metaphor: *jihad.* The tragedy of that terrorism is severe enough at the physical and material level to gain global attention and concern. However, the real tragedy of violence lies in the fact that it is a state of the soul or psyche, conditioned and twisted by specific religious archetypes. Those terrorists apparently truly believed that their action was an execution of the will and intention of God and that they would receive "exceedingly great reward."

The noted Roman Catholic scholar, René Girard, addressed at length and in depth the question of the metaphors and archetypes of violence in the Master Stories of the great religions. He analyzed the manner in which they shape human culture (Girard, 1987; see also Williams, 1996). It is his contention that murder of a key symbolic figure or group has been a crucial element in establishing and maintaining sociocultural stability since the beginning of human life.

Girard employs the ancient Greek term so important to Aristotle, *mimesis*, as the construct by which to explicate his theory. He claims that the natural human process of modeling on key historic figures or past generations produces competition regarding who in the community is most true to the ancient or historic model or tradition being remembered and celebrated. From this competition, judgments are made regarding who is good and who is bad. This mimetic and competitive process eventually becomes institutionalized in the structures of dogmas, orthodoxies, codes of social control, and rituals. Those who do not achieve well or conform are progressively valued negatively. Those who exceed the performance level of the masses may pose a threat and need to be leveled to the mean or be negatively valued as well. As these perceptions harden, the process eventually arrives at the point at which the under-performer, the nonconformist (or the threatening super-achiever), and the heretic must be eliminated. Societal justification of the murder of this singled-out person or group inevitably follows.

There are a number of implications one might draw from or use to build upon Girard's model. Let us briefly explore a few of these. The process of societal justification, mentioned above, may take the form of remembering the eliminated figure as victim of his own evil, thus as a symbol of the purification of the society; or as the heroic agent who has given his life for society's redemption. The decision between the two is a deep-structure psychodynamic decision shaped by the unconscious archetypes that prevail in the society and the Master Story metaphors that dominate the community. Which of those two roles is the one adopted in any given case depends upon which metaphor the society most needs at the time and the degree of ambiguity within the society regarding the character and quality of the person sacrificed.

Girard believed that human civilization is the product of this violent action that is designed to control the inevitable violence of the rivalry inherent in mimetic process. Thus, in the early chapters of Genesis, Cain's murder of Abel focuses and unleashes the energy for the construction of cities, industry, arts, crafts, and ordered, enriched human society. Only those who take the victim's side report this as evil. Girard contends that from the outset the mimetic process of chaotic rivalry requires a reduction of dissonance. In the Genesis narrative, this dissonance is radically reduced with one definitive act focused upon Abel, the counterforce of progress. He is murdered.

Ithamar Gruenwald, in his forthcoming work on ritual theory in cultural development, suggests that it is not insignificant that Abel is a nomadic shepherd and Cain an agrarian cultivator of fixed spaces who moves from there to urban life. Gruenwald notes that this dissonance between the idealization of the nomadic shepherd and the agrarian-urban persists throughout the Hebrew Bible and can be seen clearly in the New Testament as well. Eventually the biblical metaphor settles down as a picture of chronic tension between the pastoral-agrarian images and the urban vision. The scriptures narrate the story from the side of the victim and depict the ideal people as the remnant that harks back to the ancient nomadic model of the shepherd, those close to the earth and heavily dependent upon God moment by moment, despite the fact that the world has long since permanently passed them by in its progress from the Garden (Genesis 3) to the idealized city (Revelations 22).

Progressively the dissonance indicated in the story of Cain and Abel developed into a tension and lethal rivalry between the urban and pastoral-agrarian Israelites. This persistent dissonance played an important part in much of the history of Israel recorded in the Bible, including the conflict between the urbanized exiles returning from captivity and "the people of the land" in the narratives about the release from Babylon. Thus, among many other things, this set of scriptural metaphors and their intrinsic tensions may have contributed significantly to the disappearance of the royal line of David during the fifth century B.C.E.

Three Pillars of Violence

Girard saw three crucial elements in the mimetic process of employing violence to reduce dissonance in a society and to maintain order and peace in the face of the natural tendency to dissonance, chaos, and disorder. The first is the codification of control structures or prohibitions; the second is the creation of rituals for enacting both the event of redemptive violence and the patterns of required conformity within the society; and the third is the killing of the scapegoat. Regarding the second element, Weaver says,

> These rituals—games, dramas, animal sacrifices—provide approved outlets for expression of mimetic rivalry within a culture, and thus limit the actual violence perpetrated. While prohibitions and ritual appear as opposites—prohibition versus acting out—their function is the same. They both limit mimetic violence and contribute to the maintenance of order. But eventually a mimetic crisis develops, when prohibitions and rituals can no longer control rivalry and maintain order. At this point, the third pillar of culture and religion comes into play, the killing of a scapegoat. As problems mount, a search begins for an individual (or a group) to blame for the problem. The chosen victim must be marginal to the society as a whole and lack the ability to retaliate or seek revenge. On this scapegoat is then fixed the blame for the crisis. Because it is really believed that the scapegoat has caused the crisis, violence ceases for a time following the removal—the murder—of the scapegoat, and it seems that violence brings peace. To maintain order, the community formed on the basis of murdering the scapegoat continues to reenact that formative event through sacred rituals and by the substitution of "new victims for the original victim, in order to assure the maintenance of that miraculous peace." (Weaver, 2001, p. 47. The quotation is from Girard, 1987, p. 103)

Anyone familiar with anthropological research or with ancient mythology will realize, of course, that the scapegoat story is even more universal in the cultures of history than the narrative of the lost continent of Atlantis. Weaver summarizes the point concisely.

> The founding events of societies—the murders on which they are founded—are portrayed in myths, which contain enough historical data to locate the origins in history. At the same time, the function of the myth is to disguise the founding murder so that it does not appear as murder. The story of origins is always told from the perspective of the majority, ruling order, which enables the majority to hide the innocence of the scapegoat victim and to affix blame to it for society's problems. Removing the scapegoat then takes on the appearance of a necessary and noble deed that is done in order to preserve the society.

Killing the scapegoat becomes not an act of murder but an act of salvation. Life appears to come from death. Exposing the innocence of the victim would reveal the deed as murder, and thus undercut its efficacy as a saving event. Thus the function of ritual and of religion is to limit the violence to a single victim or single group of victims, while simultaneously disguising the fact that it is a ritual murder and providing transcendent validation of the process. (pp. 47–48)

Psychodynamics of Violence

It seems clear that within Girard's model lies a good deal of the conflict theory of Jung and Freud, as well as the fulfillment theory of Adler (Freud, 1997; see also Gay, 1988, 1993). Freud seems to have been substantially dependent upon the brief but brilliant work of a Russian psychoanalyst, Sabina Spielrein, a former student and mistress of Jung. Spielrein wrote a definitive paper in 1911 that spelled out the contours of the foundations for theories of violence as resolution of intrapsychic dissonance. It was published as "Die Destruktion als Ursache des Werdens" in the *Jahrbuch für psychoanalytische und psychopathologische Forschungen* (Spielrein, 1912). In this publication she speculated on the dynamic processes of destructive impulses contained in sexual drives, with the claim that here lie the essence and wellspring of the entire process that leads to the social necessity of violence as resolution of mimetic dissonance.

Jungian theory suggests that individuation, maturation, and wholeness in personality development require reduction of intrapsychic conflict or dissonance. Such dissonance is inherent and inevitable in the processes of birth and coping. Its reduction depends upon externalizing—acting out—the internal conflict, really or symbolically. The polarities within us, such as those between our anima and animus, must be synthesized. If they are not adequately synthesized, or are resolved in a pathological direction or manner, the dialectical process becomes destructive. In Jungian terms the atonement, or the killing of the scapegoat, is a dialectical synthesis of these polarities—for example, between justice and mercy, or between animus and anima, at the deep structure level. Conflict and violence are at the core of Jung's framework (Jung, 1997; see also Fierz, 1991; Hogenson, 1983; Homans, 1979; Jung, 1957, 1963; Palmer, 1997; Rollins, 1983).

Adler, in his fulfillment theory, illumines Jung's model by pointing out that this "constructive violence" or scapegoating is meant to end destructive violence in society by transforming violence itself into an act of grace for the community (Miles, 2002). Adler contends that the act of symbolic violence is designed to disarm the very ideologies that create the dissonance and conflict in the first place. For these theorists, the absence of conflict and of its violent externalization, or aggressive ritual sublimation, sterilizes a person, leaving that person and society in an unresolved and potentially chaos-inducing state.

Weaver acknowledges the nature of this violent scapegoat dynamic in human existence and argues, as do Gustav Aulen and J. Christiaan Beker, that the metaphor of violence at the center of the Master Story of Western tradition, namely, God's crucifixion of his Son, is designed to represent an act of grace, the purpose of which is to disarm the powers of the violent evil inherent in human persons and society (Aulen, 1969; Beker, 1980, 1982; see also Wink, 1984, 1986, 1992). However that may seem in idealistic models of theology or psychoanalysis, the case is that the disarming has failed. Moreover, the entire construct that violence quells violence is, on the face of it, absurd, whether theologized or psychoanalyzed. The violence that is supposed to afford a resolution of the mimetic competition and its consequent social dissonance provides a temporary release of the destructive human energies, at best.

Even a superficial look at the sweep of history, to say nothing of a profound study of it, informs one immediately that violence breeds violence and does not quell it. The most common and most universally agreed upon reality of history is the fact that quelling violence and social or intrapsychic dissonance by a violent or physically aggressive action that victimizes a person or a people as scapegoat merely breeds a festering and irrepressible counterforce and ferment. This eventually manifests itself in another revolution. This is true and obvious whether the conflict is adolescent individuation and disengagement from parents, or civil war, or international strife.

Jihad means struggle against evil. Humane Muslims have long interpreted this to mean the human personal struggle against the counterproductive and self-defeating forces that lie within our inner selves. However, Mohammed himself, in the process of establishing his hegemony in Arabia, at the outset called for *jihad* as a military struggle in which anyone who died in the heroic cause could be assured of the reward of immediate translation to heaven. This metaphor created an authoritative model identified with the prophet himself. There can be no doubt that it is this metaphor, which has been raised to the level of an unconscious archetype in Muslim culture, that drives the al-Qaeda terrorists in their passion to destroy the secularized Western world.

The behavior that struck down the World Trade Center towers is little different in nature, motive, spirit, and method from the Israeli extermination of the Canaanites in the biblical narrative in the Book of Joshua. Nor does it differ significantly, in any of these categories, from the Christian Crusades of the High Middle Ages. All three of these great religions of the world have at their core a religious metaphor grown into a psychological archetype that legitimates violence in the grossest imaginable forms, justifying it on the grounds of divine order and behavior.

CONCLUSION

Undoubtedly, it would be difficult to persuade the general human community, much less the perpetrators of the specific gross tragedies of human history, that their motives are unconscious and their drives are moved and shaped by a divine metaphor that works like a monster deity at unrevealed levels of their psyches.

Most of us are certain of what we are doing and confident that we know why we are doing it. Of course, this is almost never so. It is never true to the degree of clarity or transparency that we constantly and universally believe and claim.

Psychoanalytic theories have taught us a crucial thing about our role in what John F. Kennedy called "this tragic adventure" of human existence. They have given us the clue to the sources and forces at play in our psyches and societies that make violence inevitable. What their model fails to do is to provide a mechanism for exorcising the monster deity from the center of our souls or selves, an achievement that is forever unlikely as long as the function of that monster is constantly reinforced by the cultural metaphors of radical violence at the center of our Master Stories.

Until we are ready to analyze those Master Stories and eradicate from them their violent core metaphors, it is impossible for us to develop at the unconscious level—where this action is—warrantable nonviolent alternatives for our strategies in conflict resolution. Warrantable alternatives are required that carry more and better authority than we now receive automatically from the destructive metaphors of violent divine behavior that inhabit the dark caves of our individual and collective unconscious. We will never be able to accede to that better authority until we can substitute constructive metaphors for violent ones and exchange manipulative power struggles for true democracy. We cannot gain ground here until we are ready for the risks of authentic mutual acceptance of each other's needs and claims. That requires taking the time to hear and negotiate those needs and claims in good faith and, thus, to give up the notion that narcissism and justice are preeminent over grace and mercy.

This will not happen until we eliminate from our framework of thought the unconscious perceptions that atonement is a phenomenon necessary for psychosocial equanimity and transcend the notion that life is a *quid pro quo* contest. These destructive structures cannot be eradicated as long as the unconscious god in our psyches is a violent monster who cannot achieve intrapsychic stasis without killing someone, even "his beloved son."

REFERENCES

Aulen, G. (1969). *Christus Victor: An historical study of the three main types of the idea of atonement* (A. G. Herbert, Trans.). New York: Macmillan.

Beker, J. C. (1980). *Paul the Apostle: The triumph of God in life and thought.* Philadelphia: Fortress.

Beker, J. C. (1982). *Paul's apocalyptic gospel: The coming triumph of God.* Philadelphia: Fortress.

Bettelheim, B. (1984). *Freud and man's soul.* New York: Random House-Vintage.

Boccaccini, G. (2002). *Roots of rabbinic Judaism, an intellectual history, from Ezekiel to Daniel.* Grand Rapids, MI: Eerdmans.

Cox, D. (1959). *Jung and St. Paul.* New York: Association Press.

Fierz, H. K. (1991). *Jungian psychiatry.* Einsiedeln, Switzerland: Daimon Verlag.

Freud, S. (1997). *Selected writings.* New York: Book of the Month Club.

Gay, P. (1984). *The bourgeois experience: Victoria to Freud: Vol. I, Education of the senses.* New York: Norton.

Gay, P. (1986). *The bourgeois experience: Victoria to Freud: Vol. II, The tender passion.* New York: Norton.

Gay, P. (1988). *Freud, a life for our time.* New York: Norton.

Gay, P. (1993). *The bourgeois experience: Victoria to Freud: Vol. III, The cultivation of hatred.* New York: Norton.

Gay, V. P. (1983). *Reading Freud: Psychology, neurosis, and religion.* Chico, CA: Scholars Press.

Girard, R. (1987). *Things hidden since the foundation of the world.* (S. Bann & M. Metter, Trans.). Stanford, CA: Stanford University Press.

Gruenwald, I. (in press). *Rituals and ritual theory in Ancient Israel.* Leiden, Netherlands: Brill.

Guirdham, A. (1962). *Christ and Freud.* New York: Collier.

Hogenson, G. B. (1983). *Jung's struggle with Freud.* Notre Dame, IN: University of Notre Dame.

Homans, P. (1979). *Jung in context, modernity and the making of psychology.* Chicago: University of Chicago.

Jung, C. G. (1963). *Psychology and religion.* New Haven, CT: Yale University Press. (Original work published 1938)

Jung, C. G. (1957). *The undiscovered self.* (R. F. C. Hull, Trans.). Boston: Little, Brown.

Jung, C. G. (1997). *Selected writings.* New York: Book of the Month Club.

Kung, H. (1979). *Freud and the problem of God.* New Haven, CT: Yale University Press.

Miles, J. (1995). *Christ, a crisis in the life of God.* New York: Knopf.

Miles, J. (2002). *God, a biography.* New York: Knopf.

Palmer, M. (1997). *Freud and Jung on religion.* New York: Routledge.

Rollins, W. G. (1983). *Jung and the Bible.* Atlanta: John Knox.

Scharfenberg, J. (1988). *Sigmund Freud and his critique of religion.* Philadelphia: Fortress.

Slusser, G. H. (1986). *From Jung to Jesus, myth and consciousness in the New Testament.* Atlanta: John Knox.

Spielrein, S. (1912). Die destruktion als ursache des werdens. In *Jahrbuch für psychoanalytische und psychopathologische Forschungen, IV,* 465–503.

Tuchman, B. (1984). *The march of folly.* New York: Knopf.

Weaver, J. D. (2001). *The non-violent atonement.* Grand Rapids, MI: Eerdmans.

Williams, J. G. (Ed.). (1996). *The Girard reader.* New York: Crossroad.

Wilmer, H. A. (1994). *Understandable Jung, the personal side of Jungian psychology.* Wilmette, IL: Chiron Publications.

Wink, W. (1984). *Naming the powers: The language of power in the New Testament, The powers, Vol. 1.* Philadelphia: Fortress.

Wink, W. (1986). *Unmasking the powers: The invisible forces that determine human existence, The powers, Vol. 2.* Philadelphia: Fortress.

Wink, W. (1992). *Engaging the powers: Discernment and resistance in a world of domination, The powers, Vol. 3.* Minneapolis: Fortress.

7

Rebirth and Death: The Violent Potential of Apocalyptic Dreams

Benjamin Beit-Hallahmi

The impetus for the writing of this chapter is a specific historical case, and the general phenomenon of religion-related violence (Beit-Hallahmi, 2001b). My argument is that while the phenomenon is extremely complex and has to be studied with the help of various disciplines, it can be somewhat elucidated through explanations informed by a psychodynamic understanding of religion. This means looking at the paradoxical connection between dreams of salvation and dreams of violence. We will need to ask why religious love and devotion are tied to hate and destruction. Our perspective will be theoretically individualistic, but will mostly examine the reality of religious groups. Our universe of content is that of religious visions of salvation and destruction. We will look first at dreams and fantasies, while other approaches will seek to examine concrete action.

What we are looking at is the amazing association of miraculous transformations and great disasters, all created by human fantasy. We are going to look at dreams of collective rebirth, together with dreams and realities of individual rebirth, because we think that the mystery of rebirth gone wrong may be related to that of rebirth gone right and well. Successful rebirth is a mystery and a miracle. We must wonder about the internal dynamics of each such case of success, just as we must wonder about failures. What is the secret of balance and growth, in the face of deprivations and difficulties, for both individuals and groups? Cases of rebirth gone tragically wrong have come to our attention in recent years. They include the Peoples Temple, Branch Davidians, Aum Shinrikyo, the Solar Temple, and Heaven's Gate. Each case in unique. What is involved in all cases is an authoritarian leadership that sweeps the members into a cycle of violence. Where does the violence come from in these groups? How does the balance fail?

The terms apocalyptic, millenarian, and end-of-times will be used interchangeably in this chapter. End-of-times fantasies are of three kinds. There are those that are most general and most common, promising world rebirth sometime in the future. There are those promised very soon, and there are those rare cases where a date is specified. Norman Cohn defined millenarianism as "An ideology characterizing religious groups that promises imminent collective salvation for the faithful in an earthly paradise that will rise following an apocalyptic destruction ordained by the gods" (Cohn, 1970, p. 13). Ostow (1986, 1988) stated that apocalyptic fantasies consist of two elements: first, the idea that the world will be destroyed, and second, that a remnant of humanity will be rescued from the catastrophe. It is interesting to note that when the ideological content of twentieth-century fascism was being investigated by Adorno et al. (1950), the idea of world destruction was found to be a component. The Adorno et al. F scale included the following item: "It is possible that wars and social troubles will be ended once and for all by an earthquake or flood that will destroy the whole world." In this fascist vision there is no promise of rebirth, but a certainty of destruction, which brings to mind the way the three fascist regimes of Germany, Japan, and Italy ended.

We will present concrete examples of individual and collective transformations, taken from the contemporary world of salvation movements. Some of those involve growth and integration, others extreme violence. Do they have something in common? We are going to look at a progression of cases, from individual success through salvation, to group success, and then to group failure, violence, and tragedy. We will observe cases in which eschatological dreams are held central, and then we will see attempts to make them a reality through violence.

The real issue and the real mystery is why and how, following specific forms of rebirth, the psychological balance is disrupted and lost, and what solutions are sought and reached in an attempt to reestablish balance. Our most serious fear is that of the disintegration of the self, and it is clear that dreams of the coming end and the impending victory of justice and good keep the self moving on. There are probably many possible solutions, but we are interested here in those involving violent fantasies, as in the case of Brahma Kumaris, and in those involving violent acts, as in the case of Heaven's Gate and Aum Shinrikyo.

CONCEPTUAL TOOLBOX

In this chapter, we offer interpretations, speculations, and hypotheses, and our theoretical framework is largely that of psychoanalysis. Psychoanalytic writings can be recognized through their use of a common vocabulary that has become, over the years, part of everyday intellectual discourse: conscious and unconscious, id, ego, super-ego, neuroses, anxiety, and defense mechanisms. What is psychoanalytic theory? We can recognize it either through its vocabulary (to some, its "jargon") or through its bibliographic ancestry, that is, its references. In terms of interpretive tactics, what everybody knows is that psychoanalysis tells us that we need to look beneath the surface, because behind happy and loving faces sometimes there lurk madness and violence.

Two assumptions were suggested by Freud himself (1915/1916) to characterize his approach. The first assumption is that all psychic processes are strictly determined (there are no accidents, chance events, or miracles); the second is that unconscious mental processes exist, and exert significant influences on behavior. These unconscious forces shape much of the individual's emotional and interpersonal experiences. We all are ready to admit momentary, fleeting, childish, irrational thoughts, as in hypnagogic experiences. These experiences are marginal. Psychoanalysis claims that they may be more than that, and that unconscious processes are possibly the main determinants of observable behavior.

The emphasis on the unconscious part of the personality can be summed up as follows:

1. Part of the personality is unconscious, and it is quite influential.

2. The unconscious is the repository of significant early experience.

3. In the adult, unconscious ideas are often projected, creating distortions of reality, especially interpersonal reality.

Primary process, which rules the deeper, unconscious, layers of the personality, obeys the pleasure principle, starting with the baby's attempt at achieving a hallucinated reality of the desired object. The secondary process obeys the reality principle, and involves the postponement of immediate gratification and the testing of imaginary ideas against the real world. Psychoanalysis is a theory of struggle, conflict, and compromise, assuming the dynamic nature of human behavior, always resulting from conflict and change. Additional assumptions deal with over-determination and the multiple functions of behavior. The over-determination assumption states that any segment of behavior may have many preceding causes. This is tied to a developmental, or historical, emphasis, leading us to seek first causes in any individual's personal history and unique experiences. The psychoanalytic view of human motivation is often regarded as utterly pessimistic. Judging by their conscious and unconscious drives, humans are nasty and brutish, aggressive, infantile, and libido-driven. However, beyond this bleak picture of immorality and even perversity lies the capacity for sublimation, love, and culture.

Psychoanalysis is a theory of reality distortion. The psychoanalytic view of maladaptive behavior emphasizes its continuity with adaptive behavior, and leads to viewing pathology as a useful analogy of cultural structures. Psychoanalysis assumes the psychic unity of mankind, which is significant when we deal with cultural traditions. Universality is found at the most basic level of body, birth, sex, and death.

Psychoanalytic approaches of all theoretical stripes (classical, ego-psychological, and object relations) claim universal, transcultural, and a-historical validity. Universal themes in religious fantasies are the result and reflection of the psychic unity of mankind, which in turn is the consequence of common psychological structures and common early experiences, shared by all of mankind. The same basic psychological processes and complexes are expressed in individual products (dreams, stories, or daydreams) and in cultural products (art, literature, folklore, wit, religion, law, or science), because these complexes are basic and central to human experience.

What unites most strands of psychoanalytic theory is the governing metaphor of conflict. Beyond visible conflicts, invisible ones are found, even if it's hard to locate them. The family, as the locus of love and devotion, is actually a battlefield, but it only reflects the reality of both individual souls and human society as a whole. This is the source of what has to be called the tragic dimension in psychoanalytic literature, a deep recognition of human limitations and a realistic approach to one's chances of achieving happiness.

Conversion experiences start with conversion dreams. Salvation stories appear in response to dreams of a new self, a new society, a new world. It is with the help of this tradition that we approach the phenomenon of the religious imagination, and the inevitable collisions between religious fantasies and reality. The phenomenon of fantasies about self-transformation and world-transformation, which is so common among humans, plays a major role in the history of religious movements. Here we are trying to clarify its relationship to violence.

Successful rebirth means finding a way to handle aggression by directing it toward an ideal outlet, real or imaginary. The question is indeed why should a rebirth always be tied to a total destruction?

Our hypothesis is that rebirth is always tied to imagined death and violence, and that handling these fantasies is the real problem that often upsets the precarious balance in the born-again. Because the conversion solution is not truly balanced, aggression will break through.

Every successful case of individual rebirth is the result of an internal truce among opposing personality elements. One possible interpretation assumes that in conversion we see what is called a "super-ego victory" (Beit-Hallahmi, 1977; Wittenberg, 1968). An internal conflict between the conscious ego-ideal and the unconscious, archaic, parental introject is won by the latter. The child becomes more parental, and this often happens in post-adolescence, as the child grows older.

Another interpretation of successful conversion uses the concept of moral masochism (Freud, 1916). According to classical psychoanalysis, the super-ego is formed as sadistic impulses directed at the parent are recoiled and internalized. Then the super-ego, parentally derived, commands self-effacement, if not self-sacrifice, as the punishment for aggressive fantasies. In moral masochism, the super-ego is satisfied through submission and humiliation. The outer peace and happiness observed in many converts is the result of this final peace between ego and super-ego, which releases all the energy that was put into the conflict for productive use. This may be the source of many positive, altruistic behaviors. The yearning for peace and wholeness is met by religion through the internal peace between super-ego and ego. At the conscious level this is experienced as acceptance by God or Jesus, forgiveness and love, reported by converts ever since Saint Augustine of Hippo. Freud (1928) suggested that what is achieved through super-ego victory is a reconciliation with one's father and with all paternal authorities, including father gods. We forgive our parents and are forgiven by them in turn. Of course, this happens in fantasy, and we are not talking of real fathers but imagined ones, consciously and unconsciously.

Another possible explanation is that the convert has gone through the internalizing of a loved and loving imaginary object, which then supports the whole personality system. This internalized object may serve as a new super-ego, supplying the ego with a control system, which has been missing, and making possible a real control of destructive impulses. A similar process may take place in secular psychotherapy. Within a slightly different framework, Fauteux (1981) suggested that early infancy splitting of the mother into good/bad object operates in converts who reach a state of complete euphoria, denying negative impulses and negative realities, which are bound to resurface nevertheless.

What should we make of all these different and sometimes contradictory speculations? Only the realization that in cases of true self-transcendence, something important and far-reaching must be going on beneath the surface. The process is one of accepting authority, loving authority, and internalizing a loving and supportive, (but still demanding) authority. What happens in these conversion miracles is an experience of love, both giving and receiving of love. On a conscious level, this is the unconditional (or maybe conditional) love of God, and Saint Augustine has already reported on that. On an unconscious level, it is the unconditional love of the parent. The conversion experience has been viewed as ego-enhancing. Illusions and delusions may be helpful, up to a point, energizing a weak ego through narcissistic hopes.

Behind the explicit, outspoken fantasy of a new self or a new world there lie unspoken processes, which are always parallel to those on the surface. And the meaning of our fantasies about the self may not be far from that of our vision for the whole world. For in our parallel, primary-process thinking, we are the world. The invention of the new self may involve only magical gestures, but it may involve some actions as well.

DREAMS OF THE REBORN SELF

An examination of apocalyptic dreams should start with the individual search for security and wholeness and with the general idea of self-transformation. Susan Sontag, in an interview on the BBC, on May 22, 2000, said that the American dream is to reinvent yourself, be born again; but this is not just an American idea, it is a universal modern dream, and possibly a universal human dream. The broadest frame of reference we can use is the common human phenomenon of attempts to escape and transcend destiny and identity. I include here any attempt to redefine biography and identity against "objective" conditions defining that identity. Such attempts at rebirth, at identity change through private salvation, may be quite common in certain historical situations (Beit-Hallahmi, 1992). We may speak about a private utopia, as collective utopias are less and less in vogue. Dreams and actual attempts at escape and rejuvenation should be examined on the basis of context, content, or consequences, and point to a whole range of possibilities. The fantasy of escaping one's destiny, the dream of identity change, is all too human. So many people see their lives so far as a first draft. We all dream of being of becoming somebody else and something else, breaking with our destiny. This is the dream of private (and collective) salvation. More or less often, we feel "I am stuck in this life situation but I should be somewhere else."

Edouard Zarifian, in his book *Les Jardiniers de la Folie* (1988), has written about the common escape fantasy of middle-aged men, who want to give up their identities and their histories in favor of a new existence. Umberto Gallini of Milan, Italy, in 1991 opened the Alleanza Nazionale per l'Espatrio Felice, a service for individuals who wish to disappear from the real world and start a new life under a new identity. His clients have been middle-aged men who want to leave behind families and obligations. Mr. Gallini arranges for escapes to the Third World (Madagascar) with a new identity, provided you have $100,000 in savings. Of course, private salvation is a minority option. Most of us do not dare to escape from destiny in such ways and will continue to cope collectively, normatively, and realistically, possibly in quiet desperation.

In a preliminary study of escape fantasies, I have constructed a questionnaire that includes options for alternative careers and truly alternative identities ("I can imagine myself as a Tibetan monk"; "I can imagine myself as a rock singer"; "I can imagine myself as a heroin addict"). My students' favorite alternative life was "I can imagine myself winning the Nobel Prize in literature." These are fantasies without obligations, of course, but conversions are for real. Part of our own salvation fantasies are our fantasies about converts. We envy their courage to take such a step, to change in the midst of crisis, and we envy their enthusiasm, self-confidence, optimism, "wholeness," and strong convictions, once they have taken this step.

Conversions are dramatic turning points in life, tied to external or internal events (personality or trauma) leading to the reassessment of one's life, then identity change, and the "biographical break" with the past. It is higher self-esteem, or self-love, which allows us to define the new identity. During times of stress and crisis, as during times of individual distress, there is a regression to "artistic," religious, or magical ways of thinking. When realistic coping fails, magical thinking takes over. When realistic coping seems to be failing or futile, individuals may turn to magical or religious ways of coping. When all hope is lost, these ways of coping do seem worthwhile.

Magical gestures that aim at reaching a conscious break with the past and the shedding of one's identity include name changes, body changes, and "sex change." These magical or symbolic gestures are not usually sufficient for a real metamorphosis in personality. A name change does not lead to personality change, and a new nose does not do it either. Even a "sex change" often fails to bring about happiness, and these intentional scripts often end in disappointment. In many religious traditions, pilgrimage is the magical route to achieving private salvation and healing. Pilgrimage is an institutionalized way of reaching ". . . the inward transformation of spirit and personality" (Turner, 1973, p. 214). This miracle of rebirth through conversion has been described in another context: "The true believer who becomes a Muslim casts off at last his old self and takes on a new identity. He changes his name, his religion, his homeland, his 'natural' language, his moral and cultural values, his very purpose in living. He is no longer a Negro, so long despised by the white man that he has come almost to despise himself. Now he is a Black Man—divine, ruler of the universe, different only in degree from Allah himself. He is no longer discontent and baffled, harried by social obloquy and a gnawing sense of personal inadequacy. Now he is a Muslim, bearing in himself the power of the Black Nation and its glorious destiny" (Lincoln, 1961, pp. 108–109).

SUCCESSFUL REBIRTH

Every religion tells us stories of miracles and transformations. For most people, they remain stories about events that happened long ago and far away. For others, they become part of their own personal history, which they are ready to share with us. These cases of rebirth should command our most serious attention, because what they represent are indeed immensely positive transformations, which are impossible under any other conditions. The lame do not start walking, and the blind do not enjoy the sweet light of day; these miracles do not often happen. But the psychologically lame, the self-destructive and desperate, sometimes emerge from darkness and belie everything that happened earlier in their lives.

In all conversion stories a past of doubt and error is transformed into a present of wholeness in one great moment of insight and certainty. This is a new birth, leading to a new life. And the new birth often follows reaching the lowest depths of despair, and consists of ". . . an unexpected life succeeding upon death . . . the deathlike terminating of certain mental processes . . . that run to failure, and in some individuals . . . eventuate in despair" (James, 1943, p. 303). And the new birth creates a wider belief in ". . . a world in which all is well, in spite of certain forms of death, indeed because of certain forms of death—death of hope, death of strength . . ." (James, 1943, p. 305).

Our conceptual model views the source of self-reported rebirth in internal, conscious and unconscious conflicts. These conflicts are solved and a balance is reached through an attachment to a set of beliefs (delusional), specific ritual acts, changes in everyday behavior and functioning, and support by a group structure. The problem with psychological rebirth is its inherent instability. Real transformation is hard to come by. The illusion of rebirth may lead to good outcomes, but it is often insufficient to maintain balance inside a personality system that is long beset by disharmonies and imbalances. This is clear when a variety of purely secular strategies, from psychotherapy to plastic surgery, are followed on the road to self-transformation.

Testimonials of conversion tell us of a miraculous transformation, from darkness to a great light, from being lost to being found. There is a sharp contrast between earlier suffering and current improvements. The conversion narrative always includes a wide gap between the past and the present, between corruption and redemption. The power of transformation through enlightenment is proven through this gap.

To illustrate the phenomenon of psychological rebirth, we are going to present a successful, almost perfect, case, the story of H. (Beit-Hallahmi, 1992). This is a happy tale, a case in which the trauma of war is overcome through self-transformation, and no violence is contemplated. H., sitting across the table from me, as he told me his story in 1983, was unusually handsome, confident in his manner, and articulate. He was a chain-smoker, and looked more like an athlete than like the academic that he was. H. really wanted to tell me the story of his individual salvation, his conversion from great misery to great happiness, a metamorphosis that only a few may know. His life was transformed in an instant of revelation, and he was telling me about that instant. Ten years before our meeting, in October 1973, he was wounded in battle, and his injuries, while not serious, left him handicapped psychologically and physically. He simply could not do anything, could not study or work. And so he stayed home, preoccupied with his narrowing world, considering ways of getting out of his predicament, including suicide. Then, one day, in one instant of revelation, he realized that there was an answer. It was in turning to the spiritual world, which existed, invisible, above and beyond our obvious material world on earth. This world is only an illusion. It is the spirit world that determines what happens here, in the material one, through positive and negative energies. Death just means that the soul moves on. In that instant, his physical and psychological sufferings ended. He became committed to relations with the spiritual creatures inhabiting the invisible world and later formally joined one of the new religions.

Now, he was no longer a member of that group, but held to a combination of Hindu and Jewish beliefs. The other dimension of living, that of the eternal soul, colored his perceptions of others and of his own experiences. He related to people on the basis of their spirituality. Some people were recognized as having "spiritual connections" with the invisible world. Others were judged inferior, lacking in spirituality. Events in this world were determined by spiritual "forces" and "energies." Political and ideological changes were the result of positive and negative "energies," which could be stored and used over time. Thus, there had been negative political developments in Israel since the 1967 war, caused by the release of enormous negative energy, stored for centuries around the Wailing Wall in Jerusalem. These energies, left there by successive generations of praying and mourning Jews, who came to the Wall to bewail their bitter fate, were let loose when structures around the Wall were torn down in June 1967 by the Israeli government. It would take time until the negative energies dissipated. On the whole, however, things in the Middle East were moving in a peaceful direction, as positive energies were taking over. He believed that death was not such a terrible thing, because it meant a liberation of the soul from its material shackles, but suffering, which often precedes death, is a problem. His attitude toward war was ambivalent, therefore, because war brought liberation to some souls, but suffering to others. While he was no longer a member of a recognized group or a movement, he met regularly with spiritual teachers, whose identities had to be kept secret. Occult knowledge was an important part of his life, but it was not shared with his academic colleagues. Such knowledge could be shared only with the saved and the enlightened. What he told me was more in the way of a personal odyssey, a miraculous transformation, but he was not sure that I could appreciate the fine points of his occult observations of people and events.

H. was really able to overcome the weakness of his own body and his own soul, and to give birth to a new self. Following a year of dark paralysis, he emerged to become a fully functioning member of society. Eventually, he became a well-known "spiritual teacher" himself, got married, had children, and made a living. Almost thirty years after his war trauma, he can be judged an impressive story of self-transformation. Actually, H. is quite a narcissist, but a dose of narcissism may be good for you, especially when faced with a trauma as H. once was.

CONCEPTUAL INTERLUDE

The presentation of this case is necessary and important because it represents all the true believers (and especially leaders) that we are going to encounter further on as we look at various movements and their visions. The case of H. represents successful rebirth with a perfect balance. Similar individual cases may be easily found, but when we move to the group level, achieving balance is obviously much harder. Many groups of reborn individuals run into trouble sooner or later. This perfect case may still seem problematic to some. First, because of H.'s beliefs and values, which may seem immoral. But, at another level, a psychological analysis may direct us to note that cases of rebirth actually represent a way of expressing hostility toward one's parents. In terms of individual and family dynamics, every identity change is a rebellion against one's parents, who usually created the earlier identity, and against one's past. When a young individual, who grew up in the average family, joins a new religion, he is declaring a revolt against his parents. He may rebel also through finding a new, better parent in his secular psychotherapist, and psychotherapists are always better parents. The message of a child's conversion is often one of denouncing parental hypocrisy and shallowness. On a collective, generational level, finding new identities is a total ideological rebellion. The new religious identities constitute in many cases a rejection of the faith of the parents, and of the parents' everyday lifestyle.

At the same time, the rebellion against the parents may also mean the assumption of the parental role.

One great insight we were led to by classical psychoanalysis is that the child is totally confused by the notion of parenthood and family relations. Learning that we have two parents and that father and mother are also man and wife is beyond the child's comprehension at first blush. This oedipal confusion stays with all of us forever, processed, accepted, and sometimes denied. The denial of birth is no less important than the denial of death in the making of cultural fantasies. Both lead to much psychic tension, and sometimes to real violence.

The idea of individual rebirth and world rebirth is a denial of the reality of our birth and our life so far. This denial of birth is an expression of our disappointment with our parents. Not only will we give birth to ourselves and to our new selves, and not only will the oppressed minority rule the cosmos, and not only will history end, but nature itself will stop its course of death and rebirth. The end of our surrender to the body and its many weaknesses will finally come.

The eschaton is the time when human history ends and the laws of nature are abolished. Only the true believers, a small segment of humanity, have been chosen to share in the secret of total redemption and to bring it about. No wonder they feel superior to others, whose lives may be expendable, especially because the infidels are not entitled to eternal life. Sometimes our own parents and our own families are among those destined to perish on Judgment Day.

THE CASE OF THE IMMORTALS

Let us now look at another example of miraculous rebirth, this time in the form of a group. It is known as People Forever International, formerly the Eternal Flame Foundation, and also as the Arizona Immortals or the Forever People, and it is "dedicated to building a deathless world." It was founded in Scottsdale, Arizona, in the late 1960s by Charles Paul Brown (1935–), a former Presbyterian minister and nightclub singer. In the spring of 1960, Brown had a vision of Jesus Christ together with the revelation of physical immortality as a reality, or "cellular awakening." The group's doctrine is connected to Christian theology, but claims that

> . . . death is actually a fabrication or lie imposed on our minds and bodies by a ruling death consciousness in order to control the species of man and keep him in eternal bondage . . . There will never be lasting peace on earth until the LAST ENEMY OF MAN, WHICH IS DEATH is abolished . . . Most religions believe that physical immortality will eventually take place in the bodies of mankind upon the earth. However, it is always projected into some future dispensation due to misconceptions and religious dogmas. We feel the time IS NOW for an immortal species of mankind to be birthed upon the planet. (Fauset, 1944, p. 105)

Here is humanity's fondest wish, bluntly and directly expressed. And this is, of course, not unheard of in religious life. Father Divine was supposed to have given his followers everlasting life. ". . . many of us who are in this place will never lose the bodies we now have. God is here in the flesh, and he is never going away from us, and we will remain here forevermore. This is heaven on earth" (Fauset, 1944, p. 105).

In People Forever International, ancient prophecies of the end of times are supposedly fulfilled, as death is abolished. Members are reborn as immortal beings, according to their own testimony. What does this delusion do for its members? My own observations of the membership show that members who remain loyal to the group and to the idea of physical immortality are able to function quite well in society. They are far from delusional, despite the delusional nature of their beliefs, and some hold positions of power and wealth. They are totally nonviolent, and seem to have solved the problem of directing aggression. They still die, however, just like the rest of us, and explain deaths among members as evidence of insufficient faith or will power.

THE ESCHATON

To prepare for the creation of the new world, present reality needs to be destroyed and erased from memory. This will happen through trials and tribulations, whose detailed descriptions enable believers to indulge their violent imaginations and fantasize various forms of revenge on the wicked.

In the individual imagination, the creation of the world equals birth, while the end of the world equals one's own death. The apocalypse is first the denial of death. It is a miracle in which instead of death we should expect victory and rebirth in a perfect world. We will wake up in heaven, in a new reborn world. The dream of perfect rebirth demands first total destruction and only then rebirth. "For, behold, I create new heavens and a new earth: and the former shall not be remembered, nor come into mind" (Isaiah, 65:17).

Instead of facing death we reach rebirth and victory. In the words of ancient prophets "Arise and sing, ye that dwell in dust" (Isaiah, 26:19). Eschatological dreams promise us an end to the cycle of birth and death. In addition to our cosmic victory over nature, whose laws are to be abolished, there will be a human victory of our own group of the elect over all others. The believer is in ecstasy because near the eschaton he is living at the center of history and at the heart of the cosmos. This is the climax of the universal religious drama, played out on the cosmic stage. Following rebirth through blood and fire, birth and death will disappear. There will be no body, no aggression, and no sex.

Vivid fantasies about the destruction of the world are the consolation and the revenge of the downtrodden and the oppressed. The end of the old world is not only a cosmic victory over evil, but a response to frustration. Prophecies of earthquakes, epidemics, and floods, which only the elect will survive, are an immediate outlet for aggression. With the new world born, the meek shall rule, after they inherit the earth and all its riches. It seems reasonable to assume that as objective conditions become more difficult, and realistic coping does not lead to any change, humans will turn to imaginary ways of coping.

Our thoughts about the end of the world have to do with what will happen to us at the end of times and that is our death. In the group fantasy about the end of times, shared by so many religious groups, they will die, following Judgment Day, and we will live forever, and rule the world. Some of the dead will come back, but only if they are found righteous.

What unites all religious fantasies about the end of times is the denial of death and the denial of birth. The self is able to create a new world, create himself anew by sharing the group fantasy of a new heaven and a new earth. By undergoing individual transformation, one may join the elect and become part of the world-transforming project. This entails both honor and responsibility.

The religious dream is about overcoming the limitations and presses of the body in life and in death, as well as the victory of justice over evil. The dream is of the resurrection, Judgment Day, and the abolition of death. The profane world of the body and its demands must be destroyed. Who can resist the wishes for a victory of justice and life over evil and death?

In conversion and rebirth we reinvent ourselves and even try to reinvent the world. What does the individual destroy when transforming its self? An old identity, old body, old name, old social network. What do we want to destroy and get rid of? Ourselves, parts of ourselves, all others, or the world? Total destruction takes the place of pregnancy in giving birth to the new world. In the rebirth fantasy, I am the destroying and the procreating father. I am stronger than my own father, the man who created me. I am the creator. The world starts with me and it will end with me. If I die, then the world ends. I want to be reborn, but only in a new world, made to my specifications.

Religious fantasies often include ideas of bloody sacrifice *ad gloriam dei*, even when the world does not end. Cynically, we might suggest that religions advocate sacrificing others, rather than oneself, on the road to salvation. We may point out that the fantasy of a world without evil in the form of illness has cost the lives of many children. A case in point is that of the Faith Assembly, led by Hobart E. Freeman. In this group, one hundred members and their children were reported to have died between 1970 and 1990, because of their refusal to seek medical care. Freeman himself, a scholar of Hebrew and Greek and the author of ten books that were well received within the evangelical Christian community, has been described as schizophrenic, but was able to persuade and control his followers to continue risking their own and their children's lives. He died in 1984, but his ideas live on among some (Beit-Hallahmi, 1998; Hughes, 1990). Freeman's victims are less well known than those of other deranged leaders, but some of his followers were convicted and sent to prison for what some observers called infanticide. Richardson and Dewitt (1992, p. 561) note that public opinion ". . . seems to favor protection of children over parental rights and freedom of religion," as it certainly should. In fairness to some other believers and their fantasies, we should mention that self-sacrifice in the most literal sense has been a reality and an ideal in many traditions, in the form of martyrdom.

Ostow (1986, 1988) suggested that apocalyptic thinking is tied to the dynamic structure of the incipient psychotic episode, such as in schizophrenia and borderline disorder. Libido is withdrawn from the world so that the latter disappears, to be replaced by a delusional fantasy of world rebirth.

THE PREVALENCE OF APOCALYPTIC DREAMS

In addition to the well-known end-of-times historical traditions, there are several interesting cases of new religious movements, founded since 1800, where apocalyptic dreams are prominent and sometimes lead to nonviolent acts, such as the stocking of food. In the Church of Jesus Christ of Latter Day Saints (the Mormon Church), there is an expectation of upheavals and imminent disasters before the Second Coming, which would leave only the Mormons unharmed. This leads to a preoccupation with physical survival and the stocking up of emergency supplies of food and water in every Mormon home. Members are expected to have in storage one year's worth of food, in preparation for the coming global catastrophe.

The Baha'i movement, which started in the late nineteenth century as a heterodox Moslem sect and, having distanced itself from Islam, now claims to be a universal religion, preaches the religious unity of humankind, and supports the ideal of a world government and the activities of the United Nations. Its founder, Baha'u'llah, is believed to be the messianic figure expected by Judaism, Christianity, Islam, Zoroastrianism, Hinduism, and Buddhism. With the coming of Baha'u'llah, the "Manifestation of God," a new era has begun, lasting 5,000 years. It will lead to the Baha'i Cycle, lasting 500,000 years, but this will happen only after a global catastrophe and the disintegration of the present world order. Dissident Baha'i groups in the United States have predicted catastrophic floods and nuclear wars for 1963, 1980, and 1995 (Balch, Farnsworth, & Wilkins, 1983; Smith, 1987).

In the movement now known as Osho Meditation or Osho Friends International and formerly known as Rajneesh Foundation International (RFI), which was founded by Bhagwan Sree Rajneesh (real name: Chandra Mohan, 1931–1990), there were many proclamations of apocalyptic catastrophes. The movement became known for its emphasis on free sexual expression and the valuation of sexuality, described as part of the "tantric-oriented" tradition. At the same time, members were allowed no marriage and no children. There was a belief in an expected cataclysm that would end life on earth. Only Rajneesh followers would survive, and even that wasn't certain. In 1983, Rajneesh predicted an earthquake that would devastate much of the United States' west coast. In 1984, he announced that AIDS was the scourge predicted by Nostradamus, and billions would die from it within the next decade. This led to the use of various means of protection, beyond condoms, during sexual encounters. In 1985, the group's official publications predicted floods, earthquakes, and nuclear war within the next decade (Beit-Hallahmi, 1998; Belfrage, 1981; Carter, 1990; Gordon, 1987; Palmer, 1994).

A modern version of the end-of-times fantasy is the move to another planet, following the total destruction of all life on Earth. These ideas have been known for at least fifty years (Festinger, Riecken, & Schachter, 1956), and have played a role in the tragedies of Heaven's Gate and the Solar Temple, where the collective death ritual was to lead members to a rebirth on another planet. We can readily conclude that violent end-of-times fantasies are quite prevalent in thousands of religious traditions, and may be even universal. What should concern us is how often these fantasies will lead to violent actions. We may hypothesize that violent fantasies, as opposed to real acts, actually contribute to the achievement of an internal psychic balance.

The Case of the Ghost Dance: Mass Suicide?

The Ghost Dance tragedy seems to us today like a mass suicide, because here we are faced with a totally nonviolent apocalyptic dream, the opposite of the eschaton, which led to a disaster. The Ghost Dance represented a traditional response to externally imposed oppression and deprivation, and to an internal crisis of authority. Its doctrine was based on the theme of the coming triumph of the natives over the Europeans, material prosperity of the natives at the expense of Europeans, the resurrection of the dead and the return to pre-colonial blissful conditions, including the reappearance of buffalo herds. The eventual outcome would be a renewal of native existence, forever free of death, disease, and misery. To bring about this salvation, natives had to perform the sacred dance. Believers were also exhorted to discard all warlike behaviors (La Barre, 1970; Lanternari, 1963; Miller, 1985; Mooney, 1973).

The largest wave of the Ghost Dance native movement occurred in 1890 in the western United States; forty-five North American tribes were involved. At that time, the movement was inspired by the prophet Wovoka. In his visions, the native dead appeared around God's throne, and Wovoka received an assurance that he was the messenger of a messianic kingdom, soon to be established under Jesus Christ. There the natives would recover their lands and their lost way of life, while the whites would disappear. The Ghost Dance itself was designed to secure communication with the dead, hasten the coming of the messianic age, and gain further assurances for Wovoka's messages. Men and women, dressed in white, danced in circles, singing "revealed" songs and reaching ecstasy. Wovoka's followers also believed that they were immune to bullets. The Ghost Dance of 1890 ended with the massacre at Wounded Knee, South Dakota, on December 29, 1890, in which chief Sitting Bull and between 150 and 300 Sioux were killed. The Ghost Dance of North America has been compared with Cargo Cults, which is a collective term for a variety of nativist, syncretistic movements, which have appeared most often in Oceania, and promoted the belief in obtaining "cargo," i.e., manufactured goods and wealth, through spiritual means. Sometimes the expectation is that ancestors would return, delivering the "cargo" (Lanternari, 1963; Maher, 1961; Worsley, 1968). In all of these cases, as we judge them today, we regard the natives as victims of European colonization, and we recognize their deprivation and oppression. We should recall that earlier generations saw them as savages, who committed acts of what today is called terrorism (which they sometimes did).

Brahma Kumaris and the Hidden Doctrine of the Apocalypse

Sometimes, dreams of world destruction and rebirth are kept secret; in other cases, they are widely advertised. In the case of several well-known new religious movements, there has been an expectation of an apocalypse that would spare only the membership, and which is kept secret. We are going to examine one such case in detail. Brahma Kumaris (Raja Yoga), officially known as the Brahma Kumaris World Spiritual University (BKWSU) or BK, and sometimes known as RAJA YOGA or World Spiritual University, is an international Hindu revival movement, founded in 1937 in Karachi by Dada Lekh Raj (1877–1969). He was a wealthy diamond merchant, who started having visions at the age of sixty and adopted the name of Prajapita Brahma. In the early 1970s, the group opened its first branch outside India in London, and since then has spread to Europe, North and South America, Africa, and Australia. The group's international headquarters is located in Mount Abu, Rajastan, India. The group teaches the practice of what they call Raja Yoga meditation, which does not require the use of mantras, special postures, or breathing exercises, but focuses on visual contact with the founder's picture and with red lights representing the "supreme soul." The founder is regarded as divine, and members are devoted to loving him and fulfilling his commandments. Rules about ritual purity are strictly observed and they are very similar to those observed by Hindu Brahmins.

There is a total suppression of aggression and sexuality in everyday life, and an ideal of love without sex, with much social support and positive expressions in interactions among members.

The expression of any negative feelings is avoided, and there is no discussion of politics and social conflicts. Love is supposed to dominate life, even if physical love is absent, and the group advocates pacifism. It offers courses in "stress management and positive thinking" to nonmembers. Sexual activity is proscribed, and the sexes are strictly separated. It is suggested that this separation allows "released energy" to be used for meditation and good works.

Members are known as BKs or Brahmins. Most active members of the group are celibate women, and the leadership is not only exclusively female, but visibly feminist as well. While the requirements for full membership include a strict vegetarian diet, celibacy, and daily meditation, "partial members" are also recognized.

Brahma Kumaris is an example of a success story. Its members have experienced a dramatic rebirth, giving up sex and aggression, and achieving bliss and balance. They have fulfilled part of the ancient prophecies about world rebirth. To all observers, Brahma Kumaris members look impressive. They are calm, kind, forever smiling, and promoting a culture of peace and beauty. They have created a "spiritual" reality. Most members are Indian women who have been born again as Brahmins, released from the bondage of being subservient women in Indian society, and becoming independent and enterprising leaders.

But behind the bliss and human warmth lies a secret. Behind the mask of love and kindness, seething aggression hides. Brahma Kumaris' doctrine predicts a nuclear war that will come soon. Within a short time, this World War, together with a series of natural disasters, is expected to wipe out all of humanity, with the exception of Brahma Kumaris membership. Following the destruction of humanity, a new era will begin, one of peace and prosperity. Procreation will take place spiritually, and that is why sex is already superfluous. This belief in the imminent apocalypse in the form of World War III is kept secret from nonmembers.

Eschatological dreams are always like that. They include blood, fire, and heavy smoke covering the earth. Following trials and tribulations, Judgment Day leads to the destruction of the wicked. In the case of Brahma Kumaris, we observe a jarring contrast between the total commitment to love and peace, with constant smiles and meditation to the sounds of beautiful music, and the secret fantasy of world destruction behind it. The contrast is even more shocking given the feminine and feminist nature of the leadership. This secret was revealed to me by mistake in February 1994, during a visit to Mount Abu, and once the secret was out, group members and leaders were quite eager to offer detailed commentaries on world politics and military strategy.

The case of Brahma Kumaris is interesting because of the presence of both a total suppression of sex and aggression and a secret dream of total destruction. Classical psychoanalysis, in what seems today an overly mechanical fashion, assumes that aggression, as a permanent instinctual force, must find its outlet, either in fantasy or in action, if a serious imbalance in personality functioning is to be avoided (Beit-Hallahmi, 1971). If you are perfectly pacific and loving, where is your aggression going to go? Is the secret fantasy necessary for maintaining psychical balance? It should be emphasized that we have no reason to suspect that this fantasy is going to lead to any violent action.

The Case of the Branch Davidians

The tragedy of the Branch Seventh-Day Adventists, commonly known as the Branch Davidians, is well known. Its members in its various organizational forms have followed the teachings of Victor T. Houteff, who deviated from established Seventh-Day Adventist teachings in the 1930s by predicting the coming of a Davidian kingdom in Palestine, preceding the Second Coming of Christ. In the 1960s, Ben Roden (?–1978) renamed the group Branch Davidians, and was succeeded by his wife Lois (1915–1986). Their son George Roden (1938–) tried to become leader in the 1970s, but was then ousted by a new leader. This new leader was Vernon Wayne Howell (1960–1993), known after 1990 as David Koresh, who came from a Seventh-Day Adventist family and grew up in that movement. Howell joined the Branch Davidians in 1982, became the lover of Lois Roden, and then assumed the leadership in 1987, after she died.

Under his leadership, the group became known as "Students of the Seven Seals." Howell claimed a revelation that showed him to be the seventh and final angel of God. He claimed to be the Messiah, and also had exclusive sexual access to all women members and their female children. In 1989, he officially announced to the members his rights to all females. Some followers left because of this announcement. At age twelve, girls were moved to gender-segregated adult quarters, where they became available to Koresh. By 1993, there were more than a dozen women in the group who considered themselves wives to the leader. His legal wife, Rachel Howell (1970–1993), was married to him at the age of fourteen.

Koresh gathered a veritable arsenal in the 1990s—350 guns and 2 million rounds of ammunition—and gradually attracted official attention. On February 28, 1993, the Mount Carmel compound near Waco, Texas, was raided by more than one hundred agents of the United States Bureau of Alcohol, Tobacco, and Firearms (ATF), who were searching for illegal weapons. The Branch Davidians opened fire, and four agents, as well as six group members, died. This led to a fifty-one-day siege by the FBI and the ATF, around what the Davidians now called Ranch Apocalypse.

On April 19, 1993, as millions around the world watched the unfolding events on television with horror, the Mount Carmel compound went up in flames. We know now that the fire was started by group members. Eighty-six group members and their dependents died, including seventeen children. Five of the children were believed to have been fathered by David Koresh himself. Following the end of the siege, nine members of the group were sentenced to prison terms for their involvement, five of them for forty years (Beit-Hallahmi, 1998; Reavis, 1995; Wright, 1995).

In the history of David Koresh, both sex and violence were heightened and visible, as was the prediction of the coming end. One aspect of the Branch Davidians tragedy that received attention was the sexual exploitation and domination of group members and their children by their leader. In 1989, Koresh dissolved all marriages in the group. He decided on a new policy, following a divine revelation. "The sexual practices of the Branch Davidians involved a strange mixture of celibacy and polygamy" (Tabor & Gallagher, 1995, p. 66). We all know what this mixture meant: celibacy for all men in the group, and polygamy for David Koresh, who monopolized all women, just like the primal old father in Freud's primal horde (Freud, 1913). Tabor and Gallagher even quote one member of the group as saying "We as Branch Davidians aren't interested in sex. Sex is so assaultive, so aggressive. David has shouldered this burden for us" (1995, p. 72).

Regarding the leader's sexual partners, Tabor and Gallagher (1995) report the following: After arriving in Mount Carmel in 1981, he had an affair with the 67- (or 69-) year-old Lois Roden, the Branch Davidian prophetess, and announced that she would soon give birth to the Messiah. In January 1984, he legally married Rachel Jones, the daughter of a longtime Branch Davidian, Perry Jones. In 1986, he announced his "marriage" to fourteen-year-old Karen Doyle, whose father was also a group member of long standing. Later that year Koresh "married" Michelle Jones, twelve-year-old sister of wife number one. The contact with Michelle started in what seemed to some (who were told about it by Koresh himself) like a rape (Ellison & Bartkowski, 1995). Later, he took at least three more wives, aged seventeen, sixteen, and twenty, who had children by him (Tabor & Gallagher, 1995, pp. 42–43). And later on, we learn of another "wife," whose relations with Koresh started when she was thirteen. It is also clear that in some cases Koresh had sex with both a daughter and her mother. It has been alleged in the popular media that

Koresh fathered numerous children in his many liaisons. Tabor and Gallagher (1995) report that he had fathered at least twelve children in the group. "During the March 7 videotape, which the group sent out . . . Koresh affectionately introduced all twelve of his children on camera and several of his wives . . . he also held up photos of several of his 'wives' who had left the group. He had not always been so forthcoming. He realized that the practice of polygamy itself, not to mention sexual relations with girls as young as twelve or thirteen, could cause him serious legal problems" (Tabor & Gallagher, 1995, p. 66). As a result, "he even arranged sham 'marriages' for his wives with selected male members" (Tabor & Gallagher, 1995, p. 67).

There was evidence not of violent potential, but of real murderous acts in Mount Carmel long before the ATF got involved. In November 1987, Koresh, fighting for the leadership of the Branch Davidians, was challenged by George Roden (the son of the two former leaders, whose mother Lois Roden was Koresh's lover) to a final showdown. Roden dug up the body of a Davidian who had been dead for twenty years and told Koresh to raise her from the dead, if he could. This led to a forty-five-minute gun battle, in which Roden was slightly wounded. Koresh and seven of his followers were charged with attempted murder. The seven followers were acquitted, while Koresh won a mistrial, and was never retried.

George Roden left the group, and in 1989 he shot his roommate and then cut the body to pieces. He was found innocent by reason of insanity by a court in Texas and hospitalized. In 1995, he escaped to New York, but was caught and returned to Texas. The above should at least raise some doubts in your mind as to whether the Branch Davidians were just like your average Texas family as far as firearms were concerned, and indeed, "When asked about the weapons . . . Koresh defended them as part of the biblical understanding of the group" (Tabor & Gallagher, 1995, p. 65).

The confrontation between the Branch Davidians and the federal law-enforcement machinery had nothing to do with religion, and everything to do with guns. As Fogarty (1995) says: ". . . they were defending their turf with guns, protecting their messiah with an arsenal. They seemed to have stockpiled their weapons with as much ease as they stockpiled feed for their animals. . . . It does not take a prophet, or a psychologist, or even a cult deprogrammer, to see that a little gun control might have gone a long way toward preventing this pending apocalyptic confrontation" (p. 14).

The Case of the Peoples Temple Christian (Disciples) Church

Popularly known as the Peoples Temple, this U.S. Christian group was one of the most notorious religious movements of recent history, becoming the subject of worldwide horror when 913 of its members committed suicide on November 18, 1978, in Jonestown, Guyana.

It started as a typical, locally organized, lower-class U.S. congregation, founded in 1956 in Indiana as the Community National Church, by James Warren (Jim) Jones, who was born near Lyon, Indiana, on May 13, 1931. From early childhood he imitated preachers. According to some reports, he claimed to be able to perform miracles soon after becoming a minister in Indianapolis.

Jones later practiced "faith healing" and his followers claimed various miracles attributed to him. He was very active in support of integration when the concept was little favored, and he was always very popular with African Americans. In the late 1950s, Jones started developing an integrated church. He became an ordained minister of the Disciples of Christ in 1965, and then moved to California with 150 followers, first to Ukiah and then to San Francisco. Most members were poor African Americans, but Jones was able to establish ties with political leaders in the San Francisco area. Throughout its existence in San Francisco, Peoples Temple was actually a mainline Protestant congregation, belonging to the Christian Church (Disciples of Christ). At the same time, based in the Fillmore district of San Francisco, it was a community of activists fighting racism and poverty. It operated drug rehabilitation programs, soup kitchens, and daycare centers. According to some reports, Jones was influenced by the Father Divine Movement (Fauset, 1944) and was addressed later on as "Daddy" Jones.

In 1974, the group started gradually moving its members to the communal settlement of Jonestown, in Guyana, South America, and in 1977, Jones himself and several hundred followers moved there. The departure from California was caused by growing frictions with ex-members and critical media reports. During the 1970s, Jones was becoming increasingly abusive, dictatorial, and paranoid. Members were subjected to beatings, sexual abuse, and constant humiliation. In 1977, relatives of members and some ex-members described Jim Jones in more than just unflattering terms. There were reports of rehearsals for mass suicide in the Peoples Temple, which took place before 1978. There were very serious accusations, but still no one could have predicted what happened in November 1978.

When U.S. Congressman Leo Ryan traveled to Guyana to investigate claims of abuse in the group in November 1978, he was received by Jones and shown around the settlement. After leaving the site, he and members of his party were murdered by Jones's guards. This led to the final scene of death in the commune. On November 18, 1978, 913 members died in a mass suicide on orders from Jones, who was among them. Most drank poisoned Kool-Aid; a few were shot. Among the dead, 199 were over the age of 65, 300 were under 16, and 137 were under 11. It should be noted that most of the members who died with Jones were African American females, a fact that faithfully reflects the nature of the membership (Beit-Hallahmi, 1998; Hall, 1987; Kilduff & Javers, 1978; Levi, 1982; Moore & McGehee, 1989; Naipaul, 1981).

Aum Shinrikyo: Mass Terrorism and the Apocalypse

Aum Shinrikyo, or Aleph, is an international group inspired by Buddhist and Hindu ideas, with branches in Japan, South Korea, Sri Lanka, Germany, Russia, and the United States. It was founded in 1987 by Shoko Asahara (1955–), whose real name is Chizuo Matsumoto. After visiting the Himalayas, Asahara claimed he had reached the highest stage of enlightenment, and was ready to offer it to others.

The group offers its members "Real Initiation," "Astral Initiation," and "Causal Initiation." The goal is "spiritual enlightenment," and according to its publications, "After passing through Earthly Initiation which purifies one's consciousness, Astral Initiation which purifies one's subconsciousness, over 2,000 members in Japan have promoted their spiritual growth remarkably, and experienced astral projection and feelings of supreme bliss within half a year." Those who reach "spiritual enlightenment" will survive the coming global apocalypse. In the 1980s, the group's doctrine predicted the end of the world in 1997. Members still are encouraged to leave their families and adopt a monastic life. They are also expected to sign over their worldly possessions to the group.

In 1989, Tsutsumi Sakamoto, an attorney who was involved in suing the group, and his wife and his son were murdered on Asahara's orders. During the same year, according to official charges, Shuji Taguchi, a group member, was also murdered on Asahara's orders. In June 1994, seven individuals were killed in Matsumoto, Japan, as a result of a sarin nerve gas attack carried out by the group. Then, on March 20, 1995, twelve persons died and 5,000 were injured in Tokyo following another sarin nerve gas attack in the subway, attributed to Aum. According to some evidence, the sarin gas was perfumed so as to make it attractive. Huge quantities of dangerous chemicals were found at group facilities later on. Scores of Aum members were arrested. After the attack, Asahara claimed that his followers were attacked by the U.S. military using "biological weapons," and that the huge chemical stores found at one of the group's compound were used to make "plastics, fertilizers, and pottery."

Aum Shinrikyo was notorious in Japan long before the well-known 1995 terror events, and its belief system made it likely to attract less-than-friendly attention. Children in its schools were taught to regard Adolf Hitler as a living hero, and its official publications carried stories of the Jewish plan to exterminate most of humanity (Kowner, 1997). We know today that Japanese authorities were actually not just overly cautious, but negligent and deferential, if not protective, regarding criminal activities by Aum, because of its status as a religious movement. "Some observers wonder what took the Japanese authorities so long to take decisive action. It seems apparent that enough serious concerns had been raised about various Aum activities to warrant a more serious police inquiry prior to the subway gas attack" (Mullins, 1997, p. 321). Based on what we know today, the group can only be described as extremely and consistently violent and murderous. "Thirty-three Aum followers are believed to have been killed between . . . 1988 and . . . 1995 . . . Another twenty-one followers have been reported missing" (Mullins, 1997, p. 320). Among nonmembers, there have been twenty-four murder victims. There were at least nine germ-warfare attacks by Aum Shinrikyo in the early 1990s, most of which had no effect (Reuters, 1998). One triple-murder case in 1989 and another poison gas attack in 1994 that killed seven have been committed by the group, as well as less serious crimes that the police was not too eager to investigate (Beit-Hallahmi, 1998; Haworth, 1995; Mullins, 1997).

Nor is it likely that this lethal record (seventy-seven deaths on numerous occasions over seven years) and other non-lethal criminal activities were the deeds of a few rogue leaders. Numerous individuals must have been involved in, and numerous others aware of, these activities. On May 16, 1995, Asahara was arrested, and the group's many centers were raided. One raid of the headquarters showed that the group held $7 million in cash and 10 kilograms of gold. In April 1995, Hideo Murai, the group's "science department" chief, announced that the group property holdings were worth $1 billion. He was then mysteriously killed two weeks later. Fumihiro Joyu was appointed group leader following Asahara's arrest, but he himself was arrested in October 1995. As of May 1998, 192 Aum Shinrikyo members have been charged with criminal activities (Reuters, 1998). Since then, many have been convicted and sentenced for capital crimes. Aum Shinrikyo's dream was to let the apocalypse start through mass terror attacks. The destruction of society was expected to lead to a new world, born out of chaos.

The Case of Heaven's Gate

Heaven's Gate, also known as Bo and Peep, or the Higher Source, was a Christian–UFO group started in 1975 in Los Angeles by a former music professor, Marshall Herff Applewhite (1932–1997), and a registered nurse, Bonnie Lu Trousdale Nettles (1928–1985). They met in the early 1970s, when Applewhite was hospitalized in Texas, following his dismissal from his teaching job in Houston.

They called themselves Bo and Peep, and were also known as Winnie and Pooh, Chip and Dale, Do and Ti, "The Him and the Her," or "the Two," in reference to a New Testament prophecy about two witnesses. The group's doctrine was known as Human Individual Metamorphosis (HIM), aiming at the liberation of humans from the endless cycle of reincarnation. The leaders claimed that they would fulfill another ancient prophecy by being assassinated and then coming back to life three and a half days later. Following the resurrection, they would be lifted up by a UFO to the divine kingdom in outer space.

Followers agreed, in preparation for the outer space journey, to get rid of most material possessions and worldly attachments, including family and work. Members wore uniform clothing and identical haircuts. Marriage and sexual relations were also forbidden.

Group members traveled around the United States recruiting new followers and proclaiming their prophecies. Followers were promised immortality, androgyneity, and perfection, provided they followed the rules and ideas provided by the leaders. Bonnie Nettles died in 1985 of cancer, and then the group started operating in complete secrecy. Applewhite told his followers that Bonnie Nettles was actually his divine father.

In late March 1997, thirty-nine group members, including Marshall Herff Applewhite, committed suicide in Rancho Santa Fe, California, by ingesting barbiturates and alcohol. They were found lying on bunk beds, wearing cotton pants, black shirts, and sneakers. Most of them were covered with purple shrouds. They all carried on them passports and driver's licenses, as well as small change. The victims ranged in age from twenty-six to seventy-two, but twenty-one were in their forties. There were twenty-one females and eighteen males. In videotaped statements read before committing suicide, members said that they were taking this step in preparation for an expected encounter with extraterrestrials who would arrive in a spaceship following the Hale-Bopp comet. It was discovered after their deaths that some of the male group members had been castrated several years before.

The Case of the Solar Temple

The Order of the Solar Temple (Ordre du Temple Solaire) was an international Rosicrucian-Christian group, started in the 1980s by Luc Jouret (1948–1994), a Belgian practitioner of homeopathy, and Joseph Di Mambro (1924–1994), a Canadian. The group was active in France and in French-speaking areas of Canada, Switzerland, and Belgium. Jouret and Di Mambro maintained between them a wide repertoire of fraudulent practices. The official belief system of the group, combining claims about "ancient Egypt," "energy fields," reincarnation, and the "Age of Aquarius," is so widely offered in hundreds of groups all over the world (Beit-Hallahmi, 1992) as to be banal and harmless. But this was a high-involvement group, not just a series of lectures.

Members signed over their assets to the group, and according to some reports it had more than $90 million. Jouret preached a coming apocalypse, for which members had to prepare by arming themselves. At the same time, there were promises of a "transition to the future," an afterlife for members on another planet near Sirius, the brightest star in the firmament.

By the late 1980s, the Solar Temple was a target for anti-New Religious Movements groups. In 1993, it became the target of police attention (for illegal weapon charges) and sensational media reports in both Canada and Australia. In July 1993, Jouret and two associates received light sentences from a judge in Quebec for attempts to buy pistols with silencers. The early warnings were not heeded. The most sensational media reports, calling the Solar Temple a "doomsday cult," turned out to be right on the mark. On October 4, 1994, forty-six members and four children were found dead in two locations—in Granges-sur-Salvan and in Cheiry—near Geneva, Switzerland, and in one location in Morin, Quebec. The victims were shot and then set on fire; the leaders, who did the shootings, committed suicide. Five days earlier, two former members, and their infant son, had been slaughtered in Quebec.

On December 16, 1995, in a repetition of the same ritual, thirteen more members and three children met their death, laid out in a star pattern in the Vercors region of eastern France. The ritual killings were explained on the basis of the group's beliefs in a new life after death, on another planet. "We leave this earth to rediscover a Plane of Absolute Truth, far from the hypocrisy and oppression of this world," read a collective suicide note.

The killings in Quebec were explained as the result of the victims' disobedience in having a baby without the leaders' permission. It's possible that DiMambro, terminally ill, wanted to take as many with him as he could. It is clear that many of the dead at this going-away party were murdered, some for revenge, while others were willing victims (Hall & Schuyler, 1997; Mayer, 1999).

PSYCHODYNAMIC CONCLUSION

The method we follow in this chapter has been called the hermeneutics of suspicion, but suspicion about stated motives and conscious goals is not enough. It should lead to analysis, which must appreciate the complexities of internal and external realities. But choosing the interpretive strategy of suspicion seems fully justified when we discover that behind public testimonies of happiness and joy lies despair and behind vows of universal love lie murderous hate and wishes of annihilation. Dreams, innocent and pure, may give rise to madness and violence, as we cope, consciously and unconsciously, with the facts of birth and death, with the nature of our own birth to our own parents, and with the few choices we can make in our lives.

The veneer of civilization, which we all wear with pride, is awfully thin, and likely to disappear in times of crisis. We should be suspicious, cautious, but compassionate as much as possible. The human condition, which we all share, is one of suffering and frustration, much of which could be avoided by human decisions and acts. Our emphasis on psychoanalytic interpretations and internal processes should not lead us to ignore external reality, which imposes pressures and demands. Violent acts are not only the result of internal fantasies, but sometimes a reaction to external violence.

When and how do beliefs lead to action? We know that, in our secular world, religious beliefs most often predict other beliefs, rather than actions (Argyle & Beit-Hallahmi, 1975; Beit-Hallahmi, 1989; Beit-Hallahmi & Argyle, 1997). Assessing when people are going to act on their beliefs is one of our greatest challenges. Religion is defined through a unique system of beliefs that more and more often do not lead to action. When will dreams lead to action? When does peaceful and happy rebirth turn to violence? Fantasies of individual rebirth are so common as to be almost universal, and they are often not connected to religion or ideology. Religious dreams of world destruction and rebirth are also almost universal, and will rarely lead to violence. Our ability to recognize violent potential will remain limited, exactly because these cases are so unusual.

LEARNING FROM DISASTERS

What have we learned about the dynamics of destructive dreams from the recent tragedies of the Peoples Temple, Branch Davidians, Solar Temple, and Heaven's Gate? The dynamics we observe in these social movements are not just of ideological and organizational totalism, but of totalitarianism and fascism. We find total obedience to totalitarian leaders, which goes far beyond devotion (Freud, 1921). As Henderson (1975) so aptly reminds us, the recognition of evil within ourselves remains humanity's most important psychological challenge. That is why aggression is so easily externalized. In this situation, dreams of world destruction reflect disappointment and frustration. Mourning over our own misspent lives turns into aggressive fantasies. We find a leader even more deranged than anybody could imagine, at the head of a small-scale dictatorship system similar to the well-known dictatorships of the twentieth century. The questions we ask about these groups should be similar to the ones raised about historical fascist regimes (Adorno et al., 1950; Fromm, 1941).

We can only speculate about the interactions between leaders and followers, but in all the cases described above we see an extremely narcissistic leader, followed by a group of dependent, possibly borderline individuals. The feeling before the actual disaster is that the leadership, and the group, has reached the end of the road and is facing destruction or severe disruption by outside forces. For violence to appear, we need a relatively small group, totalitarian leadership, weapons, and real despair. Totalitarian leaders test their power over the membership through many displays of sadism and exploitation. The apocalypse may then follow. In the cases of Jonestown, Heaven's Gate, and the Solar Temple, suicide was the end of the world, because we, the group of the elect, were the world. Here, the price of rebirth was actual, not imagined, death. It was the leaders—Jim Jones, Joseph Di Mambro, Luc Jouret, and Marshall Applewhite—who decided to take their followers with them. Many of the victims had little choice.

What all recent cases of violence in new religious movements, starting with Jonestown in 1978 and ending with Heaven's Gate in 1997, had in common was quite simple. In all of these cases, lethal weapons and lethal chemicals were present, and later on became used. At the level of group dynamics and psychology, another common element was paranoia, whether religious or secular.

We looked closely at some new religions because it is easier to look at smaller groups, and some recent tragedies have been well-researched, but this does not mean that there is no danger in the apocalyptic dreams of old religions. Some believers in those religions are ready to die for their faith, or kill others for its glory and for promised heavenly rewards. In the real world, faith is tied to identity and action, and the lethal struggles that often ensue are not over anything metaphorical. In Israel, Palestine, Sri Lanka, India, Iran, Afghanistan, and the United States, taking seriously our apocalyptically minded neighbors should be a most practical lesson. Those who say they wish to create a Kingdom of Heaven on earth may be worth watching closely (Beit-Hallahmi, 2001a).

The saying attributed to Voltaire asserts that believing in absurdities will lead to the commission of atrocities. What Voltaire had in mind was clearly all religions, in all their manifestations. Another well-known judgment by Voltaire states that "Religion is the chief cause of all the sorrows of humanity. Everywhere it has only served to drive men to evil, and plunge them in brutal miseries . . . it makes of history an immense tableau of human follies." Always politically incorrect, Voltaire displays no respect for any religion. For Voltaire, the violent potential, and violent realities, in religion of all varieties, is not an aberration. The destructive potential is so close to the surface that we should be surprised only when it fails to appear. In the case of most groups that tell us to prepare for the end of times, we do not and should not expect anything violent to happen, but mark Voltaire's warning!

REFERENCES

Adorno, T., et al. (1950). *The authoritarian personality.* New York: Harper & Row.

Argyle, M., and Beit-Hallahmi, B. (1975). *The social psychology of religion.* London: Routledge & Kegan Paul.

Balch, R. W., Farnsworth, G., & Wilkins, S. (1983). When the bombs drop: Reactions to disconfirmed prophecy in a millennial sect. *Sociological Perspectives, 26,* 137–158.

Beit-Hallahmi, B. (1971). Sexual and aggressive fantasies in violent and non-violent prison inmates. *Journal of Personality Assessment, 35,* 326–330.

Beit-Hallahmi, B. (1977). Identity integration, self-image crisis and "Superego Victory" in post adolescent university students. *Adolescence, 12 ,* 57–69.

Beit-Hallahmi, B. (1989). *Prolegomena to the psychological study of religion.* Lewisburg, PA: Bucknell University Press.

Beit-Hallahmi, B. (1992). *Despair and deliverance: Private salvation in contemporary Israel.* Albany, NY: SUNY Press.

Beit-Hallahmi, B. (1998). *The illustrated encyclopedia of active new religions* (Revised). New York: Rosen Publishing.

Beit-Hallahmi, B. (2001a). Explaining religious utterances by taking seriously super-naturalist (and naturalist) claims. In G. Hon & S. Rakover (Eds.), *Explanation: Philosophical essays.* Dordrecht, Netherlands: Kluwer.

Beit-Hallahmi, B. (2001b). Fundamentalism. In J. Krieger (Ed.), *The Oxford companion to politics of the world.* New York: Oxford University Press.

Beit-Hallahmi, B., & Argyle, M. (1997). *The psychology of religious behaviour, belief, and experience.* London: Routledge.

Belfrage, S. (1981). *Flowers of emptiness.* New York: Dial.

Carter, L. F. (1990). *Charisma and control in Rajneeshpuram: The role of shared values in the creation of a community.* New York: Cambridge University Press.

Cohn, N. (1970). *The Pursuit of the Millennium.* New York: Oxford University Press.

Ellison, C. G., & Bartkowski, J. P. (1995). Babies were being beaten. In S. A. Wright (Ed.), *Armageddon in Waco.* Chicago: University of Chicago Press.

Fauset, A. F. (1944). *Black gods of the metropolis.* Philadelphia: University of Pennsylvania Press.

Fauteux, A. (1981). "Good/bad" splitting in the religious experience. *American Journal of Psychoanalysis, 41,* 261–267.

Festinger, L., Riecken, H. W., & Schachter, S. (1956). *When prophecy fails.* Minneapolis: University of Minnesota Press

Fogarty, R. S. (1995). An age of wisdom, an age of foolishness. In S. A. Wright (Ed.), *Armageddon in Waco.* Chicago: University of Chicago Press.

Freud, S. (1913). *Totem and taboo: The standard edition of the complete psychological writings of Sigmund Freud* (Vol. 13, pp. 1–164). London: Hogarth Press.

Freud, S. (1915/1916). Introductory lectures to psychoanalysis. In *The complete psychological works of Sigmund Freud* (Vol. 15). London: Hogarth Press.

Freud, S. (1916) Some character types met with in psycho-analytical work. *The standard edition of the complete psychological writings of Sigmund Freud* (Vol. 14, pp. 318–324). London: Hogarth Press.

Freud, S. (1921). Group psychology and the analysis of the ego. *The standard edition of the complete psychological writings of Sigmund Freud* (Vol. 18, pp. 69–143). London: Hogarth Press.

Freud, S. (1928) A religious experience. *The standard edition of the complete psychological writings of Sigmund Freud* (Vol. 21, pp. 167–174). London: Hogarth Press.

Fromm, E. (1941). *Escape from freedom.* New York: Rinehart.

Gordon, J. S. (1987). The golden guru: The strange journey of Bhagwan Shree Rajneesh. Lexington, MA: Stephen Green Press.

Hall, J. R. (1987). *Gone from the Promised Land: Jonestown in American cultural history.* New Brunswick, NJ: Transaction Books.

Hall, J. R., & Schuyler, P. (1997). The mystical apocalypse of the Solar Temple. In T. Robbins & S. J. Palmer (Eds.). *Millennium, messiahs, and mayhem.* New York: Routledge.

Haworth, A. (1995, May 14). Cults: Aum Shinrikyo. *The Guardian.*

Henderson, J. (1975). Object relations and the doctrine of "Original Sin." *International Review of Psycho-Analysis, 2,* 107–120.

Hughes, R. A. (1990). Psychological perspectives on infanticide in a faith healing sect. *Psychotherapy, 27,* 107–115.

Kilduff, M., & Javers, R. (1978). *The suicide cult.* New York: Bantam.

Kowner, R. (1997). On ignorance, respect and suspicion: Current Japanese attitudes towards Jews. The Vidal Sassoon International Center for the Study of Antisemitism, The Hebrew University of Jerusalem.

La Barre, W. (1970). *The ghost dance: The origins of religion.* New York: Doubleday and Company.

Lanternari, V. (1963). *The religions of the oppressed.* New York: Knopf.

Levi, K. (1982). *Violence and religious commitment: Implications of Jim Jones's People's Temple movement.* University Park, PA: Pennsylvania State University Press.

Lincoln, C. E. (1961). *The Black Muslims in America.* Boston: Beacon Press.

Maher, R. F. (1961). *New men of Papua: A study of culture change.* Madison, WI: University of Wisconsin Press.

Mayer, J.-F. (1999). Les chevaliers de l'apocalypse: L'Ordre de Temple Solaire et ses adeptes. In F. Champion & M. Cohen (Eds.), *Sectes et société.* Paris: Seuil.

Miller, D. H. (1985). *Ghost dance.* Lincoln, NE: University of Nebraska Press.

Milne, H .(1988). *Bhagwan: The god that failed.* New York: St. Martin's Press.

Mooney, J. (1973). *The ghost dance religion and Wounded Knee.* New York: Dover.

Moore, R., & McGehee, F. (1989). *New religious movements, mass suicide, and People's Temple.* Lewiston, NY: Edwin Mellen Press.

Mullins, M. R. (1997). Aum Shinrikyo as an apocalyptic movement. In T. Robbins & S. J. Palmer (Eds.), *Millennium, messiahs, and mayhem.* New York: Routledge.

Naipaul, S. (1981). *Journey to nowhere: A new world tragedy.* New York: Simon & Schuster.

Ostow, M. (1986). Archetypes of apocalypse in dreams and fantasies, and in religious scripture. *American Imago, 43,* 307–334.

Ostow, M. (1988). Apocalyptic thinking in mental illness and social disorder. *Psychoanalysis and Contemporary Thought, 11,* 285–297.

Palmer, S. J. (1994). *Moon sisters, Krishna mothers, Rajneesh lovers.* Syracuse, NY: Syracuse University Press.

Reavis, D. J. (1995). *The ashes of Waco: An investigation.* New York: Simon & Schuster.

Reuters News Service (1998, May 27). *Life sentence to Aum member for the poison gas attack.*

Richardson, J. T., & Dewitt, J. (1992). Christian Science, spiritual healing, the law, and public opinion. *Journal of Church and State, 34,* 549–561.

Smith, P. (1987). *The Babi and Bahai Religions: From messianic Shiism to a world religion.* Cambridge: Cambridge University Press.

Tabor, J., & Gallagher, J. (1995). *Why Waco? Cults and the battle for religious freedom in America.* Berkeley, CA: University of California Press.

Turner, V. (1973). The center out there: Pilgrim's goal. *History of Religions, 12,* 191–230.

Wittenberg, R. (1968). *Postadolescence: Theoretical and clinical aspects of psychoanalytic therapy.* New York: Grune & Stratton.

Worsley, P. (1968). *The trumpet shall sound.* New York: Schocken.

Wright, S. A. (Ed.) (1995). *Armageddon in Waco: Critical perspectives on the Branch Davidian conflict.* Chicago: University of Chicago Press.

Zarifian, E. (1988). *Les jardiniers de la folie.* Paris: Odile Jacob.

8

Entrancement in Islamic Fundamentalism

Don J. Feeney, Jr.

The shock and horrific tragedy America that endured on September 11 ignited a vast range of intense emotions, trauma, and disbelief. This stunning act of terrorism wounded, outraged, and baffled many, who questioned its sanity and purpose. Television talk show host David Letterman spoke to a bewildered nation when his show went back on the air nearly a week after the attacks. Letterman asked a question that struck the core of all America and the civilized world: "If you live to be a thousand years old . . . will that [September 11] make any goddamn sense?" (Tucker, 2001). In this chapter we will explore possible answers to this question.

Four planes were hijacked—two crashing into the World Trade Center, one into the Pentagon, and the fourth on an open field in Pennsylvania. The ringleader of the nineteen terrorists aboard the four planes was Mohamed Atta (Cloud, 2001). He was a 33-year-old, well-educated Egyptian, considered shy and nonviolent as a youth. He was fluent in three languages, held graduate degrees, and had been raised by a strict father. Those who knew him would never have predicted such behavior on his part. It was as if the terrorist leader were a different person from the man his family and friends had once known.

Contributing to the shock, trauma, and emerging confusion about these terrorists and their horrific acts were letters with the same message found in Atta's luggage and in a hijacker's car as well as in the debris of crashed United Airlines Flight 93. A partial excerpt translated from Arabic reads as follows:

> Purify your heart and forget something called life, for the time of play
> is gone and the time of truth has come. . . . God will absolve you of

your sins, and be assured that it will be only moments and then you will attain the ultimate and greatest reward.

. . . Let each find his blade for the prey to be slaughtered . . . As soon as you put your feet in and before you enter [the plane] start praying and realize that this is a battle for the sake of God, and when you sit in your seat say these prayers that we had mentioned before. When the plane starts moving, then you are traveling toward God and what a blessing that travel is. (Cloud, 2001)

In addition to such a cryptic or obtusely coded message, Atta had been described as cold and unemotional and is pictured with a staring expression, blank and far-off in focus, as if in a state of fixation. Atta was an Islamic fundamentalist who was rigidly devout in the very literal, concrete, and specific practices of the Koran. He and his sect thoroughly ascribed to the ancient teachings of Mohammed, advocating the *jihad* or Holy War against the infidels or non-Islamic believers (Cloud, 2001).

Though the Islamic religion is one that advocates love and peace, the fundamentalists have selectively concentrated their attention on a strict segment of the Koran, ignoring the symbolic, larger context of its true meaning and purpose (Bloom, 1995).

The mastermind behind the tragedy of September 11 is Osama bin Laden. His al-Qaeda terrorist organization has a weblike, worldwide network of self-organizing cells—or autonomous subgroups—of terrorists (Elliot, 2001). Bin Laden hides away in a labyrinth of underground caves and has a stoic, stone-like stare and exhibits an almost effeminate quality. It seems that the only joy he has is in the slaughter of his prey (as depicted in a video aired on December 16, 2001). With his fixed stare and shy, reticent demeanor, he seems to have similar characteristics to Mohammed Atta.

Bin Laden was born and raised as the only son of a Syrian mother. Though he is one of many sons of his Saudi Arabian father, he has been isolated and estranged from this prosperous family. While bin Laden enjoys enormous wealth (his al-Qaeda organization has received $300 million from various sources), he has been cast out by Saudi Arabia and Sudan (Riyadh, 2001). Afghanistan was the only country that offered him an enclave for terrorist training, and he joined forces there with the Taliban.

Islamic fundamentalists and their extremist beliefs are frequently characterized by what is essentially an altered state of consciousness, disconnected and out of sync with a more normal perception of reality. This particular kind of altered state is known as entrancement and can have devastating implications. It holds incredible power over human behavior if not mastered. For the psychopathic personality (Douglas, 1995; Egger, 1984; MacCulloch, Snowden, Wood, & Mills, 1983; Prentky, Burgess, and Carter, 1986; Schlesinger & Revitch, 1980), entrancement becomes a powerful force in manipulating and directing violent and destructive behavior. Further exploration of the nature of altered states and the development of entrancement is required.

ALTERED STATES AND HYPNOSIS

Arnold Ludwig (1966) coined the term "altered state of consciousness" (ASC). He used the following definition:

> Any mental state(s), induced by various physiological, psychological or pharmacological maneuvers or agents, which can be recognized subjectively by the individual himself (or by an objective observer of the individual) as representing sufficient deviation in subjective experience or psychological functioning from certain general norms for that individual during alert, waking consciousness. (p. 167)

He is suggesting that altered states be defined in terms of an individual's subjective experience and altered psychological function. These states result from changes in sensory experiences (sights, images, smells, unique sounds, tastes, feelings, and so forth). Changes in altered states can also result from various physical activities (a runner's high), focused vigilance (intensely looking out for danger or a special loved one), and physiological alterations (alcohol- and/or drug-induced). Hypnotic states are altered states that create changes in how individuals perceive themselves and their way of dealing with outer surroundings. The absorption and engrossment in what and how the individual is perceiving and experiencing are greatly increased compared with these functions in the awakened individual.

For example, hypnotized individuals can be intensely absorbed in dreams or hallucinations of people who aren't really there, or numbed to painful dental procedures. This feature can enable terrorists to hallucinate going to heaven and to be numb to the pain of a plane crash. The sense of time is greatly distorted—a five-minute childhood memory can subjectively be perceived to last all day or a twenty-minute plane ride can seem like an eternity. Individuals in these states are quite resistant to outside interruptions and distractions. A special feature of hypnotic states is that it takes energy and applied attention to induce, alter, and change states. This is an important dynamic principle of hypnosis and has significant implications for future work in releasing these bonds.

The definition of hypnosis is a special state of altered consciousness wherein select capacities are emphasized while others fade into the background. Nine out of ten people can be hypnotized. Hypnosis presents an appropriate metaphor and framework for understanding terrorist relationships. In hypnosis, there is a powerful fixation, absorption, and induction of a trance-like phenomenon. It requires people to have their conscious, critical faculties suspended as they become more and more absorbed into their personal experiences. This state has a very powerful, sensory-concentrated nature. The qualities of the hypnotic experience parallel bonding in terrorist relationships. However, to fully understand this parallel, it is essential to fully grasp the essence of the hypnotic experience.

In understanding the rationale and position of using hypnosis as a framework or structure for understanding terrorist bonding, it is important to realize that relationships among terrorists have the qualities and elements of a regressive sense of loss of control, which diffuses the sense of self. What this means is that partners feel hopeless and helpless as they intertwine in an intense, angry, isolated, and unrewarding pursuit of their hypnotic, childlike fantasies. Each person experiences reciprocal feelings of disappointment, frustration, and aggravation with his or her life situation as his or her entrancement deepens (Feeney, 1999). As entrancement serves only to intensify regressive, childlike demands while preventing constructive, responsible actions to correct the terrorist's miserable life conditions, the rage of dissatisfaction and deprivation only increases. The self-defeating and perpetuating loop creates an infinite regression as terrorists become even more entrenched in the very entrancements that blind them to what can really do to change their impoverished life conditions.

Hypnosis has a unique parallel to that type of paradigm or framework in the sense that hypnosis involves getting the individual's permission, piquing his or her interest, and narrowing his or her attention. It involves a turning inward and, at times, regressing or moving forward in time. It involves a quality of selective concentration in which individuals become intensely absorbed, focused, and fixated to the extent that they lose an outer sense of a general reality orientation. The general reality orientation (GRO) is the commonsense reality of our day-to-day conscious orientation. This involves being well oriented to time, place, person, and event.

Partners in terrorism perceive qualities in each other that seem charismatic. Such qualities may be physical features (body shape) and/or personality traits (enthusiasm, extroversion), which merge together in ways that fixate (in a narrowing of attention) partners on their perfect fantasy (which involves selective concentration). Inner, compulsive feelings (turning inward) to possess each other emerge. Partners lose track of time and daily agendas (a loss of generalized orientation). Such an encounter could be construed as a form of hypnotically induced hallucination. Hypnotized subjects can positively hallucinate or see images of their fantasies in front of them that aren't there. It can be said that partners are in a mild trance, hallucinating their idealized fantasy onto one another. Partners in terrorism are quite oblivious to the real character within themselves due to entrancement.

Another important feature of hypnosis is that it generates two types of attentional absorption, both resistant to outside interruptions and distraction. The first type is called *selective attention*, which is usually good for problem-solving on a specific skill level (dealing with educational concerns, weight loss, smoking cessation programs, and so forth). The other type is called *expansive attention* and allows a full range of stimulation and associations to be received through a stream of consciousness (witness the rush of sensations and attentional flow of riding a motorcycle at high speed, or of planes flying into the World Trade Center).

It appears that selective attention will increase the intensity of the specific experience at hand (staring at a moving watch can intensify the impact on and sensation of movement in the observer as well as any suggestions given about people, places, or things). Such staring expressions are able to be observed on some of the faces of the terrorists (such as Atta and Zacarias Moussaoui). Expansive attention will allow increases of receptivity to a stream of consciousness of feelings and memories (hearing a favorite song can open an individual to a vast range of memories, feelings, and nostalgia). Hypnotic states can be induced through application of these various types of attention and focus.

Relaxation and hypnosis are usually associated with one another, as creating a relaxed and tranquil mind occurs through a relaxed and tranquil body. Hypnosis can occur in states of physical arousal and alertness. For example, when a car's headlights shine into the eyes of a deer standing by the side of the road, it will freeze in an alert and aroused position. It is in an altered state, yet hardly relaxed. Hypnosis can occur in both relaxed hypoarousal and tense, vigilant hyperarousal.

Hypnosis also alters our GRO (Tart, 1969). When we are driving on the highway, it is our GRO that prevents us from crossing over the white line separating lanes, even when our minds are on something else. In hypnosis, the stable internal frame of reference created by GRO is diminished. Hypnotized individuals may have some awareness of outside sounds and sensations, like people talking or cars going by, but they are less acutely aware of or responsive to their presence. They are less distracted and more focused.

In deep hypnosis, in which individuals have completely relinquished their GRO, the higher cognitive functions of analysis and interpretation of here-and-now sensations are reduced. Such a reduction occurs when an individual is so attracted and absorbed by something (a great-looking car, job, house, suicide bombing, etc.) and/or someone (a well-shaped physique) that the individual unconsciously lowers his or her rational guard and impulse fantasies are entertained. At this point, sensory hallucinations and distortions may occur (there may be analgesic experiences where the pain of a toothache may be numbed). The loss of GRO is what Atta sought in urging the suicide bombers to remain focused and "think only of traveling to heaven."

Hypnosis involves dissociation, in which tranced individuals may have memories and perform acts without realizing that they are actually doing them (take the case of automatic writing, where hypnotized subjects will unconsciously write out ideas and feelings but have no recognition that they are doing it or what they wrote).

Hypnosis also creates what is known as trance logic (Brown & Fromm, 1986). This refers to the ability of hypnotized individuals to put together perceptions partially based on their real-world experience mixed and intertwined with those that are based on fantasy and imagination. The resulting perspective is that such a fusion of reality and fantasy creates hallucinations and distorted thinking patterns among hypnotized individuals. Because they are in an altered state, there is extreme tolerance for contradictions and ambiguity. An example of this is the hypnotized man believing he sees a close friend whom he hallucinates to be his mother or father. There may be distorted logic of thought. If that close friend smiles or frowns, then the individual will think that the hallucinated parent is either loving or rejecting. The trance logic of the terrorists is that the more "murders" of infidels there are, the more Allah will smile.

A further quality of hypnotized individuals is perceived involuntarism. Here, hypnotized individuals seem to be passively observing themselves act in ways that have no purpose. They feel as if things are being ruled by other forces. Hypnotic suggestion can create the effect that automatic eye closure is involuntary and beyond conscious control, leaving hypnotized individuals unable to open their eyes.

Yet, paradoxically, the hypnotized individual is utilizing a strategic trance logic to achieve the goal of hypnotic eye closure by splitting his awareness. That is, as he consciously attends to a watch moving in front of him, he is distracted from awareness of how his eye concentration causes fatigue, closure, and inner associations. When this perceived involuntarism occurs during an absorbed state of a stream of consciousness, there can be vivid imagery, memories, and changes of body image (as in "I felt like an airplane and decided to fly; my nose became the shape of a bird's beak"). Trance increases the quality and sense of realism of imaginary experiences and illusions. Because hypnotized individuals reason and think with a sensory, trance logic (the feeling of being like an airplane must mean that I am one and can now act like one), they are especially prone to feeling involuntarily controlled by inner and outer stimuli and sensations. Imagine the sense of the suicide bomber who is in an altered state literally experiencing the reality of being Allah's holy warrior, involuntarily having to kill themselves and thousands of others.

A key aspect of hypnosis is the special nature of the hypnotic relationship (Brown & Fromm, 1986). The increased availability of inner feelings, associations, images, and memories in hypnotized individuals begins to filter and shape the relationship with the hypnotist. A strong intensity and intimacy emerge between the hypnotist and the hypnotized individual. The vivid internal imagery and other highly personal sensations create a regressive affect. There is an infantilism where the individual experiences gratification of infantile wishes (attention, centeredness, and parental-like guidance). In addition, the fading of GRO that results from a restriction of input from the outside world and narrowing of the range of communication (the hypnotist is the only one the individual can contact) create a dependent, parent–child-like relationship with the hypnotist. It is not unlike the special relationship of a mother–child bond. The effects of such a special, intense bond create powerful transference effects (transferring or shifting perception and images from past significant parental figures to the here-and-now person of the hypnotist). The skillful hypnotist can utilize such regressive intensity for meaningful therapeutic change. The hypnotist realizes that his or her impact on the individual can be so intense as to seem almost magical. If the "hypnotist" is a psychopath such as Osama bin Laden, imagine the manipulative and exploitative influence he can have over such entranced terrorism.

SIGNS OF HYPNOTIC TRANCE

The signs of trance involve such concepts as depth of trance and responsiveness to suggestion. For example, arm catalepsy (when the hypnotized individual discovers his or her arm is rigid) indicates a depth of trance and responsiveness to hypnotic suggestion. Many times there are no behavioral signs of trance, only that the individual subjectively feels deeply hypnotized and intensely absorbed. Yet this same individual may not behaviorally respond because he or she is in trance. The perceptual rigidity of Islamic fundamentalists is suggestive of altered states, and it would not be difficult to begin to understand them in terms of entrancement.

Hypnotized individuals usually experience and/or demonstrate some or all of the following signs: ideomotor phenomena (alterations in physical movements caused by thinking and imagining, such as arm catalepsy) and cognitive and sensory effects (easier access to the inner world of dreams, imagery, emotions, memories, and amnesia and age regression to early childhood experiences) (Brown & Fromm, 1986).

Further signs of trance experience involve the persistent effects of posthypnotic suggestions and amnesia. Here, hypnotized individuals will be given suggestions to act or think a certain way after being awakened from the trance. They will also be given suggestions for amnesia or forgetting that such suggestions for posthypnotic behavior were ever given. For example, individuals may be given the suggestion that their understanding of conflicts and problems will become more and more clear over time after they awaken and leave the room.

Special cognitive abilities occur in trance as hypnotized individuals are capable of changing the meaning and value of words, fantasies, thoughts, and beliefs about experiences (new insights and understandings can be discovered). There can be perceptual changes in reality, illusions, hallucinations, and delusions created (factual reality can merge with fantasies, creating hallucinations, as in a real flower fantasized to be smiling; alterations in self-concept and self-esteem may be inflated or amplified by imagining self as successfully performing in school or work). Listed below are thirteen criteria for signs of trance:

1. relaxation/drowsiness
2. responsive to suggestions
3. absorption/involuntary experiencing
4. general reality orientation fading
5. vivid imagery/hallucination
6. selective or expansive attention
7. unconscious involvement
8. access to inner sensing
9. age regression
10. time distortion

11. amnesia and hyperamnesia
12. parallel awareness
13. state-dependent learning, memory, and behavior beyond waking consciousness

ENTRANCEMENT IN HYPNOSIS

A main premise advanced here is that terrorists' behavior and ways of functioning in their relationships intimately parallel similar dimensions of those in hypnotic altered states. The dimensions that are present in bonds among terrorists involve, if not require, hypnotic dynamics and forces to sustain them. The special type of altered state in such relationships is known as entrancement.

Entrancement is an alignment of matching energies and expectations at one of the deepest levels of human experience, which constitute attraction, resonance, and union between thematically similar and congruent persons (similar in thinking and believing) at many levels of their life experiences (images, feelings, characters, fantasies, chemistry, etc.). Entrancement involves suspension of critical faculties (meaning we lose our mind and surrender ourselves to some fantasy ideal way of living). It also involves selective attention filtering out incompatible information. These and many other facets suggest that the power of entrancement is hypnotic in origin. Relationship bonding among would-be terrorist and leader can be comprehended in such a hypnotic framework.

Entrancement involves a coming together or fusion of idealized images superimposed on action plans designed by terrorist leaders (Osama bin Laden) that match and merge with followers' expectations (Mohammed Atta). Each person brings to the relationship ideals or images of his or her perfection merged into the others'. Such a merger of fantasy ideals embedded into specifically designed action plans (e.g., the holy wars of the *jihad* against the Western "infidels") unleashes incredible forces for acting out catastrophic deeds in the name of God (Allah).

Entranced relationships contribute to terrorist functioning when the terrorists are unable to progress successfully from one state to the next. They experience difficulty in releasing one section or state of their relationship growth for the next one, which would assist them in continuing their journey. It is important to note that most terrorists are not aware, or are only vaguely aware, of the extent to which hypnotic entrancements operate in their significant relationships. When in entrancement, they experience chronic problems (conflicts, verbal and/or physical abuse, and other struggles). It is at this level of restrictive relating that they experience the perverse twist of merged bonding. Without learning to master, understand, and gain a perspective on hypnotic entrancement, there is great risk that the nightmarish perversion of literal, fused bonding is heightened. This can be observed when intensification of entranced fantasy ideal mergers occur. Bin Laden has portrayed himself as speaking and wearing the robe of Mohammed, who is claimed in Islamic religion to have spoken to the angel Gabriel. Bin Laden is tall, wears a long robe, and claims to, in some ways, embody the literal as well as figural presence of Mohammed (who himself was in the presence of sacredness). By association, to the Islamic fundamentalist, bin Laden could easily be construed in fantasy ideal as a deity. There is almost a love affair going on between such charismatic leaders and their followers. In some ways, the bonds between and among terrorists have such addictive alterations in states of perceiving and relating to one another. The following section describes how such entranced bondings may operate.

Partners say the perfume was hypnotizing and the personality mesmerizing. These statements are not just euphemistic terms. They access the powerful fixation and self-inductive quality of their own self-hypnotic image of what smacks of beauty, aura, and charisma. Indeed, partners create their own self-induced trance without knowing it.

In this self-talk, self-inducing trance begins a powerful journey into the deepest recesses of their own, unconscious minds. It is indeed a rapid induction. In *West Side Story*, Tony sees Maria across the dance floor, and the sudden, unexpected shock of that "perfect vision" entrances him into "love." The pair begin to induce a mutual spell over each other. Gazing into one another's eyes is the type of eye fixation that occurs in the beginning stage of hypnotic induction. The hypnotist says to his or her subject, "Let your eyes focus on some point on the wall. As you continue to stare, your eyelids could become heavy, so heavy that they may close, and you might feel more relaxed about going into trance whenever you are ready, either now or in a few moments."

Motivation and entrancement result when responding to an idealized person with the resonance of one's internal idealized thinking and imagining. This activates projection and fusion between the two. If one senses and discovers another person with his or her own unique and mysterious qualities that match one's idealized fantasies, instant rapport and absorption can develop. Everyone has some internal construct of an idealized partner. That one becomes absorbed into one's own internalized image, and in fantasy expectations of who one projects that person to be, constitutes remarkable self-deception. Such self-deception is further enhanced when an assessment of a partner is based on physical features of body shape and size. The fusion of body image with personality attributes matches the fantasized ideal projection as one and the same. The boundary between our inner and outer worlds has now dissolved and the two worlds have merged. What was perceived as fantasy is now "reality" to partners. While one sees a princess, the other sees a very plain-looking girl.

There is a slow but sure inductive quality between the "I" and the "other," which begin to mesh because of matching projections (misattributions). They make their entrance into that inductive quality of meshed oneness, which has the quality of selective attention, seeing only the best in the "other" as our ideal partner. Just such a merger of mind–body fantasy ideal and physical presence may well occur between bin Laden and his followers. Yet, as will be seen, there is a very dark, ominous side to this love affair with terrorism.

Addictive self-induction starts when partners are perceived to possess an exotic, charismatic personality associated with selective attributes that are now entranced into that addictive image of the other. Physical, sensory, and personality character-istics that partners attributed to one another create hypnotic induction. Partners see the other person as someone who reflects a fantasy of having it all. Partners are not seen as only models of fantasy. Rather, partners experience each other as a liv-ing, breathing manifestation of fantasy come true.

Embedded within entranced fantasy ideals that partners have of one another lie hidden elements of envy. While one partner may admire and idealize the other, that partner may also secretly wish that he or she too possessed such valued attrib-utes. Such hidden envy for the other's attributes is highly intensified in entrance-ment as a result of lost self-identity boundaries.

Entrancement tends to create such paradoxical, dialectical tensions in intimate relationships. The power of the hypnotic pull is the envious absorption and con-sumption of what the other has, not who the other might uniquely be as a person. Entranced partners equally lose sight of their own unique characters, falling prey to the fused, paradoxical themes that permeate entranced relationships. Partners expe-rience conflicting pulls, feeling on the one hand that they cannot live without each other, and yet on the other cannot stand to live with the other.

Entrancement encourages each partner's self-boundary toward diffusion and dis-integration. Partners lose the ability to maintain a separate and distinct integrity that attributes to each his or her own unique characteristics. Each becomes absorbed into the other's attributes. The consequences are fear, jealousy, and a lost self.

Overidentification (partners seeing themselves in each other to the point of los-ing their own sense of self), plus exaggerated admiration and envy, can mean that partners develop fear of the very unique qualities they so dearly love in each other. Partners' fear of intimacy is actually the fear of one's own uniqueness. Without uniqueness, there can be no intimacy. Entrancement creates the illusionary reality that intimacy is its own outcome. Romantic entrancement espouses the allure, pas-sion, and heat of embrace. Yet the paradox presents itself that entrancement creates the very fear and avoidance of each partner's unique qualities that are essential for intimacy. Entrancement, therefore, stands in its own way toward the path of inti-mate relating.

If entrancement interferes (by creating fears) with itself in the pursuit of intima-cy, the resulting distortions create a reality denied. Entrancement is an illusion appearing real, forever denying a partner's fulfillment of the entrancement's false promises. Illusions induce surrendering a sense of control and authority in each other's lives.

There is a rapid connection and induction characteristic in this kind of relation-ship. The problem in the beginning, as in all addictive relationships, is that the fan-tasy is expected and demanded to happen instantly. It is not seen as a journey with a desirable outcome to be nurtured and developed. It becomes a should, a must, an "ought to happen now." It becomes an irrationality of pressing partners into this neurotic, illusionary shape, fitting into the needs of the hypnotic pull. This results in denying both one's own self and the other person's identity.

Herein lies the true nature of the addiction. There is insistence that this fantasy be embodied in partners as a means of gratifying life fulfillment. The boundaries of inner thoughts and images become blurred and vulnerable to confused fixations. Partners attribute "super" powers to the other that can now supposedly change their lives.

This kind of omnipotent thinking and imaging is powerfully entrancing. It is designed to fulfill the complete induction of merging into an all-consuming, all-encompassing, larger-than-self bonding and nurturing. What is fantasized inwardly (both on a need- and idealistically based fantasy) is fused outwardly with external physical and personality attributes of our partner. There is a submergence and entrancement of inner and outer worlds fused into one. Addictive fusion through this self-induced hypnotic state begins to corrupt character.

With a suspension of critical faculties, entrancement activates mistaken beliefs stemming from distorted early childhood learning. It also engenders a suspension of volitional control, in which partners act as if they cannot help what they do. Entrancing experiences create a sense of being illusionarily taken over by the magic and wonder of this enmeshment of inner and outer worlds. Entrancement now takes on an entity all its own, so powerfully real that it now displaces common-sense logic. There is no reasoning with partners at this point.

They cannot sort out fact from fiction. Entrancement demands perfection. As quickly as times between partners can become beautiful and wondrous, they can also turn sour and stormy as rapidly as a flash flood. The slightest deviation from perfect role-playing of the ideal fantasy can result in raging jealous outbursts, accusations of betrayal, and violent attacks (verbal, emotional, and/or physical) against the "infidels." Such are the regressive effects of entrancing relationships.

These are the kinds of disqualifications of each other's fantasy needs that begin to emerge when two partners have mutually induced a trance in one another. They evoke turbulence in pulling apart, only to dive deeper into enmeshment. A temporary pulling apart creates a fear of loss, which causes partners a loss of balance (a key feature in increasing susceptibility to trance) and serves only to deepen the pull of entrancement. They are not deviant people. They are not sick. They are not ill. They are entranced. Very few people grow up without some painful, personally damaging experiences. Partners in these types of relationships do not necessarily qualify for psychiatric treatment in and of themselves. Partners in such relationships, if not "detranced" and genuinely awakened, will be driven to the point of frenzied emotional, spiritual, and eventual physical bankruptcy.

It is especially important to emphasize a unique factor of the idealized state. As in hypnosis, both parties begin to discover that by being in this type of relationship, they can now be someone that they always wanted to be but previously never believed or dreamed they could be. For example, one partner believes that, suddenly, he has found somebody who gives him all the love, admiration, and attention previously denied him. Such idealization reaches a peak level of entrancement that is narcissistic because of the nature of its self-centeredness. It results from a pyramid effect (a hypnotic technique) of one positive suggestion of specialness building upon another and another until partners believe they are each other's God. A hypnotized individual appears to behave involuntarily (as with arm rigidity). Yet, if the hypnotic induction suggests a kind of imagining and associating that has a goal-directed purpose (or it creates arm rigidity), this will be the outcome. Since critical faculties of judgment are suspended, this allows the hypnotized individual to function at a regressed level of immaturity, preoccupied with sensory gratification without conscious censorship or interference.

Such imaginary, associative, goal-directed strategy and regressed immaturity, with a suspension of critical faculties, operates in entrancing relationships. Entranced couples appear to act in involuntary, rigid ways, yet the imagery and strategy of their idealism creates a goal-directed outcome. In this case, it is a fixated, rigid way of treating each other so as to maintain the fantasized idealism of the relationship. It's a kind of "arm rigidity" of a fixated mindset. This can lead to apparent, involuntary actions and reactions from each partner. Conflicts can ensue with both being surprised at how they are acting. They are not aware of an unconscious strategy and goal-fixated behavior.

It is intriguing to note that the followers of bin Laden and the Taliban in Afghanistan entranced others into their fantasy ideals and action plans not to live together but rather to "die for Allah." An inherent betrayal, jealousy, and envy lie within terrorist schemes to obliterate whomever they entrance into their web of global cells. While they advocate a holy war against the West, the "infidels," it is their very own "lovers" whom they betray in this perfect world of entranced paradise. Followers like Richard Reid (who carried C-4 explosives inside his shoes on board an American Airlines transatlantic flight from Paris to Miami) are easily led because of their dysfunctional, weak, and impressionable nature (they are easily entranced).

Yet, there is something even more ominous about terrorist entrancements. The jealousy and rage they have regarding the West are also a characteristic of entrancement in which one partner sees the slightest deviation from the perfection of fantasy idealism, from purity, as betrayal in itself. It is quite possible that bin Laden, the Taliban, al-Qaeda, and its network of cells are rigidly obsessed and fixated on the West as the "infidels" because they are also *entranced* with us. The obsession, absorption, and demand for pure perfection of fantasy ideals leave no room for deviation or difference. It is intolerable for such entranced Islamic fundamentalists to allow the West to exist. Bin Laden refers to American support of Israel, its bombing in Afghanistan, and other actions. Yet, when the United States has withdrawn from conflict in that region of the world, this has only fanned the flames of radical fervor. Therefore, it is that we exist, that we are as a shining fantasy ideal of our own perfection, with our own physical body of manifest achievements (skyscrapers, massive commercial jet airliners, abundant wealth, technological advancement, and so forth), that threatens to consume bin Laden and his kind. How can he believe and merge with his own fantasy ideals of Allah when he himself may be obsessed with annihilation by the existence of those in the West. It is not an overt act of war that threatens bin Laden. It is the covert act of his own hidden entrancement with the West that threatens his fidelity to Islamic principles. He and his fundamentalist followers are catatonically rigid and fixated, seeking to annihilate their outer fixation on the West (and all that it has achieved and what they want in their own way but do not have) by seeking the actual physical destruction of the West.

There are multiple conditions (presented in the next section) that contribute to the presence of terrorism. Entrancement fixation is both a consequence of these conditions and a causal perpetuation of their escalation. For example, one reason we may not be liked is that someone like bin Laden perceived our military power as overwhelming in the Gulf War but lacking resolve in Somalia. The consequence is an ever-skewed fixation (entrancement) by bin Laden on the west as the "infidels" who have vast resources (which he does not) but are empty of will (which he idealizes in his terrorism). Such consequential entrancement now perpetuates further distortions of the West as imposing, restrictive, but morally "weak" infidels, which further justifies bin Laden's abusive, terrorist activities. Such interactive cycles feed into bin Laden's own entrancement with us (the ultimate infidel), which is self-conflicted and intolerable for his own existence.

Bin Laden betrays himself, his ideals, and his religion, as do all of his entranced fundamentalists who idealize what they can only have in the next life. He cannot live in his fantasy world when the seeds of his own destruction lie within him. This is not unlike a married man who is supposed to love and idealize his wife, but is tempted and entranced by the beauty across the pond from where he lives. Because his own inner entrancement with the forbidden fruit is so intense, he labels her a whore, a prostitute, and says she should be eliminated. Yet, her beauty does not harm him; only his entranced vision of her threatens him from within, tempting him to betray, to be the infidel. Bin Laden's projections onto the West betray his own introjections of infidelity and impotence he experiences in the East—what he "sees" in us is what he sees lurking in himself.

CONDITIONS OF ENTRANCEMENT

The conditions most likely to lead to terrorism simultaneously induce entrancement and are met in the Islamic fundamentalist quality of life experience. They involve environmental deprivation (of food, clothing, money, etc.), authoritarian parenting with an emphasis on strict discipline, and a limited range of choices and self-expression. In addition, there is a sense of being disenfranchised from the community and culture at large, of feeling hopeless and ineffective. Because of this restrictive range of expressions, entrancement is more likely to happen.

The Arabic and Persian countries have suffered from social, educational, and political deficits, with the masses left struggling under totalitarian regimes. Iraq is a classic example of a country with a self-serving leader who identifies himself with a stallion, seeking his own glory and oppressing the population at large when it deviates from his path. This creates disenfranchised citizens who are oppressed and limited in choices and opportunities. Islamic fundamentalists recruit from such populations of disenfranchised citizens because they are susceptible to their enticing and entrancing qualities. The fundamentalists offer a noble purposefulness that can be found in giving up one's life for one's culture. The children in Afghanistan were being educated by the Taliban to prepare themselves to sacrifice their lives (in suicide bombings and other acts of violence) in the future as a way to travel to God (Allah). They were taught that the sensory rewards and pleasures of this world were to come in the next life (seventy-two virgins in heaven, and so forth). In this way, their sense of hopelessness, futility, and lack of meaningfulness in this life could be manipulated to serve the Islamic fundamentalists' purpose of using them for mindless acts of violence. That is exactly what happened on September 11. That was clearly an act of mindless rage and violence that will never make any sense.

One can perceive the powerful effects of entrancement operating in Atta's message to the other terrorists. He says, "Purify your hearts and forget something called life." This is a powerful suggestion to fixate on some imagined (entranced), unreal, God-like holiness and to ignore the sensory world around you while you're about to murder thousands of innocent human beings. That last part he left out. Had he inserted it, it would have awakened them into the real-world experience of a general reality orientation regarding what they were going to do to themselves as well as to many others who never hurt them. By saying the time for play is over, he narrows their focus, and fixates them on a vague delusion of doing God's work, with some ultimate reward coming in the next life. The hopelessness that Atta felt, in that he believed he could never rise to any significant position in Egypt, restricted his sense of orientation to reality in this world. He was a purist and wanted his world to be perfect. This involved eliminating all injustice and unfairness. His inner fantasy-ideal of excellence in his field was so abated that he manifested his ideal into a real-world delusion that he'd rather be a "captain of a plane headed for hell than a servant in heaven." His entrancement was a ferocious and violent, perverse delusion that all of his earthly privations would be rectified in some sensory (delusional and hallucinatory) manifestation in the next life. In other words, an earth in heaven rather than a heaven on earth.

By utilizing the empowering achievements of America, vis-à-vis awesome commercial airliners colliding with its symbols of financial greatness (the World Trade Center), he was able to twist and pervert his own sense of futility on this earth into a Pyrrhic victory, "blaming the infidels" for what his own country of Egypt was actually the one preventing him from having. By distorting in entrancement the powerful achievements of the West as signs of "evil," he was able to deny his own unacceptable desires for the very things he himself so dearly wanted but believed he would never have. This is not unlike a lover who kills the one he loves so that, if he can't have her, no one can (because she was an evil harlot anyway—or so the distortion might go). The entrancing-like qualities of fixation, stone-like numbness, and flatness of emotion are all consistent characteristics of trance-like altered states. Judgment and critical faculties are temporarily suspended as the altered state is now operative in a narrow, rigid tunnel-like attentional focus. Trying to communicate in a critical dialogue with a terrorist in that state is like trying to play chess with someone on drugs.

The mixing of the afterlife into the delusional fixation feeds into the authoritarian higher-power distortion. When people feel helpless and ineffective, they are susceptible to such fixations and inculcations of altered power sources. Both Atta and bin Laden had restrictive and authoritarian family orientations, yet they were in one form or another ostracized, estranged, and/or alienated from their families. In children, such fantasy ideals of nobility, importance, and significance are quite intense. Research has shown (Schlesinger & Revitch, 1980) that violent, antisocial acts occur when so-called harmless fantasy and imagination regarding sexual scenarios are no longer contained in adulthood. The being of the perpetrator can no longer be contained within the fantasy, as it has lost its ability to satiate inner desires. The potential for abuse in these families is high and the displacement of violence and aggression from the self to others is to be expected as the child grows into adulthood. The preoccupation with restricting sexuality in Arabic cultures, the harsh discipline, and the physical beatings and oppressiveness all contribute to abusive childhood conditions. The sudden conversion of Atta in the mature adult years of his life, while on the surface surprising and atypical of terrorists, reflects the impact of entranced fantasization manifesting itself in real-world behaviors of violence and terror. All of this is experienced in the entranced delusion as noble, just, and holy as it is fused in the literal word of Islamic fundamentalists. To the terrorists, this is the literal word of Allah, and when Atta wrote that those terrorists on the plane were traveling to God, it was then that they were most fixated on this entranced fusion of the literal word of Allah with earthly actions, while with this fusion the terrorists were being manipulated with a cloaking of the horrific mayhem that was about to be unleashed.

Entrancement is easier to generate when there is no separation between fact and visions of the future. Islamic fundamentalism dissolves the boundary line between mastering the Koran and mastering *jihad* against the West. This radical form of Islam operates under delusional, or trance, logic, so that the living proof of God's validity is in the power to defeat all others.

When the United States failed to demonstrate powerful responses to Islamic attacks (the Beirut bombings in 1983, the U.S. withdrawal from Somalia, the 1993 World Trade Center bombing), the fundamentalists regarded these strategic victories as religious victories. It is not unlike children saying my dad (my God) can beat up your dad (your God). Such entranced logic of politics and religion can be seen throughout history (Hitler's dream of the thousand-year Reich, Napoleon's vision of European domination, etc.).

The Islamic fundamentalists envisioned themselves as uniting the Muslim world extending from Europe to the Philippines, and eventually throughout the world. Osama bin Laden and Mullah Omar are entranced with the vision of wearing the cloak and staff of Mohammad. In short, they see themselves as Islam's new Messiahs.

There has been a syllogistic logic attached to their formative construction of God (Allah) (Krauthammer, 2001). The construction of the Islamic warrior is:

My God is great and omnipotent. I am a warrior for God.
Therefore, victory is mine.

The caveat to this is that God is strictly and rigidly defined as a power exclusively for war, the fundamentalist's war, and nothing else. It is through this purist, self-absorbed, and ill-formed constructiveness that these fundamentalists expose their own deluded entrancement. As the United States has defeated the Taliban in Afghanistan, their formulation that might makes right has caused the voice of the fundamentalists to grow quiet. Their illusion has been shattered. Their God is not God.

Yet, entrancement (the merger of fact and fantasy) is difficult to break. The fusion of visionary fantasy ideals of world domination with terrorist activities lives on in many terrorists' minds.

The major premise of their syllogism is that God is omnipotent. Yet, everything else that follows is a sign of their deluded entrancement. First, they assume that terrorist assaults constitute what a warrior of such a God (Allah) would do. However, the glaring severity of how delusional their entrancing state actually is occurs in their conclusion: Victory is not God's, it is the terrorists'. The entrancement is so intense that these extreme radicals terrorize their own God (Allah) by claiming his/her victory (whatever that actually would be) as theirs—"victory is mine."

That is why they lost in Afghanistan. The awesome power of the United States was sustained by a world coalition of countries that enhanced and supported the war effort. Had this coalition not been gathered, the United States might have had great difficulty in delivering its overpowering forcefulness and defeating the Taliban and al-Qaeda.

The truncated and tunnel vision view of bin Laden (ironically, he lives in tunnels and caves) suffers from visionary entrancement that is devoid of judgment, reality-testing, and dealing with the real needs of the Arab people. The poverty, poor education, and oppressive political condition of Arabic and Persian people need real-world assistance in this life (Zakaria, 2001). The entranced delusional altered states of Islamic fundamentalists are so busy trying to steal victory from God (Allah) to be "my victory," sending other Arabs on suicidal, entranced "travels to God," that they have forgotten what is needed in this world. The entrancement of living to die is a dangerous, delusional perversion that makes death seem more attractive than life in this world. One can only speculate what Atta would have been like if he had achieved prominence in the field that he studied at university and had had seventy-two virgins available to him at the same time. Would that reality have served to reorient him to a more responsible moral and motivated way of life in this world?

Further signs of entrancement can be seen in how the terrorists construed (or misconstrued) their design fantasy ideal of the afterlife. It is an ideal of purist qualities (that's why it's pure fantasy) where there is an absolute and pious right and an absolute and impious wrong. An uncritical attitude can be seen in Mohammed Atta. He repeated his mantra-like set of instructions to himself and the others as the planes were being boarded. These sets of instructions reflect a pure, unchallenged, uncritical, blind acceptance of their absolute truth and validity. It is clear from such instructions that the instructions were to function more as a kind of informal hypnotic induction and deepening, placing their induced subjects in altered states of regression. What this means is that persons experiencing such mental states of alteration function at a cognitive awareness level of primary processing. This level involves literal, concrete acceptance. Whatever is described and depicted as being true in image/and or sensory-based experience will be accepted uncritically as being valid. When Atta described the steps that the terrorists would take on the plane, instead of stating the factual truth that they were all on a suicide mission and would collide with a skyscraper, he described how they would be "traveling to heaven, to God." The sensory-based experience of describing what sensations persons in such altered states will feel and what it will mean is part of their literal, uncritical fluid acceptance of someone leading them down the path. This is not to suggest that the other terrorists were unwitting conspirators and didn't know what they were doing. It does mean that they, like Atta, were already susceptible to such intense, entrancing fantasy ideals because of the deprivation and unfulfillment in their lives.

The descriptions of what heaven would hold for them (passion, nobility, forgiveness, etc.) not only titillated their imagery and fantasy but also accessed sensory experiences not gratified in their present lives. For example, Atta and others were described as visiting a pornographic shop before the tragedies were to unfold. There, they could indulge their sensory titillation of what was to be theirs in the next life. It seems curious that such soldiers of God would be preparing themselves to be in the presence of Eternal Holiness by visiting a pornographic shop. How pious and honorable is that?

The entrancement of the fantasy ideal of gaining heaven through killing people was reinforced by the literal regressive acceptance that this was the omnipotent word and will of Allah. The fusion or merger of such fantasy ideals involving terrorist activities with the infinite power of a God serves to intensity such entrancement. It is not unlike Adolf Hitler, who believed that destiny was on his side, willing him to exterminate the Jews.

Suspension of the critical faculties, accompanied by literal acceptance of highly suggestive word imagery and sensations, is an indicator of entrancing, altered states. When bin Laden and others label those in the West as "the infidels," they trigger regressive, literal altered states where blind, uncritical acceptance can occur. The very word "infidel" means unfaithful. Intense focusing and attending creates narrowed, selective tunnel vision in which regressive, literal states of suggestive acceptance are now possible. The vague reference to God and to how Westerners somehow are inherently unfaithful, betray God, evil, and therefore deserving of whatever cruelty they get, is the great hoax of entrancement. In effect, it intensely directs Arab and Persian attention and consciousness to a simple-minded, absolutist duality—"if you are not like us and thus like our God/Allah in every and all ways, then you are not one with us or our God/Allah (the One True God) and therefore you are the Evil One—the Infidel."

When the terrorists render their politics, cruelty, and subversive activities as cloaked and embedded in the entrancing word and imagery of Allah, their influence is astonishingly pervasive. The entrancing formulation that they are warriors of Allah makes for powerful imagery and uncritical acceptance. This can unleash powerful regression experiences in which childhood trauma, abuse, and other forms of personal violation can be acted out and perpetrated under the name of all that is pious and noble. This is, of course, not a new observation. How many acts of cruelty and savagery have been committed in the name of God/Allah?

To reawaken from such entrancements, the primary association needs to be broken. In the case of the terrorists, when "the warrior of God/Allah" has been defeated it becomes clear (though not all at once) that perhaps that warrior may not have been fighting in the name of God/Allah, but rather in the name of cruelty, selfish narcissism, and psychopathic tendencies.

Yet, entrancement is a powerful altered state and individuals and cultures that are limited, regressive in levels of development, and childlike in their levels of social sophistication will continue to be vulnerable. We all want to believe in ideals and we all have our fantasy and passions. Let us not forget that the suffering and crucifixion of Jesus Christ was no fantasy ideal but a realization of the real-world pain, suffering, and sacrifice involved in creating a more meaningful life in this world—before we go to the next. Arab and Persian terrorists need to reject entrancement and enrich their lives, add diversity, and adopt pluralistic ways of thinking and behaving.

The universe is evolutionary. Life builds upon itself in levels of ever-greater complexity and differentiation. If the unfolding universe is any guide, it would appear that we need to fully enrich with meaning, value, and spirituality the life we are currently in at the level we currently are at before we can hope to deserve to move onto a richer, fuller next level or dimension of existence. One life at a time, one level at a time. Maybe if the Arab and Persian cultures are nurtured, encouraged, and enriched to evolve in their own unique formative ways, there will be fewer that are eager to leave them. They need to see the world before they leave it and that means seeing hope and meaningfulness in their future in this world. There is research to demonstrate that democratic and pluralistic cultures are much less prone to engage in physical conflict and war. Perhaps a chess game (or whatever is its equivalent in Arab and Persian cultures) would be a healthier alternative to work out our conflicts than the massive destruction of societies. The time has come for regressive entrancements such as "my God can beat up your God" to be removed from the maiming and killing of innocent human beings (whether they are different from us or not). Actually, this sounds as if it could be the name of a new video game. It certainly would be a welcome relief and a more spiritual elevation toward the next life—in this life.

REFERENCES

Bloom, H. (1995). *The Lucifer principle*. New York: Atlantic Monthly Press.

Brown, D. P., & Fromm, E. (1986). *Hypnotherapy and hypoanalysis*. Hillsdale, NJ: Lawrence Erlbaum.

Cloud, J. (2001, October 8). Atta's odyssey. *Time*, pp. 64–67.

Douglas, J. (1995). *Mind hunter*. New York: Pocket Books.

Egger, S. A. (1984). A working definition of serial murder and the reduction of linkage blindness. *Journal of Police Science and Administration, 12*, 348–357.

Elliot, Michael (2001, November 12). Hate club. *Time*, pp. 58–74.

Feeney Jr., D. J. (1999). *Entrancing relationships*. Westport, CT: Praeger Press.

Krauthammer, C. (2001, December 24). Only in their dreams. *Time*, pp 60–61.

Ludwig, A. M. (1966). Altered states of consciousness. *Archives of General Psychiatry, 15*, 225–234.

MacCulloch, M., Snowden, P., Wood, P., & Mills, E. (1983). Sadistic fantasy, sadistic behavior and offending. *British Journal Psychiatry, 143*, 20–29.

Prentky, R., Burgess, A., & Carter, D. (1986). Victim responses by rapist type: An empirical and clinical analysis. *Journal of Interpersonal Violence, 1*, 73–98.

Riyadh, S. M. (2001, November 19). The near misses. *Time*, p. 57. Schlesinger, L. B., & Revitch, E. (1980). The criminal fantasy technique: A comparison of sex offenders and substance abusers. *Journal of Clinical Psychology, 37*, 210–218.

Schlesinger, L. B., & Revitch, E. (1980). Criminal fantasy technique: Comparison of sex offenders and substance abusers. *Journal of Clinical Psychology, 37*, 210–218.

Tart, C. T. (1969). *Altered states of consciousness*. New York: John Wiley and Sons.

Tucker, K. (2001, November 2). The importance of being Dave. *Entertainment*, p. 26.

Zakaria, F. (2001, October 15). Why do they hate us? *Newsweek*, pp. 22–40.

9

Terrorists and Cultists

Arthur A. Dole

THE ISSUES

To what extent, if any, can one hundred years of psychological research into cults, sects, and religion help in understanding, preventing, and opposing terrorists? Specifically, are bin Laden and al-Qaeda cultists? The answers to these questions are particularly important because of conflicts in the Middle East and Afghanistan and the attacks of September 11, 2001. In the longer run they may also be pertinent to unimagined events. Religious zealots have gone to war throughout history in the name of Jesus, Allah, Jehovah, Zeus, God, and various other deities. Unfortunately, it is likely that religious zealots will continue to terrorize.

Bin Laden and al-Qaeda

Who is Osama bin Laden and who are his followers? To answer these questions I read Peter L. Bergen's *Holy War* (published in October 2001), scanned the Internet in December, thumbed the *Dictionary of Cults, Sects, Religions, and the Occult* (Mather & Nichols, 1993), and absorbed various accounts in the current media. Here is some of what I learned.

Bin Laden was born in 1957 in Saudi Arabia, one of the many children of a wealthy contractor. During his childhood in a primitive village, the prevailing religion was fundamentalist Islam. Islam, now one of the world's major religions, was founded in the sixth century A.D. Although there are many Islamic sects, they share the belief that " 'There is no God but Allah and Muhammad is his prophet.' . . . a

Moslem who hopes to escape the wrath of Allah and the tormenting fires of hell must diligently strive to fulfill the requirements set forth . . ." in the Koran (Mather & Nichols, 1993, pp. 139, 143). As a university student, then an engineer and contractor in Saudi Arabia, bin Laden was exposed to the Saudi Arabian Wahhabi, "the strictest and most conservative of all Moslem sects . . . founded in the eighteenth century" (Mather & Nichols, 1993, p. 145). Thus, the roots of bin Laden's religious orientation are extremely authoritarian and militant.

As a volunteer in the Afghan forces during the war with the Soviet Union in the late 1980s, bin Laden became a hero, a charismatic figure noted for his bravery and serenity in combat. According to the U.S. Department of State (2001), bin Laden established al-Qaeda

> to bring together Arabs who fought in Afghanistan against the Soviet invasion. Helped finance, recruit, transport, and train Sunni Islamic extremists for the Afghan resistance. (p. 1)

When he returned to Saudi Arabia after the war, he was profoundly outraged by the corruption of the ruling class and by the American military presence. The current goal of al-Qaeda is (U.S. Department of State, 2001)

> to establish a pan-Islamic Caliphate throughout the world by working with allied Islamic extremist groups to overthrow regimes it deems "non-Islamic" and expelling Westerners and non-Muslims from Muslim countries. Issued statement under banner of "the World Islamic Front for Jihad Against the Jews and Crusaders" in February 1998, saying it was the duty of all Muslims to kill US citizens—civilian or military—and their allies everywhere. . . . May have several hundred to several thousand members. Also serves as a focal point or umbrella organization for a worldwide network that includes many Sunni Islamic extremist groups. . . . Bin Laden . . . is said to have inherited approximately $300 million that he uses to finance the group. Al-Qaida also maintains moneymaking front organizations, solicits donations from like-minded supporters, and illicitly siphons funds from donations to Muslim charitable organizations. (pp. 1–2)

TERRORIST, CULTIST, MIND CONTROL

Terrorist, cultist, and *mind control* are slippery terms that often shift depending upon the preference of the user.

Terrorist

According to *Webster's Deluxe Unabridged Dictionary* (McKechnie, 1979), the root word *terror* is based on the Latin *terrere,* "to frighten," and is defined in part as "1. Intense fear."

Terrorism is ". . . n. 1. A terrorizing; use of terror and violence to intimidate, subjugate, etc., especially as a political weapon. 2. Intimidation and subjugation. . . ." It follows that a terrorist is "n. A person who practices or favors terrorism." Examples are those participating in the French Reign of Terror and the extreme revolutionary societies in Czarist Russia. (p. 443)

From the American point of view, the nineteen men who smashed into the World Trade Center towers, the Pentagon, and the ground of Pennsylvania were terrorists, as were their suspected supporters—bin Laden, al-Qaeda, and the Taliban. On the other hand, from the point of view of those hostile to the United States, the bombers were martyrs and the Americans are the terrorists. As Michael Kinsley has written (2001), defining terrorism is essential; it's also impossible. I propose to use the term *terrorist* in the following sense: Given a conflict, a terrorist is an extremely hostile opponent. And the psychology of conflict resolution may be useful, especially if Americans realize they themselves are not mediators, not neutral interveners, but participants in a struggle.

Cultist

Cultist is also a tricky term. Returning to my old but reliable dictionary (McKechnie, 1979), I find:

> Cult. n. (Fr. culte, L. cultus from colere to cultivate, worship)
> 1. worship, reverential honor, religious devotion. (Obs.)
> 2. the system of outward forms and ceremonies used in worship; religious rules and formalities.
> 3. devoted attachment to or extravagant admiration for, a person, principle, etc., especially when regarded as a fad.
> 4. a group of followers, sect. (p. 443)

Ask a sociologist, a lawyer, a theologian, an anthropologist, or a scholar in American studies to define cult and one would in all probability hear five rather different replies. Because I am a psychologist, I find the most useful elaborating on the term in *The Illustrated Encyclopedia of Active New Religions, Sects, and Cults*, by Benjamin Beit-Hallahmi (1993), a professor of psychology at the University of Haifa.

Beit-Hallahmi lists more than nine hundred groups. He classifies them in three categories. An active new religion is a group displaying some novelty, distinctiveness from existing religions, new leadership, and new claims to divine truth. A sect was once connected with another religious organization. And a cult "is in a way more deviant. . . . outside the religious establishment. . . . Use of the term implies nothing pejorative."

For a thoughtful discussion on using the term *cult*, see also a recent essay by Herbert Rosedale and Michael Langone (1998). They remark that even though it has limited utility, it is the best term we have for group psychological manipulation.

Mind Control

Abusive religious, political, and other groups are characterized by many cult watchers (AFF, 1998) as using "mind control." For example, they apply deception, intensive persuasion, covert hypnotic techniques, and extreme flattery to recruit converts. They control devotees through confession, induced guilt, a totalistic organization, and absolute adherence to a theology or dogma. The individual's freedom is sharply reduced; during the conversion process, the leaders have control of the recruit's environment (Lifton, 1961).

SELECTED RELEVANT RESEARCH

Anecdotal

The work of a number of psychologists and psychiatrists is helpful in understanding very abusive groups. Using anecdotal evidence from many sources, William James (1902) was a pioneer in describing "subliminal consciousness" as a factor in religious conversion. An altered state of consciousness was common to a variety of sects and creeds. Often in the nineteenth and early twentieth centuries conversions were induced by charismatic leaders—some of whom were frauds or emotionally disturbed. Religion offered believers comfort and certainty in times of social unrest.

Clinical

During the Korean War a number of mental health specialists—including Robert J. Lifton (1961), Margaret Singer (1979), and Edgar Schein (Schein, Schneier, & Barker, 1961)—had the opportunity to interview military and civilians who had been imprisoned by the Chinese Communists. Some had converted to communism. Once released, most of these former prisoners reverted to their previous belief system. In his influential book, *The Psychology of Totalism*, Lifton (1961) detailed the formula for mind control. Under deliberately designed conditions, absent physical coercion, the Communists, for example, converted Catholic priests and U.S. Army officers to a new belief system, distinctly different from their previous loyalties.

As a practicing clinical psychologist, Margaret Singer (1979) saw a large number of patients who had been members of various small religious and political groups. Recalling her previous experience with former prisoners of war, she recognized that the ex-cultists were the victims of mind control. Many of her patients had been young, bright, emotionally normal, Jewish or Protestant college students at the time they were deceived, converted, manipulated, and exploited by a new religion.

Relying heavily on her patients' accounts in therapy, Singer has published extensively (Singer, 1979; Singer & Lalich, 1997; Singer & West, 1980) and has testified frequently as an expert witness. Her insights into the misuses of mind control by abusive groups have influenced countercultists, exit consultants, and rehabilitation workers assisting cult victims. They have been criticized by some psychologists (Amitrani & Di Marzio, 2000), because her views have yet to be fully substantiated.

It is a commonplace among psychologists, psychiatrists, and stage magicians that some subjects, obeying posthypnotic suggestion, will act in unusual and uncharacteristic ways. In the trial of Patty Hearst, the heiress who turned bank robber, the late Martin Orme, who was both a psychologist and psychiatrist, testified as an expert witness to support the defense argument: Under the hypnotic influence of her captors, he argued, she had converted to their cause. Orme (Karlin & Orme, 1996) has also discussed how an abusive satanic group misused hypnosis and social influence.

Hindu movements such as Divine Light Mission and Hare Krishna (Beit-Hallahmi, 1993) expect devotees to chant, to repeat an assigned mantra. Clinicians have observed that this practice can lead over time to cognitive impairment. Recently psychologist Steve Hassan (2001) videotaped a role play of a Scientology training session. The trainer (a former member of the group) repeated the same exercise daily over a period of weeks. Once the trainee was in a trance state, he was prepared to withstand argument and questioning of his new belief system.

When recruits to the neo-Islamic groups Taliban and al-Qaeda attend training schools, they are taught to memorize the Koran in Arabic (Bergen, 2001), even though for some that language is foreign. Perhaps this practice explains in part their loyalty to their group. Mind control.

Experimental

How does it happen that ordinary people, such as Germans during the Holocaust, torture innocent victims? Social psychologist Stanley Milgram provides a possible answer: They were just following the orders of an authority. In his experiments (Milgram, 1974; Miller, Collins, & Brief, 1995) an imposing "authority," dressed in lab white and formal in manner, asks a paid volunteer subject to participate in a study of learning. The volunteer is told that when the learner (actually a confederate) fails an assigned task, the volunteer is to administer an electric shock. (In fact, there is no harm to the learner, no shock, and the task is rigged.). As the shocks "increase in intensity," the "learner" begins to writhe in agony, and the scientist prods the "experimenter" to continue increasing the voltage. Milgram reported that 65 percent of the participants obeyed the scientist's orders to the maximum extent, even though the victim protested. This experiment has been repeated with many variations (Miller et al., 1995). Consistently, the contrived situation exercised remarkable power over ordinary participants.

One partial explanation, then, for the abusive acts of cult members—theft, deception, drug sales, suicide, and worse: They are following orders of their guru.

The work of Philip Zimbardo, a professor of psychology at Stanford University and president of the American Psychological Association in 2001–2002, demonstrates dramatically how assigned roles within an environment influence interpersonal behaviors (Zimbardo, 1996). Certain rooms within Zimbardo's lab were adapted to resemble cells within a prison. Paid volunteer undergraduates were assigned at random the role of prisoner or of guard. Within a short time, the guards dominated and verbally abused the prisoners, and the prisoners organized a rebellion. This experiment illustrates how much a person's behavior is shaped by the role he or she is playing.

Given an abusive religious group that sends its missionaries into college dormitories or door to door into the homes of strangers, Zimbardo's experiment may explain in part missionaries' behavior toward prospective converts. Some cultists term their conversion efforts "heavenly deception" or "transcendental trickery." So too the power of a role assigned by a charismatic leader may explain in part why apparently ordinary Middle Eastern young men become martyrs.

Are cultists crazy, emotionally disturbed? In one longitudinal study, clinical psychologist Paul Martin (Martin, Langone, Dole, & Wiltrout, 1992) administered the Millon Clinical Mutiaxial Inventory (MCMI), a self-report inventory designed to assess personality and clinical symptoms of psychiatric patients, to sixty-six residents of a rehabilitation facility immediately after they left an abusive group and again six months later, following treatment. Most scores on MCMI scales dropped substantially and significantly from abnormal toward normal. Martin and his collaborators concluded that dissociative processes are central to the cult experience.

Malinoski, Langone, and Lynn (1999) compared former members of the International Churches of Christ (ICC) with former Catholics and with InterVarsity Christian Fellowship graduates on a battery of standardized measures of psychological distress. The former ICC members scored higher than the non-cultic comparison groups on depression, anxiety, dissociation, and symptoms of avoidance and intrusion, supporting clinical reports of important levels of psychological symptoms in former cult members.

Conceptualizations

Drawing on theory and years of clinical experience with cult victims, psychologists Steven Hassan (2000) and Michael Langone (1993) have described how cults may misapply psychological principles, especially in recruiting, converting, and controlling their members.

Scholars in sociology, religious studies, and anthropology also have made valuable contributions to knowledge about new religions (their term). For example, Bromley and Shupe (1979), using observations and structured interviews, have analyzed in detail the operations of the Unification Church.

Bromley (2001) and others have criticized the concepts of mind control and brainwashing as well as the medicalization of countercultism. In response, Langone (2000), long a leader in the countercult group, has called for a dialogue between the two camps in cultic studies.

INTERVENTIONS

Among the distinguishing characteristics of cultists is their resistance to external pressures from parents and friends to reject their new religions. Through trial and error over many years countercultists have developed techniques for persuading cultists voluntarily to leave their groups. Kidnapping and involuntary deprogramming are now rarely applied.

Steven Hassan, an exit consultant, psychologist, and author (2000), bases his counseling of voluntary cultists on theory and research. To combat destructive mind control, he has developed the Strategic Interaction Approach. This approach is designed to free the cult member from the group's control over his or her life.

CASE STUDY

In a rare study of a voluntary deprogramming, Dubrow-Eichel (1989; 1990) applied psychotherapy process methodology. With permission he audiotaped, transcribed, and analyzed the interactions over three days of a team of three deprogrammers and a Hare Krishna devotee. The devotee decided finally to leave the group. In this single case the Hare Krishna changed his loyalty to the group slowly; within a respectful atmosphere, cognitive interventions were effective. As Dubrow-Eichel (1990) summarizes,

> . . . this deprogramming was a persuasive conversation and moral discourse in which the primary activities were asking for and receiving information (education) and self-disclosing (affiliation). The cultist's decreased attentional motility and increased ideational activity suggested improved concentration and implied a change in consciousness. (p. 174)

This successful deconversion—a single, case-intensive study—might serve as a model for studies of al-Qaeda captives. Of course, interventions would need to be adapted to the Afghanistan situation.

Surveys

In what respects, if any, are religions, sects, and cults harmful to their own members and to the public? Under the leadership of its executive officer, Michael Langone, who has a doctorate in counseling psychology, the American Family Foundation (AFF) has sponsored a series of opinion surveys. The AFF describes itself as follows (1998):

> AFF is "a secular, nonprofit, tax-exempt research center and educational organization founded in 1979" . . . Its "mission is to study psy-

chological manipulation and cultic groups, to educate the public and professional and to assist those who have been adversely affected by a cultic experience." (p. iii)

According to surveys of former cultists (Chambers, Langone, Dole, & Grice, 1994); of AFF advisory board members (Dubrow-Eichel & Dole, 1986)—that is theologians, lawyers, mental health specialists, and others with expertise about cults; of skeptical scientists (Dole, Langone, & Dubrow-Eichel, 1993); and of New Age observers (Dole et al., 1993), religious, political, and New Age groups varied from benign to very harmful. Those rated most harmful applied mind control in recruiting and controlling members.

Langone and his associates also have developed the Group Psychological Abuse Scale (GPA) (Chambers et al., 1994). Respondents are asked to rate a group for each of twenty-eight descriptions of an abuse on a five-point scale from "not characteristic" to "very characteristic" (see Appendix). After they administered this inventory to 308 former members of 101 different groups, Langone and collaborators (Chambers et al., 1994) identified four factors that they called Compliance, Exploitation, Mind Control, and Anxious Dependence. Once again the cultic groups varied from benign to abusive and also were characterized by distinctive profiles on GPA sub-scales. "Reliability and validity findings suggest the GPA should be useful in characterizing the varieties of abuse and in differentiating cults from innocuous groups." (Chambers et al., 1994, p. 88.) Later in this paper I will consider whether or not a version of the GPA is characteristic of bin Laden and al-Qaeda.

INCIDENTS OF CULT VIOLENCE

It is tempting to equate the September 11 attacks in which nineteen young men martyred themselves with three widely publicized incidents: the People's Temple at Jonestown, the Branch Davidians at Waco, and the Aum Shinrikyo group in Tokyo. Here is a brief description of each group from Beit-Hallahmi's encyclopedia (1993), followed by a summary of media reports about each incident:

People's Temple Christian (Disciples) Church. Popularly known as the People's Temple, this Christian group was one of the most notorious religious movements of recent history, becoming the subject of worldwide horror when more than 900 of its members committed suicide. Founded in 1956 in Indiana as the Community National Church by Jim Jones (1931–1978), it started as a typical lower-class congregation. Jones practiced faith healing, and his followers attributed various miracles to him. He became an ordained minister of the Disciples of Christ in 1965 and then moved to San Francisco with 150 followers. Most members were poor African Americans, but Jones was able to establish ties with political leaders in the area. Throughout its existence there,

People's Temple was actually a mainline Protestant congregation belonging to the Christian Church (Disciples of Christ). In 1974 the group moved to Guyana, South America. In November 1978, 912 members died in a mass suicide on orders from Jones, who was among them. It should be noted that most of the members who died with Jones were African American females. (p. 226)

Because of complaints by some of his constituents who were concerned about family members, in 1978 U.S. Rep. Leo J. Ryan flew to Guyana to investigate. Ryan was murdered. Only then, perhaps fearing retaliation, Jones, agitated, called on his followers to join him in taking their lives.

Branch Davidians (Branch Seventh Day Adventists). Adventist group started near Waco, Texas, in 1935. Members of the Branch in its various organizational forms have followed the teachings of Victor T. Houteff, which deviated from those of the Seventh Day Adventist Association. After Houteff's death and the discrediting of his wife because of the failure of a prophecy, Ben Roden (d. 1978) renamed the group the Branch Davidians. Roden's son, who took over from his mother, was challenged in 1987 by Vernon Howell, an ousted member. Howell's trial on charges of attempted murder ended in mistrial; the charges were later dropped.

Howell in 1990 changed his name to Koresh. He recruited intensively, combining biblical exhortation with rock music. He fathered numerous children by women members. He stockpiled Mount Carmel with a formidable arsenal. On February 28, 1993, more than 100 federal officers attempted to arrest Koresh on a weapons charge. After a 34-minute gun battle, four officers were dead and many wounded. A 51-day standoff ensued, punctuated by hours of telephone negotiations and intermittent release of children and a few adults. On April 19, the F. B. I. began firing tear gas into the compound. Within hours, members of the cult set frame buildings afire. Of some 80 persons, including at least 17 children, only nine persons escaped the inferno. The compound was utterly destroyed. (p. 38)

Despite considerable controversy, subsequent Senate hearings exonerated the FBI. Allegedly blaming the government for this incident, Timothy McVeigh bombed the Murrah Federal Building in Oklahoma City in 1995.

Aum Supreme Truth (Aum Shinrikyo). International Buddhist-Taoist-Hinduist group with branches in Japan and the United States, founded in 1986 and led by Shoko Asahara. It offers its members "real Initiation," "Astral Initiation," and "Causal Initiation." The goal of the group is "spiritual enlightenment." According to its publications, "After passing through Earthly Initiation which purifies one's consciousness, Astral Initiation which purifies one's subconsciousness, over 2,000 members in Japan have promoted their spiritual growth remarkably, and experienced astral projection and feelings of supreme bliss within half a year." Members are encouraged to leave their families and adopt a monastic life. In 1989 Shoko Asahara ran unsuccessfully in the elections for the Japanese parliament. (p. 23)

A year after this description was published in 1993, Aum members unleashed the nerve gas sarin in the Matsumoto subway. Seven people died and many more were sickened. In 1995, Aum again released nerve gas, this time in a Tokyo subway. Twelve people died and about five thousand were sickened. According to recent news summaries in the *Cult Observer* ("State intervenes," 2000; "Aum," 2000), an AFF-sponsored review of press reports on cultism and unethical social influence, some Aum Shinrikyo cultists have been arrested for fraud, another member of the group has been sentenced to life imprisonment for the Matsumoto attack, and the chief of the group's Osaka office was sentenced in November 2000 for complicity in the murder of a man who was planning to quit the sect in 1989.

Interpretations

The following interpretation of these three incidents from a psychological perspective needs further intensive analysis for verification.

A "killer cult" led by a charismatic religious psychopath recruits ordinary devotees with intensive persuasion and the promise of a certain and blessed future, then secures their loyalty through covert hypnosis and other mind-control techniques. Posthypnotic suggestion may account for their rigid, irrational adherence to hero/martyr roles. Upon command they kill. In the episodes at Waco and Jonestown the groups were cornered and retaliated with homicide and suicide. At Waco particularly, the Branch Davidians violently resisted arrest and physical force.

In my estimate, apologists for new religions, including sociologists (for example, Shupe & Bromley, 1980; Bromley & Hadden, 1993), consider the concept of mind control to be unproved. These scholars assume that cult members are responsible for their beliefs unless influenced by threat and physical force. They ignore any psychology that emphasizes states of consciousness. In their view, the Branch Davidians, People's Temple, or Aum were justified in their actions; they were provoked into defending their right to practice their faith.

Killer Cults

How common are killer religious cults? Although the ex-members surveyed by Chambers and collaborators (1994) rated 101 different groups in the United States on the GPA, none was associated with homicide or suicide on a large-scale basis. A review of all reports published by the *Cult Observer* in 2000 and 2001 revealed only one instance of mass death in the United States and other countries. In March 2000, up to one thousand people associated with the Movement for the Restoration of the Ten Commandments of God, led by self-styled prophet Joseph Kibetere, perished in a Uganda church fire ("Trying," 2000). According to this AFF publication's report, the evidence is ambiguous as to whether or not the group was like a classic cult. Whether or not they killed themselves or were murdered is unclear.

In a variety of groups here and abroad in the same two-year period, however, there were instances of fraud, neglect and starvation of members, child abuse, corporal punishment, manipulation, exploitation, excessive control, illegal enticement, and more. Yet, except for the ambiguous report from Uganda, apparently no other mass killing occurred.

IS BIN LADEN A CULT LEADER?

Is bin Laden a cult leader? Some expert observers have termed bin Laden and al-Qaeda a cult. For example, professional exit consultants Steve Dubrow-Eichel and Linda Dubrow (Diament, 2001), after examining in detail the available media reports about those associated with the September 11 terrorists, have concluded that al-Qaeda is indeed a cult.

One way to identify a harmful group is to ask former members to complete the GPA. As a method of gauging public opinion shortly after September 11, I asked a group of ten students in a non-credit brief course concerned with war and peace to rate al-Qaeda on the four factors of GPA (Chambers et al., 1994). First I presented the eight items associated with each factor. For example, the characteristic "The group approves of violence against outsiders" is one of the items assigned to Exploitation. "Members are expected to serve the group's leaders" is an example of the Compliance factor. "The group believes or implies its leader is divine" is one of the eight items assigned to the Anxious Dependency sub-scale. And "Members are just as capable of independent critical thinking as they were before they joined the group" (reversed in scoring) represents the Mind Control factor (see Appendix for GPA items).

The class of well-informed adult students concurred that bin Laden and followers as described in national media were characteristic of an abusive religious group. If the cultic nature of al-Qaeda can be verified by further analyses, especially by field studies, important implications for prevention and control follow.

In other words, the public image of bin Laden and his followers shortly after the suicides was that they resembled a very abusive group. It is important to stress that an accurate GPA rating by former members with intimate knowledge is not currently obtainable. Rather, as a psychologist I could argue that the U.S. opponent had been successfully demonized.

Are Terrorists Cultists?

On the other hand, the argument that all terrorists are cultic in character is more difficult to sustain. If we accept the literal definition of terrorist, one who uses threats and violence, and if we apply the interpretation that in a conflict the term *terrorist* may be used to demonize the opponent, we enter a discussion confounded by politics and semantics. Thus, all sides in Northern Ireland or in Chechnya may complain about "terrorists," yet none of the combatants resembles very closely a religious cult.

Political Cults

The psychology of political cults deserves separate consideration. Tourish and Wohlforth (2000) have described a number of harmful activist groups (e.g., Lyndon Larouche and Synanon). They are distinctive in their attempt to address economic and social problems with an extreme creed or manifesto (right or left). They do have in common with religious groups loyal, dedicated, single-minded members under mind control who have a strong commitment to a manipulative leader. The authors maintain that these political groups are similar in modus operandi to religious cults. Although abusive, those described by Tourish and Wohlforth have not committed mass murder. In contrast, Hitler and Nazism can be likened to a killer political cult.

TENTATIVE CONCLUSIONS

My conclusions are tempered by the fact that as a psychologist I have considerable firsthand knowledge about cultists' behavior but what I know about terrorists depends on the national media—TV, magazines, books, and newspapers. I have limited my attention largely to a single group—al-Qaeda—because not enough information is available about alleged terrorist groups such as Hamas in Israel or the Tamil Tigers in Sri Lanka, which may also resemble killer religious/political cults.

According to this analysis, bin Laden and al-Qaeda resemble in their behaviors, beliefs, and cognitive structures members of an abusive political/religious killer cult. However, other abusive groups rarely commit mass homicide and suicide even though they apply mind control, coercive persuasion, manipulation, and the like, and even though some use fraud, deceit, child abuse, and more. Therefore, generalizations about the prevention and control of abusive groups may or may not apply. Furthermore, so-called terrorists may not be cultists but simply participants in a political conflict. For example, Palestinians may accuse Israelis of terrorism.

RECOMMENDATIONS

Prevention and Control

I suggest the following possible actions that may be valuable in the prevention and control of groups such as bin Laden and his followers. These are my opinions and should be interpreted as such.

When religious leaders preach hatred and murder in the name of God, watchdog groups should respond immediately. Such watchdog groups could include investigative journalists, international bodies such as the United Nations, or nongovernmental organizations such as Amnesty International and other nonprofit agencies that emphasize peace and justice.

The first step is to identify a specific, potential/alleged dangerous religious group and then to analyze in depth its history, dynamics, motivation, cognitive structures, grievances, theology, and the like. At this point, psychologists and other scholars should be introduced as consultants. And former members should be interviewed by specialists who speak the group's language.

Such identification and analyses should form the bases for two kinds of preventive action: publicity and education directed at prospective converts, and interventions to reduce the threat of harmfulness. In the case of bin Laden, hindsight suggests that books, TV documentaries, radio broadcasts, and newspaper reports might have been circulated to hot spots years ago, accompanied by remedial diplomatic and economic actions.

The following is part of a statement by one hundred Nobel laureates (2001) that was published two months after September 11:

> The most profound danger to world peace in the coming years will stem not from the irrational acts of states or individuals but from the legitimate demands of the world's dispossessed. . . . The only hope for the future lies in co-operative international action, legitimized by democracy. (p. A21)

The international community faces a formidable challenge. How to counteract the social, economic, and political conditions that foster killer cults. Much, it seems to me, depends upon the effectiveness over a period of decades of a complex network of organizations designed to address particular global problems. The United Nations—with such agencies as the United Nations Children's Fund, United Nations Special Commission, and the United Nations Educational, Scientific, and Cultural Organization—is one example among many. Can organizations like the AFF or the Leo J. Ryan Foundation, also a countercult group, provide models of prevention and intervention in counteracting killer cults like al-Qaeda? Yes, in the sense of demonstrating the importance of identifying dangerous groups early in their development, of initiating research, and of encouraging publicity and public education that inoculates the target population.

A major difficulty arises when the potentially extremely harmful group origi-
nates in a foreign country. Obviously it is fellow citizens, who speak the language
and know the culture, who are in the best position to take appropriate actions.

Falun Gong

An example is the Falun Gong. According to an official of the People's Republic
of China ("Why China," 2000), group leader Li Hongzhi claims to "possess
absolute authority and power . . . Falun Gong is a cult which has committed a host
of serious crimes. . . . obstructing justice, causing human deaths and illegally
obtaining state secrets" (pp. 13–14). Rahn (2000) recommends independent verification of such information coming out of China and a broader investigation of the
topic.

In the United States, Falun Gong is protected by the legal system and traditions
of religious freedom. In China, according to *Cult Observer* ("Torture," 2001), the
government has moved forcefully to gain the upper hand, using "torture and high-
pressure indoctrination . . . in its protracted battle against the banned Falun Gong
spiritual movement" (p. 12).

Al-Qaeda

Al-Qaeda's attacks on the United States pose unusual problems because some of
its members are ready to kill opponents and themselves, because it has cells in
many countries, and because bin Laden and thousands of followers have been shel-
tered by the Taliban in Afghanistan.

It may be too late to borrow the kind of countercult measures developed in this
country (Hassan, 2000; Langone, 1993; and Singer & Lalich, 1997) and in some
European countries. However, if, for example, the Saudi government captures
some civilian al-Qaeda members, it might be fruitful first to train selected Saudi
Arabians as exit consultants. Drawing on intimate knowledge of Saudi culture and
Islam, these Saudi consultants might then adapt such deconversion techniques as
Hassan's (2000) Strategic Interaction Approach. Perhaps family members of the
cultist and rehabilitated former terrorists could participate.

If al-Qaeda is indeed a killer cult, another important implication concerns the
nature of mind control. Not only does religious conversion lead to murder and
martyrdom, it also prepares the devotee to endure extreme measures. Thus, while
some Taliban officers and soldiers surrendered when defeat was clear, al-Qaeda
fighters persisted. Torture, threats, imprisonment, and violence rarely change the
minds of cultists. If opponents in an understandable thrust for justice use violence,
the cycle spins downward. How can the cycle of violence be broken?

Consultation

In response to this question, I have no magic bullets. However, one possible
path to an answer is consultation with intimately informed experts. When police or
military face members of a killer cult in difficult circumstances, they might profit

from prior training in the appropriate responses to a specific dangerous group by consultants familiar with its language, motivation, culture, and history. In the case of the Branch Davidians, for example, a skillfully designed quarantine and messages from former members might have been more effective than direct assault.

Research

Another potential answer is research. Well-designed studies of the complex phenomenon of terrorism, including how to identify, prevent, and contain killer cults, and how to counter mind control, can be justified as a part of national defense, perhaps part of a Manhattan Project for the Social Sciences. For instance, investigations of the personality structure of bin Laden and his followers would be invaluable.

Such studies should include both qualitative and quantitative methods, and laboratory and field studies, as well as intensive clinical case histories.

REFERENCES

AFF (American Family Foundation) (1998). *Cults and psychological abuse: A resource guide.* Bonita Springs, FL: Author.

Amitrani, A., & Di Marzio, R. (2000). "Mind control" in new religious movements and the American Psychological Association. *Cultic Studies Journal, 17,* 101–121.

Aum, now "Aleph," still live issue (2000). *Cult Observer, 2,* 11.

Beit-Hallahmi, B. (1993). *The illustrated encyclopedia of active new religions, sects, and cults.* New York: Rosen.

Berger, P. L. (2001). *Holy war: Inside the secret world of Osama bin Laden.* New York: Free Press.

Bromley, D. G. (2001). A tale of two theories: Brainwashing and conversion as competing political narratives. In B. Zablocki & T. Robbins (Eds.), *Misunderstanding cults* (pp. 318–348). Toronto: University of Toronto Press.

Bromley, D. G., & Hadden, J. K. (Eds.) (1993). *The handbook on cults and sects in America.* Greenwich, CT: Jai Press.

Bromley, D. G., & Shupe, A. D. (1979). *"Moonies" in America.* Beverly Hills, CA: Sage.

Chambers, W. V., Langone, M. D., Dole, A. A., & Grice, J. W. (1994). The group psychological abuse scale: A measure of the varieties of cultic abuse. *Cultic Studies Journal, 11,* 88–117.

Diament, C. (2001). The cult of terror. *Weekly Press, 1,* 9.

Dole, A. A., Langone, M. D., & Dubrow-Eichel, S. K. (1993). Is the New Age harmless? Critics vs. experts. *Cultic Studies Journal, 10,* 53–77.

Dubrow-Eichel, S. K. (1989). Deprogramming: A case study. Part I: Personal observations of the group process. *Cultic Studies Journal (Special Issue). 6 (2).*

Dubrow-Eichel, S. K. (1990). Deprogramming: A case study—Part II: Conversation analysis. *Cultic Studies Journal, 7,* 174–216.

Dubrow-Eichel, S. K., & Dole, A. A. (1986). Some new religions are dangerous. *Cultic Studies Journal, 2,* 17–30.

Hassan, S. (2000). *Releasing the bonds: Empowering people to think for themselves.* Somerville, MA: Freedom of Mind Press.

Hassan, S. (2001, August). How cults use hypnotic methods to indoctrinate their members. Paper presented at the annual meeting of the American Psychological Association.

James, W. (1902). *Varieties of religious experience.* New York: Longmans, Green.

Karlin, R. A., & Orme, M. T. (1996). Commentary on Borawick v. Shay: Hypnosis, social influence, incestuous child abuse, and satanic ritual abuse: The iatrogenic redaction of horrific memories for the remote past. *Cultic Studies Journal, 13,* 42–94.

Kinsley, M. (2001, October 5). Defining terrorism. *Washington Post,* p. A37.

Langone, M. D. (Ed.) (1993). *Recovery from cults: Help for victims of psychological and spiritual abuse.* New York: Norton.

Langone, M. D. (2000). The two "camps" of cultic studies: Time for a dialogue. *Cultic Studies Journal, 17,* 79–100.

Lifton, R. J. (1961). *Thought reform and the psychology of totalism.* New York: Norton.

Malinoski, P. T., Langone, M. D., & Lynn, S. J. (1999). Psychological distress in former members of the International Churches of Christ and noncultic groups. *Cultic Studies Journal, 16,* 33–48.

Martin, P. R., Langone, M. D., Dole, A. A., & Wiltrout, J. (1992). Post-cult symptoms as measured by the MCMI before and after residential treatment. *Cultic Studies Journal, 9,* 219–150.

Mather, G. A., & Nichols, L. A. (Eds.) (1993). *Dictionary of cults, sects, religions, and the occult.* Grand Rapids, MI: Zondervan Publishing House.

McKechnie, J. L. (Ed.) (1979). *Webster's deluxe unabridged dictionary.* New York: Simon & Schuster.

Milgram, S. (1974). *Obedience to authority: An experimental view.* New York: Harper & Row.

Miller, A. G., Collins, B. E., & Brief, D. E. (1995). Perspectives on obedience to authority: The legacy of the Milgram experiments. *Journal of Social Issues, 31,* 1–19.

Nobel laureates, statement by 100 (2001, December 7). *Toronto Globe and Mail,* p. A 21.

Rahn, P. (2000). The Falon Gong: Beyond the headlines. *Cultic Studies Journal, 17,* 168–186.

Rosedale, H. L., & Langone, M. D. (1998). On using the term "cult." In *Cults and psychological abuse: A resource guide* (pp. 67–72). Bonita Springs, FL: American Family Foundation.

Schein, E., Schneier, I., & Barker, C. H. (1961). *Coercive persuasion: A sociopsychological analysis of the "brainwashing" of American civilian prisoners by the Chinese communists.* New York: Norton.

Shupe, A. D., & Bromley, D. G. (1980). *The new vigilantes.* Beverly Hills, CA: Sage.

Singer, M. L. (1979). Coming out of the cults. *Psychology Today, 12,* 72–82.

Singer, M. L., & Lalich, J. (1997). *Cults in our midst.* New York: Jossey-Bass.

Singer, M. L., & West, J. (1980). Cults, quacks, and non-professional therapies. In *Comprehensive textbook of psychiatry* (Vol. 3). Baltimore: Williams & Wilkins.

State intervenes in Aum activities (2000). *Cult Observer, 4,* 11.

Tourish, D., & Wohlforth, T. (2000). *On the edge: Political cults right and left.* Armonk, NY: M. E. Sharpe.

Trying to understand Uganda "Holocaust" (2000). *Cult Observer, 2,* 18–19.

Torture and "brainwashing" decimating Falun Gong (2001). *Cult Observer, 3*, 12–13.
United States Department of State (2001, October). *Patterns of global terrorism.* Al-Qaida. Retrieved from http://library.nps.navy.mil/home/tgp/qaida.htm.
Why China calls Falun Gong a "cult" (2000). *Cult Observer, 2*, 13–14.
Zimbardo, P. (1996). *The psychology of mind control.* Palo Alto, CA: Stanford University Course Reader.

APPENDIX

The Group Psychological Abuse Scale (GPA)

This inventory is designed to evaluate certain aspects of religious, psychotherapeutic, political, commercial, and other groups. Please rate, as best you can, the degree to which the following statements characterize the group under consideration. Rate each item according to your experience and observations (in retrospect) of how the group actually functioned. If your group had different levels of membership (within which the group's dominant features differed), please apply the ratings to the level with which you have the greatest familiarity. Circle the best answer, using the following ratings: 1 = not at all characteristic; 2 = not characteristic; 3 = can't say/not sure; 4 = characteristic; 5 = very characteristic.

1. (R) The group does not tell members how to conduct their sex lives.
2. Women are directed to use their bodies for the purpose of recruiting or of manipulation.
3. The group advocates or implies that breaking the law is okay if it serves the interest of the group.
4. Members are expected to postpone or give up their personal, vocation, and educational goals in order to work for the group.
5. (R) The group encourages ill members to get medical assistance.
6. Gaining political power is a major goal of the group.
7. Members believe that to leave the group would be death or eternal damnation for themselves or their families.
8. The group discourages members from displaying negative emotions.
9. Members feel they are part of a special elite.
10. The group teaches that persons who are critical of the group are in the power of evil, satanic forces.
11. The group uses coercive persuasion and mind control.
12. The group approves of violence against outsiders (e. g., "satanic communists," etc.).

13. Members are expected to live with other members.

14. Members must abide by the group's guidelines regarding dating and intimate relationships.

15. People who stay in the group do so because they are deceived and manipulated.

16. The group teaches special exercises (e.g., meditation, chanting, speaking in tongues) to push doubts or negative thoughts out of consciousness.

17. Medical attention is discouraged, even though there may be a medical problem.

18. Members are expected to serve the group's leaders.

19. Raising money is a major goal of the group.

20. The group does not hesitate to threaten outside critics.

21. (R) Members re expected to make decisions without consulting the group's leader(s).

22. (R) Members are just as capable of independent critical thinking as they were before they joined the group.

23. The group believes or implies its leader is divine.

24. Mind control is used without conscious consent of members.

25. (R) Members feel little psychological pressure from leaders.

26. (R) The group's leader(s) rarely criticize members.

27. Recruiting members is a major goal of the group.

28. Members are expected to consult with leaders about most decisions, including those concerning work, child rearing, whether or not to visit relatives, etc.

Note: (R) items are reversed in scoring.

Researchers wishing to use the GPA Scale should contact Michael D. Langone (AFF, P.O. Box 2265, Bonita Springs, FL 33959). Scale adapted from Chambers et al., (1994).

Afterword

Harvey Langholtz
Series Editor
Psychological Dimensions to War and Peace

In the four edited volumes of the *Psychology of Terrorism,* Dr. Chris Stout and forty-three contributing authors have explored terrorism from the perspectives of psychological theory, therapy, history, sociology, political science, international relations, religion, anthropology, and other disciplines. These authors have brought differing viewpoints and they offer different views. In some cases the reader might even wonder if these authors have been addressing different subjects and different realities.

But this is the fundamental anomaly in the study of terrorism. On the one hand, it is easy to oversimplify and explain terrorism. On the other hand, recent events show us how difficult it is truly to understand terrorism, much less to know how to deal with it both reasonably and effectively. There is no universally agreed-upon definition of terrorism. Views on terrorism are often politically driven and it seems to be easier to cloud the discussion than to agree on an understanding. The issue urgently demands immediate solutions but these solutions appear to be a long way off.

As we look back over the ten years that preceded September 11, 2001, it seems we all missed the signals—the bombing of the Khobar Towers in Saudi Arabia, the U.S. embassies in Kenya and Tanzania, the USS *Cole,* and the federal building in Oklahoma City; the gas attack on the Tokyo subway; and of course the 1993 attack on the World Trade Center itself. Did our world actually change on that one day or were we only coming to realize as we watched the events in helpless disbelief that our understanding of the world had been wrong?

In the long view of history, September 11 will be remembered as a day when we were forced in fear and pain to reexamine some of our fundamental assumptions. And in this long view scholars will look to see what the serious and well-considered reactions were in the months following the event as psychologists and others took the time to reflect on the events of the day. That is what the contributing authors to these four volumes have sought to do in the immediate aftermath of the event: To consider terrorism, the causes of terrorism, people's reactions to terrorist acts, interventions to prevent or contain terrorism, and the possible role psychologists can play in understanding, explaining, and limiting terrorism and its effects.

Index

ideology of, 46–47; firearm ownership stance of, 47

Millenarianism, defined, 164. *See also* Apocalyptic fantasies

Millennium (Attali), 85, 108

Millon Clinical Multiaxial Inventory (MCMI), administered to former cultists, 216

Mind control, 214–15, 218; and conversion to communism, 214; in Hindu movements, 215; through posthypnotic suggest, 215, 220; and religious conversion, 214; research, 214–16

Minority group identity: in aftermath of September 11 attacks, 23–25; and group generalization of cultural differences, 23–24; public, stereotyping and metasterotyping in, 24–25; and shifts in private identities, 25

Misogyny: in Arab cultures, 123–27; and cycle of abuse, 126; and fantasy distorting of women, 123; and neglectful mothering, 123; psychology of, 124–25

Moro, Aldo, 70

Movement for the Restoration of the Ten Commandments of God, 221

Murder: in new religious movement, 180, 182–83, 184; and sociocultural stability, 156–57

Muslim culture: authoritarianism family orientation, 205; entrancement in, 203–5; environmental deprivation in, 203–4; globalization and, 49–50; inclination toward violent conflict in, 34; liberalism and tolerance in, 19–20; misogyny and abuse of females in, 123–25; perceived Western threat to, 14–15; symbolism of the veil in, 49–50

Muslims, post-September 11 bias toward, 23, 24–25. *See also* Arab women

Napoleon, entranced logic of, 205

Nationalism, and patriotism, 21

Native Americans, nonviolent apocalyptic dream of, 176

Nazism, as killer cult, 222

Neglectful mothering, pathological consequences of, 122–23

New religious movements, 175–84, 213;

altered states of consciousness in, 214; apocalyptic fantasies in, 175–84; cultic violence in, 218–20; mass suicide in, 181, 183–84, 186; murderous violence in, 180, 182–83, 184; paranoia in, 186; sexual exploitation and domination in, 178–79, 181; totalitarianism in, 185–86. *See also* Cultists; Cult(s)

Nonstate terror: anti-state and vigilante violence as, 4; twentieth-century deaths from, 4

North American Free Trade Agreement (NAFTA), militia movement and, 46–47

Omar, Mullah, 205

Oppression: cycle of constraint in, 87; and empathy, 122

Osho Meditation, apocalyptic proclamations of, 175

Pakistani *madrasahs*, religious indoctrination in, 69

Palestinian terrorists, 33; material motivations for, 8; origins and motivations of, 8

Patriotism: constructive versus blind, 21–22; and nationalism, 21

People Forever International, physical immortality vision of, 172–73

People's Temple Christian (Disciples) Church: and end-of-times group fantasy, 180–81; Jonestown mass suicide of, 218–19, 220; racial integration and activism of, 181

Pol Pot, death toll of, 4

Political action, group interest versus self-interest in, 9

Political terrorism, history of, 3–4

Psychoanalytic theory: apocalyptic fantasy in, 164–67; conflict as governing metaphor in, 166; and conversion experiences, 166–67; psychic unity in, 166

Radical-socialist terrorist groups, 12

Raj, Dada Lekh (Prajapita Brahma), 177

Raja Yoga, Hindu revival movement of, 177–78

Rajneesh Foundation International (RFI), apocalyptic proclamations of, 175

Rebirth and conversion: in apocalyptic fan-

About the Editor and Advisory Board

CHRIS E. STOUT is a clinical psychologist who holds a joint government and academic appointment in the Northwestern University Medical School, and serves as the first Chief of Psychological Services of the state of Illinois. He served as an NGO Special Representative to the United Nations, was appointed by the U.S. Department of Commerce as a Baldrige Examiner, and served as an advisor to the White House for both political parties. He was appointed to the World Economic Forum's Global Leaders of Tomorrow. He has published or presented more than three hundred papers and twenty-two books. His works have been translated into five languages. He has lectured across the nation and in sixteen countries and has visited more than fifty nations. He has been on missions around the world and has reached the top of three of the world's Seven Summits. He was Distinguished Alumni of the Year from Purdue University and Distinguished Psychologist of the Year, in addition to receiving more than thirty other postdoctoral awards. He is past President of the Illinois Psychological Association and is a member of the National Academy of Practice. He has been widely interviewed by the media, including CNBC, CNN, Oprah, *Time*, the *Chicago Tribune*, and the *Wall Street Journal*, and was noted as "one of the most frequently cited psychologists in the scientific literature" by Hartwick College. A distinct honor was his award as one of ten Volunteers of the Year in Illinois, and both the Senate and House have recognized his work by proclamation of "Dr. Chris E. Stout Week."

DANA ROYCE BAERGER is a practicing clinical and forensic psychologist in Chicago. She specializes in issues related to children, families, mental health, and the legal system. She is on the clinical faculty of the Department of Psychiatry and Behavioral Sciences at Northwestern University Medical School, and is also a staff member of the Children and Family Justice Center at Northwestern University Law School. In her private practice she provides psychotherapy services to individuals, couples, and groups; consults with attorneys regarding clinical and forensic practice standards; and consults with mental health professionals regarding ethical and risk management issues.

TERRENCE J. KOLLER is a practicing clinical psychologist in Chicago. He also serves as Executive Director and Legislative Liaison of the Illinois Psychological Association. He is Clinical Assistant Professor of Psychology in the Department of Psychiatry at the University of Illinois Medical School in Chicago. His areas of expertise include attachment and loss, parent-child interaction, and ethical and legal issues relating to the practice of psychology. He was the 1990 recipient of the Illinois Psychological Association's Distinguished Psychologist Award, and received an honorary doctor of humane letters degree from the Chicago School of Professional Psychology in 1995.

STEVEN P. KOURIS is associate chairman of the Department of Psychiatry at the University of Illinois College of Medicine in Rockford and medical director of the Jack Mabley Developmental Center in Dixon, Illinois. A medical graduate of Des Moines University, he interned at the Mayo Clinic and served clinical residencies at the University of Michigan and Detroit Medical Centers. He also completed an epidemiology research fellowship at the Minnesota Department of Health, and earned degrees in environmental health from the University of Minnesota and in preventive medicine from the University of Wisconsin. An accomplished clinician, teacher, and researcher, he is certified in multiple areas of psychiatry and medicine, and specializes in pediatric and developmental neuropsychiatry.

RONALD F. LEVANT is Dean and professor of psychology at the Center for Psychological Studies at Nova Southeastern University. He chairs the American Psychological Association (APA) Committee on Psychology's Response to Terrorism, and is a Fellow of APA Divisions 1, 12, 17, 27, 29, 31, 39, 42, 43, and 51. He has served on the faculties of Boston University, Harvard Medical School, and Rutgers University. He has authored or edited thirteen books and more than one hundred refereed journal articles and book chapters. He has served as Editor of the *Journal of Family Psychology*, is an Associate Editor of *Professional Psychology: Research and Practice*, and is an advisory editor or consulting editor to the following journals: *American Journal of Family Therapy, Journal of Marriage and Family Therapy, Men and Masculinities, Psychology of Men and Masculinity, Journal of African American Men, Journal of Trauma Practice, In Session: Psychotherapy in Practice*, and *Clinical Psychology: Science and Practice*.

MALINI PATEL is clinical associate professor of psychiatry and behavioral sciences at Finch University of Health Sciences/Chicago Medical School, and Acting Medical Director at a state psychiatric facility. She is board certified with added qualifications in addiction psychiatry. She is actively involved in resident and medical student training programs and has received awards for her teaching and contributions to psychiatric education. She also practices in a community mental health clinic where she sees patients in the Dual Diagnosis and Assertive Community Treatment Programs. She has published and presented on topics related to court-ordered treatment, administrative psychiatry, and substance abuse.

About the Contributors

SHARIF ABDULLAH is an adjunct faculty member at Marylhurst University and Portland State University. An author, proponent, and catalyst for inclusive social, cultural, and spiritual transformation, his work as a humanistic globalist has taken him to more than two dozen countries and to every continent. He received a B.A. in psychology from Clark University and a J.D. from Boston University. He has appeared on several international globalization forums. His writings include *The Power of One: Authentic Leadership in Turbulent Times.* He is founder and president of Commonway Institute in Portland, Oregon.

RUBÉN ARDILA is Professor of Psychology at the National University of Colombia (Bogota, Colombia). He has published twenty-three books and more than one hundred and fifty scientific papers in different languages, mainly Spanish and English. He founded the *Latin American Journal of Psychology* and has been the editor of this journal for several years. His main areas of research are the experimental analysis of behavior, social issues, peace psychology, and international psychology. He has been a visiting professor in the United States, Germany, Spain, Argentina, and Puerto Rico. He is a member of the executive committee of the International Union of Psychological Science.

BENJAMIN BEIT-HALLAHMI received his Ph.D. in clinical psychology from Michigan State University in 1970. Since then he has held clinical, research, and teaching positions in the United States, Europe, and Israel. He is the author, coauthor, editor, or coeditor of seventeen books and monographs on the psychology of religion, social identity, and personality development. In addition, he has a special interest in questions of ethics and ideology in psychological research and practice. In 1993, he was the recipient of the William James Award for his contributions to the psychology of religion.

FRED BEMAK is currently a Professor and the Program Coordinator for the Counseling and Development Program at the Graduate School of Education at George Mason University. He has done extensive work in the area of refugee and immigrant psychosocial adjustment and mental health. He has given seminars and lectures and conducted research throughout the United States and in more than thirty countries in the areas of cross-cultural psychology and the psychosocial adjustment of refugees and immigrants. He is a former Fulbright Scholar, a Kellogg International Fellow, and a recipient of the International Exchange of Experts and Research Fellowship through the World Rehabilitation Fund. He has been working nationally and internationally in the area of refugee adjustment and acculturation for the past twenty years as a researcher, clinician, and clinical consultant and has numerous publications in the area. He has recently written a book in collaboration with Rita Chi-Ying Chung and Paul Pedersen, *Counseling Refugees: A Psychosocial Approach to Innovative Multicultural Interventions*, published by Greenwood Publishing.

BRENDA ANN BOSCH is Clinical and Research Coordinator, Senior Clinical Psychologist, and Lecturer in the Department of Medically Applied Psychology, Nelson R. Mandela School of Medicine, University of Natal, Durban, South Africa. She is a member of several scientific organizations and professional societies. She is a consultant in clinical neuropsychology/disability, dissociative disorders in forensic psychology, traumatic stress, and peer supervision. Her current research and publication thrusts include the relationship between stress and neuropsychological deficits, stress and psycho-oncology, the intensive care unit, and mortuaries/law enforcement.

HENRY BREED has worked more than a decade in the United Nations, having been a Humanitarian Affairs Officer, Assistant to the Under-Secretary-General for Peacekeeping, and Assistant to the Special Representative of the Secretary-General to the former Yugoslavia and to the North Atlantic Treaty Organization. He is currently Political Affairs Officer in the Office of the Iraq Programmed. In past posts, he has been called upon to go to Mozambique, Rwanda, and the former Yugoslavia. In his current post, he has been closely involved in a broad range of international activities within Iraq. He has worked as a consulting editor for UNESCO on issues including education, development, and cultural preservation, and he has been actively involved in a range of environmental activities related to the Earth Summit. Born in Norway and raised in New York, he received undergraduate degrees in music and fine arts from Indiana University in Bloomington. He also holds a master's degree in public administration from Harvard University, a diplôme in international history and politics from the Graduate Institute of International Studies in Geneva, and a master's in international affairs from Columbia University. A member of the Council on Foreign Relations and of the International Institute of Strategic Studies, he was awarded the Beale Fellowship at Harvard and was admitted to the academic fraternity Pi Kappa Lambda at Indiana University. He is also a Fulbright Scholar, a "boursier de la Confédération Suisse," and a Regents Scholar. He lives in New York.

GIOVANNI CARACCI is a Clinical Associate Professor of Psychiatry at the Mount Sinai School of Medicine and Director of Residency Training and Medical Student Education at the Mount Sinai School of Medicine (Cabrini) Program. He is the Chair of the World Psychiatric Association on Urban Mental Health and a member of the Commission on Global Psychiatry of the American Psychiatric Association. He represents the World Psychiatric Association at the United Nations in New York, where he is Chair of the Non Governmental Organizations Executive Committee on Mental Health and Treasurer of the NGO Executive Committee of HABITAT (Center for Human Settlement). His main fields of expertise are international mental health, education, and cultural issues in mental health.

RITA CHI-YING CHUNG received her Ph.D. in psychology at Victoria University in Wellington, New Zealand. She is currently an Associate Professor in the Counseling and Development Program in the Graduate School of Education at George Mason University. She was awarded a Medical Research Council (MRC) Fellowship for postdoctoral work in the United States. Following the MRC fellowship, she remained as a Project Director for the National Research Center on Asian American Mental Health at the University of California, Los Angeles. In addition, she has been a visiting professor at the Federal University of Rio Grande do Sul in Brazil, Johns Hopkins University, and George Washington University, and a consultant for the World Bank. She has conducted research and written extensively on Asian immigrants and refugee mental health and has worked in the Pacific Rim, Asia, Europe, and Latin America. She has recently written a book in collaboration with Fred Bemak and Paul Pedersen, *Counseling Refugees: A Psychosocial Approach to Innovative Multicultural Interventions,* published by Greenwood Publishing.

JOHN M. DAVIS is Professor of Psychology at Southwest Texas State University. He completed advanced work at two German universities and received his Ph.D. in experimental/social psychology from the University of Oklahoma. He has lived and worked as a psychologist in Germany, China, England, and the United States. He has researched and published in the areas of interpersonal relations, refugee stress/adaptation, health psychology, and international psychology. Recent publications include a book chapter (1999) on health psychology in international perspective and an invited article (2000) on international psychology in the prestigious *Encyclopedia of Psychology* (APA/Oxford University Press). His current research interests include international terrorism from the perspectives of social and international psychology, and the influences of ethnic self-identity and attitude similarity on interpersonal and intergroup attraction.

ARTHUR A. DOLE is Professor Emeritus at the University of Pennsylvania Graduate School of Education, and former Chair of the Psychology in Education Division. He is a member of the Board of Directors of AFF, a nonprofit organization that encourages education and research about abusive groups, and a consulting editor of the *Cultic Studies Journal.* His research has focused on the harmfulness of cultic groups.

BORIS DROZDEK is a psychiatrist working at the GGZ Den Bosch/Outpatient and Daytreatment Centre for Refugees, the Netherlands. He is researching, publishing, and teaching in the field of psychotrauma and forced migration.

JONATHAN T. DRUMMOND is a doctoral student in social psychology at Princeton University. Prior to beginning doctoral work, he taught at the United States Air Force (USAF) Academy in the Department of Behavioral Sciences and Leadership as a major in the USAF. His research interests include psychological construction and attributions of legitimacy about political and judicial institutions in the United States and South Asia, retaliatory violence, white separatism, and divergent Aryan identity narratives (present and historical) in Indian Hindutva, Sinhalese Buddhism, and Euro-American Wotanism.

SOLVIG EKBLAD, a clinical psychologist, is Adjunct Associate Professor in Transcultural Psychology at the Karolinska Institutet, Department of Neurotec, Section of Psychiatry, Stockholm, Sweden. She is also Head of the Unit for Immigrant Environment and Health at the National Institute of Psychosocial Factors and Health, Solna, Sweden. She is in charge of the research group "Transcultural Psychology" and supervises Ph.D. and master's level students. At present, she has research grants from the National Swedish Integration Office, the European Refugee Fund, and the Stockholm County Council. She is collaborating with several foreign and local research teams. She is Co-Chair for the International Committee of Refugees and Other Migrants (ICROM), World Federation for Mental Health. She has written many articles and book chapters and has presented papers at international and national conferences in the field of migration and mental health.

SALMAN ELBEDOUR received his Ph.D. in school psychology from the University of Minnesota. After working at Ben-Gurion University, Israel, for six years, and at Bir Zeit University in the Palestinian Authority, he joined the School of Education at Howard University. He is currently an Associate Professor and the Coordinator of the School Psychology Program. His research and clinical interests are focused on psychopathology, maltreatment, child abuse, and neglect. He has published in the areas of cross-cultural and developmental studies of young children and adolescents placed at risk, specifically children exposed to political unrest, family conflict, and school violence. He has published extensively on the impact of the Israeli-Arab conflict on the development and socialization of children in the region. His Ph.D. thesis, "Psychology of Children of War," investigated the traumatic risk, resilience, and social and moral development of Palestinian children of the uprising, or *intifada.*

J. HAROLD ELLENS is a retired Professor of Philosophy, Theology, and Psychology, as well as the author, coauthor, and/or editor of 68 books and 148 professional journal articles. He spent his professional life on the issues involved in the interface of psychology and theology, served for fifteen years as Executive Director of the Christian Association for Psychological Studies, and as Founding Editor and Editor-in-Chief of the *Journal of Psychology and Christianity.* He holds a Ph.D. from Wayne State University in the psychology of human communication, a Ph.D. from the University of Michigan in Biblical and Near Eastern Studies, and master's degrees from Calvin Theological Seminary, Princeton Theological Seminary, and the University of Michigan. His publications include *God's Grace and Human Health* and *Psychotheology: Key Issues,* as well as chapters in *Moral Obligation and the Military, Baker Encyclopedia of Psychology, Abingdon Dictionary of Pastoral Care,* and *Humanistic Psychology.* He is currently a research scholar at the University of Michigan, Department of Near Eastern Studies. He is also a retired Presbyterian theologian and minister, and a retired U.S. Army Colonel.

TERI L. ELLIOTT is a clinical psychologist in New York City, specializing in children and adolescents. She is an Assistant Professor at the Disaster Mental Health Institute (DMHI), where she focuses on children and violence, bullying interventions, disaster response and preparedness, and psychological responses to weapons of mass destruction. She teaches and consults nationally and internationally on topics including children and trauma, crisis intervention, psychological support, and refugee mental health.

STEPHEN D. FABICK is a consulting and clinical psychologist in Birmingham, Michigan. He is past President of Psychologists for Social Responsibility (PsySR), past Chair of the PsySR Enemy Images program, and current Chair of its Conflict Resolution Action Committee. He is also Chair of the Conflict Resolution Working Group of the Society for the Study of Peace, Conflict and Violence (Division 48 of the American Psychological Association). His interest has been in conflict transformation and prejudice reduction. He authored *US & THEM: The Challenge of Diversity,* a Workshop Presenter's Manual. The program was included in President Clinton's Initiative on Race Relations and selected by the Center for Living Democracy as a model program in their book *Bridging the Racial Divide.* The program focuses on transforming group prejudice and conflict.

DON J. FEENEY, JR., is a clinical psychologist and Executive Director of Consulting Psychological Services in Chicago. In practice for more than twenty-five years, he has authored books including *Entrancing Relationships* (Praeger, 1999) and *Motifs: The Transformative Creation of Self* (Praeger, 2001).

RONA M. FIELDS is a clinical psychologist and Senior Associate at Associates in Community Health and Development and Associates in Community Psychology, in Washington, D.C. She has been an Assistant Professor at California State University, a Professor at the California School of Professional Psychology, and an Adjunct Professor at George Mason University and the American School of Professional Psychology. Her research includes studies of terrorism, violence and prejudice, peace-keeping operations and hostage negotiations, and treating victims of torture.

TIMOTHY GALLIMORE is a certified mediator, facilitator, and third-party neutral in conflict resolution. He researches and writes on trauma healing and reconciliation and on violence prevention. He earned a Ph.D. in mass communication from Indiana University in 1992. He was a consultant to the United Nations Development Program for Women and on the USAID Rwanda Rule of Law project to institute a community restorative justice system for trying genocide suspects.

TED G. GOERTZEL is Professor of Sociology at Rutgers University in Camden, New Jersey. His books include *Turncoats and True Believers, Linus Pauling: A Life in Science and Medicine,* and *Fernando Henrique Cardoso: Reinventing Democracy in Brazil.* His articles include "The Ethics of Terrorism and Revolution" and "Myths of Murder and Multiple Regression," and can be found on his Web site at http://goertzel.org/ted.

EDITH HENDERSON GROTBERG, a developmental psychologist, works for the Civitan International Research Center at the University of Alabama, Birmingham, and with the Institute for Mental Health Initiatives, George Washington University, Washington, D.C. Through the International Resilience Research Project (IRRP), she found many answers to the role of resilience in understanding and enhancing human health and behavior. Her articles have been published in *Ambulatory Child Health* and *The Community of Caring,* and some of her books on resilience have been translated into other languages.

RAYMOND H. HAMDEN is a clinical psychologist and Director of Psychology Services at the Comprehensive Medical Center in Dubai, United Arab Emirates. Born in the United States, he was a 1986 Visiting Fellow at the University of Maryland, College Park, Center for International Development and Conflict Management. His research and consultations focused on the psychology of the terrorist and hostage situations. He earned a Ph.D. at Heed University, Department of Psychology, and continued postgraduate study in psychoanalysis at the Philadelphia School of Modern Psychoanalysis. In 1990, he moved to the United Arab Emirates and established his own practice. He holds adjunct faculty positions at institutions including the University of Indianapolis, and has taught at the American Universities in Dubai and Sharjah. He holds Diplomate and Fellow status at the American College of Forensic Examiners and the American Academy of Sexologists. He is licensed by the Dubai Department of Health and Medical Services, as well as by the Board of Psychology Examiners in Washington, D.C. He is also a member of the International Society for Political Psychology and the International Council of Psychologists. He is an ACFE Diplomate, American Board of Psychological Specialties.

FADEL ABU HEIN is a community and clinical psychologist on the faculty of Al Aksa University in Gaza. He was for many years the senior psychologist at the Gaza Community Health Center, where he developed the research program and also instituted a broad outreach service for a traumatized population that had no other mental health resource. He has more recently established his own clinical practice in Gaza in conjunction with his teaching responsibilities at Al Aksa University.

CRAIG HIGSON-SMITH is a research psychologist employed in the Child, Youth and Family unit of the Human Sciences Research Council of South Africa. He is a specialist researcher in the fields of violence and traumatic stress. Previously, he cofounded and managed the KwaZulu-Natal Programme for Survivors of Violence, a nongovernment organization dedicated to supporting communities ravaged by civil conflict in Southern Africa. More recently, he cofounded the South African Institute for Traumatic Stress.

J. E. (HANS) HOVENS is a clinical psychologist and psychiatrist. He has published extensively on the subject of post-traumatic stress disorder. Currently, he is a lecturer on psychiatry at the Delta Psychiatric Teaching Hospital in Poortugaal, the Netherlands.

NIRA KFIR is a clinical psychologist who received her Ph.D. in social psychiatry at the Université de Paris, Sorbonne, Center for Social Psychiatry. She is the Director of Maagalim-Institute of Psychotherapy and Counseling in Tel Aviv. In 1973, she developed a Crisis Intervention program adopted by the Israeli Ministry of Defense, and it is still in use for group work with bereaved families. She developed the psychotherapeutic diagnostic system of Personality Impasse/Priority Therapy.

OLUFEMI A. LAWAL is a Ph.D. candidate at the University of Lagos, Akoka-Yaba, Lagos, Nigeria. He has been a teacher and coordinator at St. Finbarr's College in Lagos, and is now an instructor at Quantum Educational Services, Ilupeju, Ibadan, Oyo.

JOHN E. LeCAPITAINE is Professor and former Chair of the Department of Counseling and School Psychology, University of Wisconsin, River Falls. He has a doctorate in counseling psychology (Boston University), a doctorate in metaphysics, a master of science in school psychology, and a bachelor of science in mathematics. He is a Diplomate Forensic Psychologist and a member of the International Council of Psychologists, the American Psychological Association, the American College of Forensic Examiners, the Institute of Noetic Sciences, the National Association of School Psychologists, and *Who's Who in the World*. He has written a number of articles, receiving the Special Merit award from *Education* for *Schools as Developmental Clinics: Overcoming the Shadow's Three Faces*.

JOHN E. MACK is a Pulitzer Prize–winning author and Professor of Psychiatry at Harvard Medical School who has explored how cultural worldviews may obscure solutions to social, ecological, and spiritual crises. He is the founder of the Center for Psychology and Social Change. He also founded the Department of Psychiatry at the Cambridge Hospital in 1969. In 1983 he testified before Congress on the psychological impact of the nuclear arms race on children. He is the author or coauthor of ten books, including *A Prince of Our Disorder*, a Pulitzer Prize–winning biography of T. E. Lawrence, and, most recently, *Passport to the Cosmos*.

SHERRI McCARTHY is an Associate Professor of Educational Psychology at Northern Arizona University's Yuma campus. She has published research in international journals on a variety of topics, including developing critical thinking skills, anger management training, substance abuse counseling, and the role of psychology in improving society. She has also written books in the areas of special education and grief and bereavement issues. She is active in the International Council of Psychologists' Psychology and Law interest group. She is also active in the American Psychological Association, serving as the Division 2 Teaching of Psychology liaison to the Council on International Relations in Psychology and as the leader of the P3 Global Psychology Project.

CLARK McCAULEY is a Professor of Psychology at Bryn Mawr College and serves as a faculty member and Co-Director of the Solomon Asch Center for Study of Ethnopolitical Conflict at the University of Pennsylvania. He received his Ph.D. in social psychology from the University of Pennsylvania in 1970. His research interests include stereotypes and the psychology of group identification, group dynamics and intergroup conflict, and the psychological foundations of ethnic conflict and genocide. His recent work includes a new measure of intergroup contact, "the exposure index."

STEVE S. OLWEEAN is a psychotherapist with a degree in clinical psychology from Western Michigan University. He is President of the Association for Humanistic Psychology (AHP), and Founding Director of Common Bond Institute. Since 1990, he has served as AHP International Liaison and Coordinator of International Programs. His principal treatment area is trauma and abuse recovery and reframing negative belief systems. His primary international focus is conflict transformation, forgiveness, reconciliation, and humanitarian recovery efforts. He cofounded and each year coordinates the Annual International Conference on Conflict Resolution held in St. Petersburg, Russia. He also developed an integrated Catastrophic Trauma Recovery (CTR) treatment model for treating large populations experiencing trauma due to war, violence, and catastrophe.

DIANE PERLMAN is a clinical psychologist in Pennsylvania, with a special interest in political psychology. She is Co-Chair of the American Psychological Association Committee on Global Violence and Security within Division 48, the Society for the Study of Peace, Conflict, and Violence. She is also a research associate with the Citizens Panel on Ultimate Weapons at the Center on Violence and Human

Survival. She is Vice President of the Philadelphia Project for Global Security, and Liaison to the psychology community for the Global Nonviolent Peace Force. She is also Founding Member of and a research associate for the Transcending Trauma Project, studying adaptation of Holocaust survivors and their children. She is a Fellow of the Solomon Asch Center for Study of Ethnopolitical Conflict at the University of Pennsylvania and was a speaker for two decades for Physicians for Social Responsibility.

MARC PILISUK is a clinical and social psychologist. He is Professor Emeritus of the University of California and a Professor at the Saybrook Graduate School and Research Center in San Francisco. He is a past President of APA Division 48, the Society for the Study of Peace, Conflict, and Violence; a member of the steering committee of Psychologists for Social Responsibility; and one of the founders of the first teach-in.

JERRY S. PIVEN is a Professor of Psychology at New School University and New York University, where his courses focus on the psychology of religion, death, and sexuality. He is a member of the National Psychological Association for Psychoanalysis and author of *Death and Delusion: A Freudian Analysis of Mortal Terror*. He is editor of the series Psychological Undercurrents of History and is presently working on a psychoanalytic exploration of the madness and perversion of Yukio Mishima.

WILLIAM H. REID is a Clinical and Adjunct Professor of Psychiatry at the University of Texas Health Science Center, Texas A&M College of Medicine, and Texas Tech University Medical Center. He is past President of the American Academy of Psychiatry and the Law. He is a fellow of the Royal College of Physicians, American College of Psychiatrists, and American Psychiatric Association. He is also past Chair of the National Council of State Medical Directors, and a U.S. Observer for the Board of Presidents of the Socialist Countries' Psychiatric Associations, Sofia, Bulgaria. He was U.S. Representative, Ver Heyden de Lancey Conference on Psychiatry, Law, and Public Policy at Trinity College, Cambridge University, as well as visiting lecturer, Hunan Medical College, Changsha, Hunan.

LOURENS SCHLEBUSCH is Professor and Head of the Department of Medically Applied Psychology, Nelson R. Mandela School of Medicine, University of Natal, Durban, South Africa. He is a suicidologist, stress management and medico-legal/disability consultant, Chief Clinical Psychologist for the Hospital Services of the KwaZulu-Natal Provincial Administration, and Chief Consultant in Behavioural Medicine at various hospitals in Durban, South Africa. He is a member of many scientific editorial boards, organizations, and societies, and is a reviewer of scientific publications both nationally and internationally. He has many professional listings, honors, and awards. He has made many significant research contributions to his field and has published widely. He is currently researching various aspects of traumatic stress and suicide prevention.

KLAUS SCHWAB is Founder and President of the World Economic Forum, an organization committed to improving the state of the world, and based in Geneva, Switzerland. He has worked in several high-level roles with the United Nations and is now a Professor at the University of Geneva. He studied at the Swiss Federal Institute of Technology, the University of Fribourg, and the John F. Kennedy School at Harvard University.

KATHY SEXTON-RADEK is Professor of Psychology at Elmhurst College and Director of Psychological Services, Hinsdale Hospital/Suburban Pulmonary and Sleep Associates. She has designed conflict resolution and stress management curriculums for elementary and secondary school children and has implemented these programs with inner-city students at risk for violence and substance abuse. She has also constructed and taught anti-violence workshops for teachers. She is the author of more than thirty peer-reviewed articles in the areas of behavioral medicine, applied cognitive behavior theory in school settings, and psychology pedagogy. She is an elected member of her local school board, and a member of the American Psychological Association, Sigma Xi, and the Sleep Research Society.

ERVIN STAUB is Professor of Psychology at the University of Massachusetts at Amherst. He has published many articles and book chapters and several books about the influences that lead to caring, helping, and altruism, and their development in children. His upcoming book is *A Brighter Future: Raising Caring and Nonviolent Children.* He has also done extensive research into and writing about the roots and prevention of genocide and other group violence, including his book *The Roots of Evil: The Origins of Genocide and Other Group Violence.* Since 1999, he has been conducting, with collaborators, a project in Rwanda on healing, reconciliation, and other avenues to the prevention of renewed violence. His awards include the Otto Klineberg International and Intercultural Relations Prize of the Society for the Psychological Study of Social Issues. He has been President of the Society for the Study of Peace, Conflict, and Violence (Division 48 of the American Psychological Association) and of the International Society for Political Psychology.

MICHAEL J. STEVENS is a Professor of Psychology at Illinois State University in Normal. He is a Fellow of the American Psychological Association, serving as Chair of the Committee for International Liaisons of the Division of International Psychology. He is also a member of the Advisory Board of the Middle East Psychological Network. He is an honorary professor at the Lucian Blaga University of Sibiu, Romania, where he completed Fulbright and IREX grants. In 2000, he received the Recognition Award from the American Psychological Association for his work in international psychology.

TREVOR STOKES is Professor of Child and Family Studies, Professor of Psychology, Professor of Psychological and Social Foundations of Education, and Professor of Special Education at the University of South Florida, Tampa. He received his bachelor's degree with first-class honors in psychology at the University of Western

Australia, a Ph.D. in developmental and child psychology from the University of Kansas, and Ph.D. Clinical Psychology Augmentation at West Virginia University. His research, teaching, and clinical activities involve the behavior analysis and developmental assessment of aggression within families, with a focus on techniques for interception of violent repertoires by children.

TIMOTHY H. WARNEKA treats adolescents and children in a community mental health center near Cleveland, Ohio. He specializes in working with sexually aggressive and/or aggressive juveniles. He has studied the martial art of aikido for more than twelve years and incorporates aikido principles into his psychotherapeutic work. He is President of Cleveland Therapists, Ltd. (www.clevelandtherapists.com), a referral site for mental health professionals. He is President of Psyche & Soma Consulting, Ltd., an organization that offers training and consultation on a variety of mental health subjects.

MICHAEL WESSELLS is Professor of Psychology at Randolph-Macon College and Senior Technical Advisor for the Christian Children's Fund. He has served as President of the Division of Peace Psychology of the American Psychological Association and of Psychologists for Social Responsibility. His research examines psychology of terrorism, psychosocial assistance in emergencies, post-conflict reconstruction, and reintegration of former child soldiers. In countries such as Angola, Sierra Leone, East Timor, Kosovo, and Afghanistan, he helps to develop community-based, culturally grounded programs that assist children, families, and communities affected by armed conflict.

ANGELA WONG is a University of California student in sociology and social welfare. She is a research assistant and an intern providing assistance at homeless shelters.